COMMUNISTS CONSTRUCTING CAPITALISM

MANCHESTER
1824

Manchester University Press

ALTERNATIVE SINOLOGY

Series editors: Richard Madsen and Yangwen Zheng

This series provides a dedicated outlet for monographs and possibly edited volumes that take alternative views on contemporary or historical China; use alternative research methodologies to achieve unique outcomes; focus on otherwise understudied or marginalized aspects of China, Chineseness, or the Chinese state and the Chinese cultural diaspora; or generally attempt to unsettle the status quo in Chinese Studies, broadly construed. There has never been a better time to embark on such a series, as both China and the academic disciplines engaged in studying it seem ready for change.

Previously published

The advocacy trap   Stephen Noakes

Communists constructing capitalism

State, market, and the Party in China's financial reform

Julian Gruin

Manchester University Press

Published by Manchester University Press
Altrincham Street, Manchester M1 7JA
www.manchesteruniversitypress.co.uk

British Library Cataloguing-in-Publication Data
A catalogue record for this book is available from the British Library

ISBN 978 1 52613 532 2 hardback
ISBN 978 1 5261 3534 6 paperback

First published 2019

Typeset in Monotype Fournier by
Servis Filmsetting Ltd, Stockport, Cheshire
Printed in Great Britain
by TJ International Ltd, Padstow

To my parents, Rick and Yeats Gruin

Contents

Figures

Tables

Series editors' foreword

The study of China has in recent decades seen an explosion as many universities have begun to offer modules ranging from Chinese history, politics and sociology to urban, cultural, and Diaspora studies. This is welcome news; the field grows when the world is hungry for knowledge about China. Chinese studies as a result have moved further away from the interdisciplinary tradition of Sinology towards more discipline-based teaching and research. This is significant because it has helped integrate the once-marginalised Chinese subjects into firmly established academic disciplines; practitioners should learn and grow within their own fields. This has also, however, compartmentalised Chinese studies as China scholars communicate much less with each other than before since they now teach and research in different departments; the study of China has lost some of its exceptionalism and former sheen.

Alternative Sinology calls for a more nuanced way forward. China scholars can firmly ground themselves in their own perspective fields; they still have the advantage of Sinology, the more holistic approach. The combination of disciplinary and area studies can help us innovate and lead. Now is an exciting time to take the study of China to new heights as the country has seen unprecedented change and offers us both hindsight and new observations. Alternative Sinology challenges China scholars. It calls on them to think creatively and unsettle the status quo by using new and alternative materials and methods to dissect China. It encourages them to take on understudied and marginalised aspects of China at a time when the field is growing and expanding rapidly. The case of China can promote the field and strengthen the individual discipline as well.

Zheng Yangwen and Richard Madsen

Preface

On 8 November 2008 in the heart of Beijing's 'financial street' [金融街], an executive at one of China's 'big five' state-owned commercial banks (SOCBs) received a phone call from the head of one of the bank's offices in a city in Shandong province. The provincial bank head had dined the night before with a local Party official, and one topic dominated discussion: how they could maintain confidence in the financial system, free up liquidity and investment capital, and stimulate domestic demand. Three days previously, the Central Committee of the Communist Party of China (CCP) had issued Document No. 18, laying out ten policies to 'further expand domestic demand and assure stable rapid growth' in the midst of global economic downturn, and cadres across the country were tripping over themselves to gear up plans and projects for investment (Liu Zebang 2008). One dilemma presented itself, however: since its establishment in 2003 the China Banking Regulatory Commission (CBRC) had also been leading the 'modernization' of China's banking sector in macro-prudential regulation, corporate governance, and financial supervision, aspects of which were at risk of being ridden over roughshod in the frenetic drive to shore up growth. The Beijing executive's opinion was clear: the Party centre was under no illusions as to the need for clear macroeconomic direction, and if those at lower levels started second-guessing, 'no-one would know what to do and economic disorder would ensue'. Unity [团结] was the order of the day, and the CBRC would also do what the Party required of it.[1]

When I sat down with this executive in late 2012, sipping green tea in a corner office, the financial crisis had brought Western economies to their knees, and the triumphalism that had accompanied China's much-feted stimulus package and 8.7 per cent gross domestic product (GDP) growth in 2009 had begun to fade amidst growing awareness of wasteful investment projects, a further consolidation of economic power within the largest state-owned enterprises (SOEs), and a perception that ordinary households were amongst the last beneficiaries of the stimulus spending. We talked about this concept of economic disorder [*jingji hunluan* 经济混乱] – what it means, what causes it, and its implications. I asked about the lessons he drew from the 2008 financial crisis, and he said interesting but not entirely unexpected things about reducing inefficient state bureaucracy, about managing moral hazard, about limiting the innovation of complex financial products; but then he surprised me. He mentioned a different word for disorder [*dongluan* 动乱], and said that neither the state nor the market were capable of managing this kind of disorder. This is a political word, not an economic one, and it connotes turmoil, unrest, *upheaval*. As China was accelerating financial reform, as the 'transformation of the state' was gathering pace, the lesson that this banker took from the crisis was that it was neither the regulatory state nor the free market that prevented *dongluan*. It was the Party.

This vignette highlights three puzzling aspects of China's reform-era trajectory of development: (1) the embrace of 'the market'; (2) the rationalization of 'the state'; and (3) the undisputed political-economic authority of the CCP. As Xi Jinping's administration now confronts the mounting pressures of global economic turbulence and uncharted domestic economic terrain, important questions remain unanswered about how these features of China's political economy are connected, and how they are likely to evolve in the years to come. Simplifying somewhat, the core argument I develop in this book is that to understand these trends we have to look beyond the concepts of the state and the market as we have understood them in the liberal tradition of political economy, and instead theorize the politico-economic agency of the CCP itself, and in particular the ideas and conceptions of order that underpin this agency. Such factors have been largely neglected in existing accounts of China's financial development and reform, which remain focused on the more micro-level dynamics of political contestation *within* the state and market environments, without pausing to consider more broadly how these political and economic logics have interacted so as to produce a remarkably stable, if unbalanced and as yet potentially unsustainable, set of mechanisms for economic growth and the accumulation of capital. As I argue in this book, without accounting for the ideational cohesion that generated a powerful basis for CCP authority and control over the flow of capital throughout the economy, it becomes very difficult to understand both the resiliency of Party control and the commitment to market-based institutional reform. Although Chinese financial policymaking and development since the early 1990s has embodied a capitalist logic of economic growth and accumulation, the manifestation of this logic elides the traditional analytical dichotomy between the state and the market. Rather, this logic manifests in the CCP constituting the central feature of a system of socio-economic risk management that has functioned both to support economic growth, at the same time as a mechanism of political control. That is to say, the process of financial reform involved the construction of a system that would enable state-regulated and market-based economic growth at the same time as preserve CCP authority over the nature and structure of that growth.

The motivation for probing the sociological role of the CCP arose inductively from numerous discussions in the field amongst academics and bankers in Beijing, where it rapidly became apparent that in order to understand the role of the financial system in China, one must look beyond traditional notions of market liberalization and state regulation. In the wake of the 2008–09 crisis, it was an opportune time not just to consider how China's development was affecting global finance, but perhaps more importantly, to reflect more deeply and critically upon some of the axiomatic assumptions that underpinned the development of Western finance. Interrogating these conceptual and theoretical underpinnings of Western political economy in turn would provoke a reassessment of how these intellectual lineages had informed – and indeed tainted – resulting perspectives on Chinese economic development. What I discovered during two years of residence and fieldwork in Beijing was not just that Chinese finance was subject to state intervention, the politics of which obstructed market liberalization. Rather, my findings would reveal that the Chinese path of financial development was the product of an understanding of the relationship between market competition, bureaucratic regulation, and political authority that was fundamentally different to that which had led Western economies to financial near-meltdown. This itself was no normative judgement – China's financial capitalism is unsustainable and crisis-prone just like any other – however it raised important questions for how we understand contemporary capitalism in comparative context. In contrast to a complex intertwining of socio-political rights with both the redistributive and regulative function of the state as well as the liberating competition of the market mechanism, Chinese political economy embodied such rights in the relationship between society and the CCP itself, whilst the social institutions enabling state regulation and market competition constituted tools – to be directed and shaped towards political ends but which give rise to little normative authority themselves. From this perspective, Xi Jinping's consolidation of the CCP's ideological and organizational authority is far from a rupture with the course of reform and opening but rather marks a deepening of a political tradition deeply embedded in Chinese history and society. It represents a determined effort to construct a viable authoritarian capitalism – one that harnesses the power of both state and market in pursuit of the deeper political objectives of CCP-led socio-economic development and national rejuvenation.

The majority of the book was then written in Oxford under the astute guidance of Andrew Hurrell, whose advice and support throughout was invaluable in establishing the core intellectual concerns and tone of the project. At Oxford, I was the beneficiary of a deep and diverse intellectual community stretching across the fields of international relations and Chinese Studies. In particular Shaun Breslin, Sarah Eaton, Kalypso Nicolaïdis, and Eric Thun provided insightful and invaluable feedback at various stages, improving the final manuscript considerably. St Antony's College itself was not just a vibrant and multi-faceted hub of intellectual activity that I was fortunate to be a member of, but also provided financial support via the Wai Seng Senior Research Scholarship in Asia-Pacific Studies for which I am particularly indebted. Beyond St Antony's I have received financial support from many sources, but in particular I am also extremely grateful to the Chiang Ching-Kuo Foundation for funding the latter stages of the project, to the University of California at Berkeley for funding language studies in Beijing at the Inter-University Program for Chinese Studies, and to the Department of Politics and International Relations for funding fieldwork throughout the project. The receipt of a Future Research Leaders Fellowship from the UK Economic and Social Research Council (ES/N001982/1) also made further research and revisions possible on the manuscript.

Beyond Oxford, a number of institutions and individuals were instrumental in enabling the course of research. My discussions and seminars in Cologne whilst visiting the Max Planck Institute for the Study of Societies were particularly valuable in establishing the theoretical parameters of the project and opening up new lines of inquiry to me, and I would like to thank the staff and researchers at the institute not only for their financial support, but also for making my time in Cologne such an enjoyable one. In the course of revisions, I benefited considerably from the manuscript development sessions held at the University of Warwick, and the valuable feedback and support provided by those attending. It has also been a pleasure to work with Manchester University Press, and I am particularly grateful also to the two reviewers whose comments on the text helped improve it considerably. Since I began working on this project, a number of scholars and practitioners have generously shared their insights, networks, and suggestions with me. Amongst others still, Jamil Anderlini, Bilal Baloch, Quentin Bruneau, Tobias ten Brink, Greg Chin, Martin Chorzempa, Jerry Cohen, Rogier Creemers, Claire Du, Matt Ferchen, Rosemary Foot, Thomas Gold, Sandra Heep, Sebastian Heilmann, Huang Wei, Scott Kennedy, Chris Kutarna, Wendy Leutert, Tracy Li, Vic Li, LJ Liu, Kun-Chin Lin, Anton Malkin, Christopher McNally, Miguel Otero-Iglesias, Lou Pauly, Simon Rabinovitch, Chris Sampson, Henry Sanderson, Vivienne Shue, Wolfgang Streeck, Marc Szepan, Carl Walter, Ann Wang, Logan Wright, Wang Jue, Wang Yingyao, Wang Yong, Xiao Geng, Xu Jiajun, Xu Qiyuan, and Lea Yu all did their part in shaping the course of the research.

My lengthy stint of fieldwork in China was possible only with the help of a number of people. Zhu Tianbiao at the Peking University School of Government and Gao Haihong and Zhang Ming at the Chinese Academy of Social Sciences all provided invaluable institutional support and intellectual guidance, and their efforts were complemented by many others at both institutions. This extends especially to all those within the various institutions and organizations of China's financial ecosystem who shared their time, opinions, and hospitality with me during those months of talking, not just in airless meeting rooms but also over tennis, hotpot, or *baijiu*, sometimes all three. Some I now count as friends as well as spirited interlocutors, but to all of them I can only say that this research would not have been possible without you, and I want to express my heartfelt gratitude. My teachers at the Inter-University Program at Tsinghua University were all wonderful, especially 许老师 who was an endless source of motivation and support. The inestimable Peter Knaack also arrived in my life at this time as both a wonderful friend and inspiring colleague. My Beijing existence proved full of surprises, and Kirie Stromberg and Rosalyn Shih were especially treasured companions along this path. I'm grateful to them and many other friends for making my life in Beijing the enriching experience that it was.

Finally, I thank my family – Rick, Yeats, and Adrian – for shaping, supporting, and surviving my intellectual career in too many ways to describe with any eloquence here. Above all, they encouraged me always to follow my own path and provided the love and support with which I was able to do this. Despite the distances across which the Gruins are now dispersed around the world, they are always close to my heart.

Note

1   Interview 14 December 2012, Beijing – Bank of China.

Abbreviations

ABC	Agricultural Bank of China
ADBC	Agricultural Development Bank of China
AFC	Asian financial crisis
AMC	Asset management company
BIS	Bank for International Settlements
BOC	Bank of China
BOCOM	Bank of Communications
CASS	Chinese Academy of Social Sciences
CBRC	China Banking Regulatory Commission
CCB	China Construction Bank
CCP	Communist Party of China
CDB	China Development Bank
CFDIWC	Central Financial Discipline and Inspection Work Commission
CFELG	Central Finance and Economic Leading Group
CFELSG	Central Finance and Economic Leading Small Group
CFWC	Central Financial Work Commission
CIC	China Investment Corporation
CISP	Credit Information Sharing Platform
COD	Central Organization Department
CRC	Credit Reference Center
CSRC	China Securities Regulatory Commission
DFS	Digital financial services
EIBC	Export-Import Bank of China
FDI	Foreign direct investment

GDP	Gross domestic product
GITIC	Guangdong International Trust and Investment Company
HKSE	Hong Kong Stock Exchange
ICBC	Industrial and Commercial Bank of China
ICT	Information and communications technology
ITIC	International trust and investment company
JSCB	Joint-stock commercial bank
LGFV	Local government financing vehicle
MOF	Ministry of Finance
NBCI	Non-bank credit intermediation
NBFI	Non-bank financial institution
NDRC	National Development and Reform Commission
NIFA	National Internet Finance Association
NPL	Non-performing loan
NSSFC	National Social Security Fund Council
PBOC	People's Bank of China
PRC	People's Republic of China
PSC	Politburo Standing Committee
RCC	Rural credit cooperative
REER	Real effective exchange rate
RMB	Renminbi
RRR	Reserve ratio requirement
SAFE	State Administration of Foreign Exchange
SCS	Social Credit System
SHSE	Shanghai Stock Exchange
SME	Small and medium enterprise
SOCB	State-owned commercial bank
SOE	State-owned enterprise
SZSE	Shenzhen Stock Exchange
TIC	Trust and investment company
WMP	Wealth management product
WTO	World Trade Organization

1

State, market, and the Party
in Chinese capitalism

Whether a little more plan, or a little more market; this is not the
fundamental difference between socialism and capitalism. The plan
and the market are both economic tools.

Deng Xiaoping (1993)[1]

The Party is everywhere, in all institutions, and [with] influence
over all people. But the way it works is invisible, like in that
American movie *Fight Club*. The first rule is that you don't talk
about it.

Beijing investment banker[2]

Since Deng spoke at the outset of the reform era of the construction of 'real' banks (Han 1995), the ongoing reform of the
financial sector has left it unclear to many – observers and participants alike – exactly what this role is and what it should be.
Nevertheless, the CCP's pursuit of an increasingly efficient economy whilst guarding against any political risk has been premised
upon its capacity to retain control over the flow of capital and the
related preservation of monetary and fiscal autonomy. In this way,
the course of market-oriented economic reform, even as it has
redefined the relative role of the state, has simultaneously intensified the political-economic importance of the CCP. Out of an
analysis of how the financial system has been deployed by the CCP
since the conception of the socialist market economy following
the 1989 Tiananmen Square protests, this book sheds light on how
the CCP has constructed capitalism. This is a capitalism that has

1

not only reshaped but itself has also adapted to the social structures of contemporary China, and in ways that now defy the traditional analytic categories of Western political economy.

I examine how this process of 'communists constructing capitalism' has been underpinned by historically distinctive cognitive frames concerning the relationship between financial capital and socio-political authority. These frames are a product of deeply embedded social norms and structures coalescing with the opportunities and constraints – both discursive and material – generated through China's interaction with the global political economy. Accordingly, the financial system has continuously occupied a unique position at the centre of the broader political economy. Through analysis of the path of financial reform since the early 1990s, I trace the implications of the duality of the role that it fulfilled under the aegis of CCP control, firstly as an economically effective mechanism for financial intermediation within the real economy, and secondly as a politically effective mechanism for preserving centralized power and authority over the benefits of that financial intermediation. The institutional and regulatory reforms that took place during the 1990s and 2000s do not overshadow the continuity of this function. Indeed, as will be discussed in later chapters, those reforms were in many ways structured specifically around the need to preserve the integrity of this duality.

The development of the banking system is less a story of obstructed or stalled reform, but more one of a commitment to pressing against the limits of the growth model and engaging in a form of brinksmanship with the financial crisis in an effort to secure enough material wealth in order to ameliorate the effects of capitalist accumulation. This effort to 'buy time' through accumulation, and to 'do enough' to address social conflict and preserve social stability, is what distinguishes the modern epoch of capitalist accumulation from either a traditional conception of free market laissez-faire capitalism or of the true ideal of the developmental state. This was the guiding principle that has accompanied reform since the early 1990s, and it can still be witnessed today as the

2

CCP continues to actively engineer the process of development in a way that ameliorates the worst excesses of capitalist growth. More broadly, it serves ultimately as a demonstration of just how antithetical capitalism is to democracy. The role of the CCP in constructing an authoritarian capitalist society illuminates not just how the development of capitalism has affected China, but how China affects our conceptions of capitalism.

These arguments engage two long-standing conceptual fractures in contemporary political economy. The first concerns the relationship between the domestic (or the local) and its relationship to the international (or the global), the second that between the political logics of the state and the economic logics of the market. How the political problem is resolved in China via the economic, and moreover how the economic solution is in turn underpinned by the political, is one of the most central and intriguing aspects of China's path to reform and opening.[3] This process is in turn connected intimately to the evolution of the global political economy, as capitalist development has come to form the central objective of reform-era Chinese society. Recognizing the extent of the interpenetration of the political and the economic transforms the question of how China 'became' capitalist. Rather than one of the waxing and waning of state economic power and the political agency of private economic actors as China embarked on a new era of development, it becomes one of how structurally entrenched imperatives – both domestic and international – are constraining certain individuals, networks, and institutions whilst generating political resources for others, within an increasingly interdependent global system.

The book therefore addresses these fractures between the universal and the local, and the political and the economic, by approaching the 'China question' from an alternative perspective – one that de-emphasizes the state versus market dichotomy and instead focuses on the socio-economic foundations of power and authority that manifest through the financial system. At the core of a global political economy that has given rise to these analytical fractures reside multiple systems for mediating the flow of capital and resources necessary for modern economic activity and production. Finance – and more specifically financial capital – penetrates the political realm as well as the economic, whilst also forming a critical set of linkages between the domestic and the international within the global political economy. This leads to the question of finance and its duality of purpose – as a system of financial intermediation as well as political control. It further points towards how the role of China's financial system is crucial in China's emergence into the global political economy as breaking down barriers between not only the political and the economic, but also between the local and the universal. This book speaks not only to the study of China's political economy and the theoretical and conceptual debates that surround this endeavour, but also to more fundamental questions concerning how the universal coalesces with the local at the point of what remains fundamentally but not exclusively the international.

In this manner the book seeks to answer Kellee Tsai's call for scholarship to better 'show what China can do for political science, both empirically and analytically' (Tsai 2013, 860). It does so in three related ways. First, it provides an insight into the nature of China's socialist market economy, probing China's development as a resiliently non-liberalized *political* economy that underpinned stable, rapid, and yet unsustainable economic growth. This is an empirical paradox that has not yet been adequately addressed, and I place the role of the CCP at the heart of this examination. The role of the financial system in China's development has, as for all other financial systems in the world, been underpinned by a set of ideas and institutions that enable socio-political uncertainty to be evaluated, financial risk to be managed, and economic activity to be undertaken. The book shows how this process in China has revolved, not around an equilibrium reached between state regulation and market freedom, but around the role of the CCP as the primary source of confidence and faith in financial stability and economic growth.

This gives rise to the book's second objective, which is to explore how such a perspective overcomes some of the limitations

4

of studying the political economy of financial capitalism that arise through a focus upon the distinct institutional categories of the state and the market. The role of the CCP as conceptualized in this book illustrates the difficulties of relying upon these categories to understand the intersection of universal logics of economic development and the particular social institutions through which these logics manifest. The study represents an attempt to overcome these conceptual limitations and provide a means of grappling with the empirical problem of explaining paradoxical trends in China's politico-economic development at the same time as generating insight into what China's post-1989 financial development can tell us about the nature of contemporary political economy as contemporary *capitalist* political economy.

The third objective of the book is accordingly to place these investigations in the context of the long-run evolution of the global political economy and to destabilize conceptions of China as 'just another actor' that is still comprehensible on the basis of concepts and theories of socio-economic action rooted in 'Western political economy'. China's experience of financial reform and economic growth demonstrates the significant scope for reconfiguring understandings of how financial systems affect the course of socioeconomic development within contemporary global capitalism. The distinctiveness of the interaction between political authority and financial capital in China has the potential to profoundly disrupt the presumed resilience of the global liberal order, even as capitalism itself as a mode of social organization comes to be increasingly entrenched within this global order.

An ongoing puzzle: the socialist market economy

Xi Jinping's remarkable political ascent, reaching its peak at the Nineteenth Party Congress in late 2017, has starkly highlighted the twin faces of China's evolving capitalism: a resiliently illiberal authoritarian political system in conjunction with increasingly market-oriented economic reform and restructuring. He has emerged as not only the most powerful Chinese leader in decades, but also the most committed ideologically to the intertwining of the CCP's fate with that of the Chinese nation. In addition to contributing his eponymous philosophy to the CCP's constitutional canon and embarking on a historic campaign of both Party-cleansing and Party-building, he rapidly consolidated his dominance over the policymaking institutions of Party, state, and military with his creation at the 2013 third plenum of two new central leading groups – one for State Security [国家安全领导小组], another for Comprehensively Deepening Reform [全面深化改革领导小组]. Through his leadership of these two crucial bodies, he therefore obtained 'omnipotent power' (Zheng and Gore 2015), which he has wielded across all areas of society, media, and the Party itself. Amongst a plethora of others, these groups at the apex of the Party's policymaking apparatus symbolize the concurrent enmeshment of political and economic issues under Xi's sole authority. The separation of politics and economics, at most a tenuous conceptual fiction in the most liberal or laissez-faire of societies, is now thoroughly non-existent in Xi's China.

Although heated debates continue around the nature of China's 'intra-party democracy' [党内民主主义] (Bell 2015), the overall trend towards a deepening of centralized authoritarian control under the CCP is clear to see. There is considerable evidence of the institutionalized underpinnings of the CCP's resilience (see Gore 2014; Zeng 2014; cf. Li 2012; Fewsmith and Nathan 2018), and Xi Jinping's efforts to further consolidate personalized political power should be viewed in terms of continuity of a long-standing trend, rather than a rupture with it. At the same time as clamping down on political expression and other civil liberties, Xi Jinping entered office committed to economic reform, vocally exclaiming 'market decisiveness' [市场的决定性] as a core element of China's future economic trajectory (Naughton 2014). On top of this is the drive towards 'national rejuvenation' [国家复兴] and the aspirational sloganeering surrounding the realization of the 'Chinese Dream' [中国梦]. Even though the ideological thicket of the political discourse emanating from Beijing can often seem as if it is deliberately intended to obfuscate as much as clarify, the common thread remains the leadership and unquestioned authority of the CCP.

The dilemma of Chinese governance to which the CCP is responding in such fashion was posed by Wang Huning (1988, 1) in his early writings on centre–local relations:

If power is not transferred to the lower level it will be impossible to invigorate the economy and move it toward modernization; but the transfer of power to the lower level brings with it extremely great difficulties to the regulation and control by the political system.

As I argue in this book, any system of Chinese governance inevitably has roots in the historical development of Chinese society and is deeply embedded in Chinese cultural norms and attitudes towards financial capital itself. Although the CCP has marshalled increasing and enhanced authority over the institutions of state and market, it is by no means a recent development, and the Party's current organizational and ideological reinvigoration under Xi Jinping can be seen as the latest incarnation of the attempt to grapple with a long-standing dilemma of Chinese governance.

These intertwined paths of political and economic change are embodied in the evolving concept of the 'socialist market economy' [社会主义市场经济], and particularly in the nature of the financial capital at its heart. Much scholarly and popular discourse tends not to provide very good answers to the question of how and why the financial underpinnings of this system operate as they do. Although recent work has explored these deeper ideational underpinnings of economic reform in the state-owned sector and strategic industries (Eaton 2016), there is a peculiar lack of similarly rigorous analysis that homes in on the role of the financial sector in supporting this process. Both in China and throughout Western commentary, the dynamics of financial reform and of restructuring the state-owned industrial and manufacturing sectors are often perceived in terms of the challenge of identifying and realizing rational developmental principles. According to this view, political power struggles between 'conservatives' and 'reformers' in Beijing are relevant insofar as they may threaten to derail or delay these efforts, but do not determine what is considered to be the most rational developmental policy (Lardy 1998; Huang 2008; Shih 2008; Walter and Howie 2011; Nee and Opper 2012). These accounts tend to analyse the development of China's political economy against an implicit counterfactual of (for example) the World Bank's nine components of what is 'generally considered to constitute a comprehensive reform program' (Hellman 1998, 223), and in so doing come to conflate reform with market liberalization.

Yet it is increasingly clear that change in China's political economy, and especially within China's financial sector, is not necessarily predicated on a teleological conception of a system that will eventually come to resemble a liberal market democracy. The assumptions underlying these mainstream analyses deflect attention away from more nuanced consideration of the kind of market economy that reform is directed towards. This book presents evidence that a key underlying reason for the unique and peculiar path of financial reform since the early and mid-1990s has been the CCP's active and deliberate construction of a financial system that would serve both the economic function of economic growth and accumulation as well as the political function of continued CCP control. In making this argument, this account complements existing partial explanations, militating against relying exclusively upon interest-based and institutional frameworks in order to explain the dynamics of financial reform. It was neither factional stalemate between Jiang Zemin and Zhu Rongji (Shih 2008), the urban biases of the increasingly technocratic leadership (Huang 2008), nor vested interests entrenched in the under-performing state-owned sector (Lardy 1998), that should be considered the root cause of 'illiberal' financial reform. These existing narratives each miss elements of the overall trajectory of reform and, more importantly, miss the profound implications of what was in fact a much more concerted intersubjective understanding of the bases for growth, reform, and development that were embodied within the financial system.

Shih's factional account of elite politics in the 1990s rests upon the observation that, 'unlike the usual portrayal of technocrats who were either agents to political principals or "insulated" technocrats operating beyond the pull of politics, technocrats in China were highly politicized' (Shih 2008, 160). However, the political and economic demands upon the top leadership came to produce as much a cohesiveness of perspective as much as factional infighting. Shih's factional model generates a degree of insight into how personal political priorities sewed discord between members of the CCP elite in the waning years of Deng Xiaoping's authority. However, it provides very little sense of how the CCP was capable of so effectively mitigating the excesses of these inflationary cycles, the extent to which its approach to reform of the financial system itself was crucial to this success, and why this would ultimately produce a political economy that bound together the interests of both state, market, and society in the uninterrupted pursuit of economic growth. As Cheng Li (2016) has observed in discussing China's peculiar brand of 'bipartisanship':

> From a collective perspective, both [factional] camps share fun-
> damental goals: maintaining China's political and social stability,
> promoting continued economic growth, enhancing China's status
> as a major international player, and, most important, ensuring the
> survival of CCP rule.

As a result, almost entirely missing from this literature is the unpacking of the deeper connection between the social and cultural context out of which these political debates emerge and how this context redefines the very basis upon which economic and political rationality is constructed and pursued. Political power struggles are themselves rooted in and resolved by ideological contests (Tu 1993). Indeed, as Misra (1998, 8) has argued, 'the interaction between ideas, ideology, power conflicts, and policy formation is much more complex than is conceded by the power-interest and bureaucratic politics approaches'. One must turn to a deeper

9

stratum of analysis in order to understand the social, discursive, and ideological foundations of China's economic development.

Approaching the study of China's political economy in this manner therefore does not directly challenge other theories of decision-making in contemporary China. Accounts of China's reform trajectory derived from concepts of the developmental state, models of bureaucratic power politics, complementarities of institutional design, or bargaining dynamics of central–local relations each offer useful insights into China's historical and current path of development. However, if the goal is instead to explain not just economic growth and macroeconomic stability, but also the broader question of how these dynamics are embedded in a longer-run trajectory of sociocultural and politico-economic evolution, then it is necessary to develop a dynamic theory that could 'capture the forces producing change in the system' (Oksenberg 2001, 28). In his attempt to do more than simply provide a static description of that system, Oksenberg (2001, 28) could do little more than point to idiosyncratic and ad hoc factors that were 'generating an evolution of the system, but in an incoherent and uncoordinated fashion', concluding that 'increasingly, the system has a disjointed, byzantine quality to it'. In developing a theory of the CCP and its relationship to financial capital, the goal is therefore not to entirely supplant other frameworks of Chinese political economy, but to generate a greater analytic coherence to the diverse multitude of factors that are driving China's political economy.

The CCP's sinews of financial governance

The central importance of the CCP in the increasingly modern and rationalized institutional fabric of contemporary Chinese society thus comes more sharply into focus. The principles through which the CCP underpins Chinese society have a systemic quality; they permeate the institutions of the political economy and its governance, such that the operation of formal institutions is infused and overlaid with what amounts to a non-state and non-market set of institutional dynamics. As it has presided over an increasing

10

rationalization of the various structures of governance, the CCP has also rationalized itself as a 'governing party' (Heath 2014), embracing such concepts such as 'scientific management' [科学管理], 'system-building' [体系建设], 'regularization' [正规化], and 'institutionalization' [制度化]. The process of building a modern capitalist state bureaucracy in no way entails what many believed to be an eventual withering away of the Party's central role, but rather involves enhancing the function of the state as a tool – itself in turn overseeing the market as a tool – in service of the CCP's overarching developmental mission and vision of society.

China's banking system has increasingly come to resemble the institutional configuration of any other modern system of financial intermediation, and yet the core feature of financial institutions in China remains their duality of function under the authority of the CCP (Gruin 2013), transforming in turn the nature of financial markets and the broader institutional fabric of capital itself. Modes of technical management through 'Western' concepts of banking supervision and regulation are established, but Chinese institutions and principles distinctively influence the manner in which they work. Capital is transformed from a tool for the exercise of ostensibly market power, into a tool for the market-situated exercise not of state power, but the power of a group of actors whose role is inextricably bound up with both the productive functions of the market but also the governance functions of the state. Stent (2017, 20) describes the resulting hybrid character of Chinese banks as:

> neither wholly a creature of the market, nor wholly an agent of the state ... they are viewed by the government ultimately in instrumental fashion. Banks exist to play a role in the overall economy, the financial intermediation role. They are a means to an end, not the end in itself. In creating this hybrid culture of banks, China attempts to have its cake and eat it too – realize the efficiency of market-driven, competitive management, while at the same time retaining ultimate control of the banking sector and guiding bank operations at the macro level in support of broad economic policy.

11

To achieve this, the CCP functions as an organizationally distinct and coherent system of policy development, promulgation, implementation, and enforcement. As it has embraced the conceptual framework and institutional architectures of a socialist market economy, the CCP has nevertheless adapted itself and its relations to other governance structures in order to consolidate its real authority over a rapidly evolving political economy. Developing the effective duality of the financial system as a mechanism for macroeconomic governance and financial intermediation, and thus as a mechanism for economic growth and political control, has relied heavily upon the ability of the leadership to diffuse its policy preferences and priorities. Party discipline was at the core of Zhu Rongji's (2013 [1993], 134) emphasis upon the 'unification of thinking' [统一思想] and reconciling the disparate elements of the newly emerging institutional function of the banking system. Although the state apparatus continued to fulfil its functional role in crafting industrial policy, drawing up the credit plan, and issuing guidance to bank managers, it was the CCP that was necessary to set the underlying objectives and parameters of these functions, as well as ensure that the state fulfilled them.

The Party operates through horizontal and vertical networks of coordination and hierarchy intended to provide a uniform set of understandings of central CCP priorities and objectives, which are then reinforced through overlapping networked bonds of *guanxi*, meaning dyadic social ties (关系), and reciprocal obligation. This is evident throughout China's financial elites, who constitute a dense and overlapping network of Party cadres that connect all the important entities in the financial system and comprise the core of China's governance regime for finance.[4] As the process of marketization unfolded, the need to establish modern institutions of finance came to clash and then be resolved with the system of 'parallel rule' that had been adopted from the Soviet model of 'police-patrol' oversight (Shirk 1993, 57–8). Parallel rule ensures that the Party is responsible for all important appointments of officials within the financial system, that it possesses a strong organizational presence in the form of Party committees in every financial institution, and that financial institutions can be directed to pursue national economic objectives (Stent 2017). As Pistor (2013, 3) has argued in relation to the control over appointment of financial elites by the CCP,

> [Human resources management] has become a substitute to direct state control, which was still pervasive in China until the end of the 1990s, and a complement to the new rule-based formal mechanisms of control. The CCP's control over [HRM] intensified as the state apparatus loosened its direct control over the financial system.

The para-institutional network that is the CCP cadre system is rooted in the Party's 'position-list' [职务名称表] system, at its core a list of positions for approximately 5000 Party officials [中共中央管理干部职务名称表].[5] It is administered by the Organization Department of the CCP, a highly secretive yet incredibly influential Party organ.[6] As one Ministry of Finance (MOF) official stated in relation to the contemporary role of financial elites, 'the chairmen of the large banks cannot be said to be purely bankers. They are politicians.'[7] At the heart of this remains a focus on the incentive structure for banking management and behaviour. The social responsibility *and* political fidelity of senior banking management must be achieved, whether through informal moral persuasion or through overt material measures, and constitutes a fundamental component in achieving a balance between profit and responsibility. As Liu Mingkang, then head of the CBRC, pointed out in 2008, 'whether the incentives for increased performance are sourced in market profits or social advancement, regulatory and governance structures must be capable of achieving this balance' (Liu Mingkang 2008a).

Horizontally, during the 1990s, the appointment of all leading financial cadres was overseen by the Central Organization Department (COD) under the 1990 position-list.[8] The capacity of the Party to control the transfer and promotion of these cadres was strengthened, as cadres such as Zhou Xiaochuan, Wang Qishan, Dai Xianglong, Liu Mingkang, Guo Shuqing, and Shang

Fulin were rotated progressively through the primary financial institutions that were emerging in the early 1990s: the five SOCBs, three policy banks, the People's Bank of China (PBOC), the CBRC, the China Securities Regulatory Commission (CSRC), and the State Administration of Foreign Exchange (SAFE). One former SOCB party committee member described this process of rotation and placement in the following terms:

> They don't think the same way, but all of the top financial guys have spent their careers being moved around by the Party, through the central bank, the state banks, the regulators. They have different ideas about how to do it, but they all know that their careers depend on protecting the Party. And the ones who are at the top now, they were groomed beginning in the early 1990s.[9]

Vertically, they functioned through hierarchical injunctions and the instillation of Party discipline amongst cadres. After every major Party meeting or financial work conference, comprehensive Party-led study meetings were convened in order to determine how to implement the objectives and realize the intentions of central leaders. For example, in 1993 following the Fourteenth Party Congress at which the goal of constructing a socialist market economy was proclaimed, the Bank of Communications organized meetings for all branch managers to meet, at which the Bank President Dai Xianglong, who would later be appointed governor of the PBOC in 1995, gave a speech that laid out his vision of a 'socialist commercial bank' (Dai 1993). The role and duty of cadres within state-owned firms is thus to provide moral and political leadership, frequently through political and ideological study sessions, a role that has not only retained its salience through the reform era but which has been progressively upgraded and enhanced since the late 1990s (Heath 2014). Another former SOCB Party committee member recalls the manner in which they were compelled to read, study, and then debate Dai Xianglong's 'instructional handbook' (Dai 2001) for leading cadres involved in financial work.[10]

These organizational features are necessary but insufficient elements of economic governance that also secure the CCP's political endurance. Functions are not objectively assigned to institutions and organizations, nor are they structurally immutable. Rather, it is the social acceptance of these institutions and, crucially, the terms of that acceptance that are significant. CCP authority rests ultimately on the ideological integrity of its status as the sole guarantor of Chinese economic and social development. As later chapters explore, when transposed into the context of financial development it is this status that reduces uncertainty, generates confidence and faith, and thereby generates an underlying basis for financial activity and investment. At a general level, the guiding ideology of 'socialism with Chinese characteristics' constitutes a sociologically performative system of thought that not only provides substantive guidance on the principal contradictions of Chinese development, but also justifies the CCP's undisputed authority to define and resolve these contradictions.

China's challenge to contemporary political economy

Integral to any attempt to understand the process by which China's communists constructed capitalism is the challenge of identifying the drivers of change in China's political economy. The second major argument I develop in this book is that the difficulties encountered in making adequate sense of China's political economy reflect deeper issues in dominant perspectives in political economy. These issues revolve largely around how we conceptualize the state and the market, recognized as the 'key controversy' (Zhao 2017, 7) at the centre of debates over China's economic development. At its core, this can be distilled to a problematic broader tendency to view political economy as largely constituted by a mutually antagonistic relationship between a regulatory state and a competitive market.[11]

Although recent advances in the political economy of development have enabled much more nuanced perspectives on the interrelationship between state regulation and market

15

competition, China's experience of development provokes us to further examine the concepts that we use as proxies for these political and economic dynamics. Abrams (1988, 58) describes this problem of reification elegantly: 'The state is not the reality which stands behind the mask of political practice. It is itself the mask which prevents us from seeing political practice as it is.' Although market actors and state actors are real, markets and states themselves are not. They possess agency only as conceptually delimited bundles of individuals, institutions, and ideas. Given that markets and states are not immutable, objective facts, it makes sense to think of them not as 'real', but 'as if real' (Hay 2014), an ontological distinction that passes with little fanfare in everyday practice, but which comes to be analytically important when developing social scientific concepts that travel across both space and time.

Although these are conceptual issues that afflict analytical frameworks across the fields of international and comparative political economy (see Underhill 2000; Underhill and Zhang 2005), they are especially acute in the case of China, for which there is a temptation to regard much of the actual operating practices of governance as anomalous and analytically insignificant, insofar as they fail to fit more or less neatly into one of the existing foundational conceptual categories of political economy: the state or the market. State intervention is either praised as an effective developmental mechanism, or it is condemned as a harmful obstacle to an efficient set of market mechanisms. These prevailing perspectives are simplified and depicted in Table 1.1. An orthodox 'competitive markets perspective' account of China's banking reform generally traces the gradual uncoupling of the banking sector from direct state control, arguing for the incompleteness of this process of graduating from state-directed lending to profit-driven capital allocation (Lardy 1998; Pei 1998; 2006; Kwong 2011; Walter and Howie 2011). Rooted in a linear and unidirectional market transition theory (Nee 1989; Nee and Opper 2012), the competitive markets perspective assumes that increasing marketization, consolidation of property rights, and the assumption of financial risk

16

Table 1.1. Perspectives on Chinese economic development

	Driver of economic growth	Driver of economic distortion
Competitive markets	Economic entrepreneurship	Rent-seeking/corporate monopoly
Developmental state	Developmental technocracy	Corruption/state monopoly

by private actors within the financial sector will deliver greater economic efficiency and greater social equality.[12] Much of this literature on the role of the financial system in affecting the path of socio-economic development focuses upon the relationship between financial liberalization and economic growth (McKinnon 1973; Shaw 1973), and evidence of the positive correlation between the two (Roubini and Sala-i-Martin 1992; Levine 2005). However, as a result of this focus, such approaches approach the paradox of China's development by addressing only two cells of Table 1.1: growth-generating competition on the part of private actors, and growth-retarding corruption or monopoly on the part of public actors (Lü 2000; Bernstein and Xiaobo 2003). The existence of effective state capacity, and the financial elites that underpin it, are regarded as epiphenomenal at best, and as accentuating corruption and vested interests at worst.

Alternative accounts of China's banking and financial reforms, under the label of the 'developmental state perspective', dispute that China's financial sector has necessarily performed in such a suboptimal manner as is commonly argued. The developmental state perspective also places analytical emphasis upon only two of the cells of the table; however, conversely this time it is active state developmentalism that is viewed as largely responsible for facilitating such rapid economic growth (Knight 2014). These perspectives are problematic because they are each characterized by the assumption that the institutions of the market and the state are inherently driven by distinct logics of action, leading them to unjustified predilections for either emphasizing the negative (the competitive markets perspective) or the positive (the developmental state perspective) outcomes of a state-controlled and financially repressed banking sector.

By problematizing the concept of the state as a macro-holistic actor, China scholars have taken valuable steps in probing the nuanced balance between state and market forces in China's economic development. Walder (1995) and Oi (1995) have identified the importance of local state actors in driving China's growth, thus adding another dimension to the market transition theory, one which involves a transfer of economic power from central to local authorities. This strand of literature rightly draws attention to the fact that the devolution of both authority over both capital and policy development has been a crucial factor in catalysing local institutional adaptation and accelerating economic development (Naughton 1995). Yet these arguments nevertheless do not directly address a key question of the relationship between these two dimensions of institutional change in the reform era: whether decentralization entails more market or merely a reconfiguration of state authority. Notwithstanding significant devolution to lower levels of government and the accompanying competitive dynamics between local authorities, the role of the state vis-à-vis the market is still considered to remain largely intact. With her 'co-evolutionary' framework of directed improvisation between state bureaucratic institutions and entrepreneurial competition, Ang (2016) has made a significant contribution to our understanding of how economic growth necessarily entails an iterative dynamic between institutional development and market dynamism. Nevertheless, she pays less attention to the sociological glue that binds and guides actors across both the state-market and centre–local divide.

One of the central objectives of this book is to provide an alternative to the conceptual antimony between state and market, by pointing to the way in which *capitalist* economic development – as distinct from some timeless and ahistorical conception of either *state-led* or *market-led* development – rests upon contingent foundations that are both socially embedded and historically situated. Such social embeddedness enables actors straddling the public and the private – thus fusing together the state and the market – to coordinate social action in ways that can produce dynamic economic growth, yet also produce a concentration of power that shapes how that growth takes place and whom it benefits. Examining this social embeddedness in the context of the CCP and its relationship to the socialist market economy enables us to refine our theories of Chinese political economy, and to more effectively draw upon the Chinese experience and reflect on theories of political economy that have emerged out of the Western historical experience.

Jettisoning these assumptions involves a recognition that even as the integration of global production and the transnationalization of financial activity has brought 'transitional' and 'developing' countries firmly within the realm of the global capitalist system, the experience of reform-era China serves as a clear reminder that the processes of capitalist production can take place through socioculturally variegated and historically contingent institutional structures. As such, capitalism is a constellation of logics of action and cognitive dispositions, not a set of preordained economic arrangements that may be deductively conceived and assessed in a reductionist manner. Consequently, whilst the ideas and practices of capitalism transform those societies with which they come into contact, the historical lineages and cultural norms of societies in turn have profound consequences for the manifestation of capitalist ideas and practices.

This opens up the possibility of exploring an alternative perspective that recasts the political economy as displaying significant functional similarities between the institutions of the state and the market. On this view, China's banking sector constitutes a set of both discursive and structural institutions that fuse together state and market actors, embodying a substantially different confluence of rationalities from either that of a commercially oriented system of intermediation premised on the underlying stability and efficiency of profit-seeking market actors, or of a banking sector rationally engineered by a group of wise and visionary bureaucrats. From this vantage point, the institutional reorientation of China's financial system towards the prioritization of economic growth over social egalitarianism is not understood exclusively as

19

the commercialization of lending practices and/or as a process of structural liberalization to open up the system to private capital. Nor should it be understood exclusively as retrenching state-controlled entities as the beneficiaries of directly political exchanges. Rather, the economic and political functions of the financial system conjoin, such that the increasingly commercialized structure of the financial system and the increasingly rationalized activities of financial institutions are directed towards strengthening not just the market economy, but a market economy over which the CCP ultimately remained 'paramount leader', with the ability to 'bang the table' [拍桌],[13] and end the discussion.

In circumstances where such ambiguity exists as to the role of a state-controlled banking sector, it is not enough to retell the story of banking reform in China as simply one of state-embedded bureaucratic politics or of the inexorable pull of market forces. Rather, one must question the timeless quality of these concepts and the largely reified analytic weight that is placed upon them. Contrary to much mainstream political economy, social action cannot be conceptually black-boxed within either the state or the market. To theoretically demarcate these two categories – even for the purposes of studying their interaction – is to assume that for analytic purposes the behaviour of one actor is relevant *insofar* as it contributes to the explanatory significance of either the state or the market as a driver of economic outcomes. The level of institutional interpenetration apparent in Chinese governance as its leaders seek to simultaneously maintain political integrity and generate economic activity should motivate us to dispense with these epithets as theoretical ideal types and instead to look towards new conceptual horizons.

Reconceiving Chinese capitalism

As Chapter 2 of this book makes clear, this begins with placing the current dynamics of Chinese financial reform in the context of a historical process of economic development in which the relationship between the state, the market, and their relationship to patterns of power and authority held different meanings, which were utilized for different purposes. Only upon this basis does it become feasible to undertake a more fundamental conceptual redescription of the financial landscape of contemporary Chinese capitalism and its role within the broader transnational political economy, an objective at the heart of this book.

The central organizing concept for doing so is that of socio-economic uncertainty, the subject of Chapter 3. The challenge of understanding financial governance in circumstances where the dividing lines between public and private are blurred forces us to return to some fundamental questions of how logics of economic activity are generated, changed, and sustained. Focusing on how socio-economic uncertainty affects ideas, institutions, and interests enables the observer to analytically deprioritize the state and the market as proxy independent variables in and of themselves, but instead to treat them as intervening institutional fields through which logics of action can be played out. From this vantage point, the flow of capital through the political economy comes to be seen as modulated in terms of its relation to the socio-political authority of the CCP. Through the exercise of such authority, an ideologically robust and institutionally sophisticated organizational structure at the nexus of state governance and market-active financial institutions is capable of both *managing* socio-economic uncertainty so as to enable productive economic activity whilst also *exploiting* socio-economic uncertainty in order to shape the nature of that activity whilst also preserving political control. The CCP appears thus at the core of a coherent and institutionally flexible system of capitalist accumulation, rather than as either a rigid and ossified authoritarian organization encircled by capitalist market forces or as a committed adherent to the financial and economic liberalization that is often assumed to inevitably accompany economic commercialization and growth.

Socio-economic uncertainty is therefore a concept that takes us a long way in understanding how financial systems are implicated in processes of generating socio-economic stability, as well as variegated socio-political outcomes. The key to CCP control

21

over the broader trajectory of economic development in China has been at once to embrace and control uncertainty. Mechanisms of CCP control reduce uncertainty, even as they concentrate the ability to do so within a particular social grouping. The need for these cognitive and institutional mechanisms for mediating (and thus translating) the social world into a comprehensible environment for action has traditionally been conceived of as being satisfied either by the structures of state regulation or structures of market exchange. In China's emergence as a capitalist political economy, the role of the CCP disturbs these traditional categories of state and market as concepts capable of carrying serious analytical weight, not because the functional characteristics of hierarchical control or contractual exchange as a means of organizing socio-economic reproduction have been eliminated or even necessarily transformed, but rather because the imperatives of power-infused capitalist accumulation find expression in how the CCP itself constructs mechanisms for orienting action towards economic growth as a basis for satisfying the priorities of social stability and order.

Out of this conception of the CCP emerges an alternative means of telling the story of China's financial reform. Rather than pitting mutually opposed logics of the state and market against each other, this book offers an account of economic growth, of financial stability, and of the concentration of political power as the product of what makes society and the political economy hang together, even if only in temporary and unstable constellations of interests and power. In this narrative, reform-era China has been marked by a series of socio-historically contingent critical junctures that have instilled and then retrenched economic growth as a fundamental policy priority, and catalysed a course of ideational and institutional change that has not only enabled economic growth and political authority to coexist, but has also produced a self-reinforcing relationship between a discourse of economic growth and a discourse of stable social development and progress under the political leadership and authority of the CCP. In the aftermath of the political and ideological turmoil of both the Cultural

22

Revolution and the societally traumatic repression of the 1989 protest movements, economic growth came to be viewed as the primary, if not sole, basis for legitimacy. The opening of China's economy during the 1990s, combined with the 1997 Asian financial crisis (AFC), came to reinforce this particular political logic of economic reform (cf. Shirk 1993), and despite the deepening of fundamental imbalances within China's economy during the 2000s, the intertwining of political and economic objectives further propelled efforts to 'build' [建设], 'strengthen' [加强], and 'perfect' [完善] the CCP's central role, even as economic and financial reform proceeded apace.[14] Accordingly, economic activity has flourished, but at the heart of this growth has been the deployment of capital in a particular manner, one that enfolds the power of capital within the political structure.

This role of the CCP emerges out of a historical social order, the 'rationality' of which has been largely occluded in both the historiography of economic development, as well as the theoretical architecture of contemporary political economy. Zheng Yongnian has labelled the CCP the 'organizational emperor', the nature of which as socioculturally embedded has been downplayed as either epiphenomenal or analytically residual in the study of the state and the market from a Western politico-economic perspective.[15] I do not claim that China's contemporary socialism is essentially just the most recent incarnation of the country's age-old tradition of absolutist state power (see Blecher 2003, 1), but argue for the need to adopt a dialectical approach to the rise of the CCP and the patterns of political authority at the centre of which it has come to exist. That is to say, neither the cultural-philosophical foundations of Confucianism that underpinned imperial rule from 221 BCE (Fairbank and Goldman 2006, 51–3), nor a transplanted system of political thought giving rise to a largely endogenous organizational dynamic of CCP rule, should be seen as exclusively responsible for the structuring of contemporary Chinese politics.[16] Rather, the CCP reflects the deep rootedness of *Chinese* modernity within the enduring social orders that have and continue to characterize Chinese society and culture.

Organization of the book

These arguments are based on qualitative fieldwork that took place over the two-year period between April 2012 and April 2014, and between September 2016 and October 2017. Over sixty interviews were conducted with members of the Beijing financial elite. These interviews were conducted in Chinese and English with individuals currently working in or retired from the central ministries and regulatory agencies, the central bank, commercial banks including all of the 'big five' SOCBs, recently emergent information and communications technology (ICT) firms, and a number of government think tanks and universities. These semi-structured interviews lasted on average one hour, and generated direct insights and information about the process of financial policymaking, the role of the CCP networks in the financial system, and the function of the legal and social institutions underpinning financial and economic activity in China. Cumulatively, they provide a rich source of information as to how financial elites and policymakers in China came to manage the ambiguous relationship between state and market by extending the reach of financial capital, but simultaneously consolidating the persistently illiberal authority of the CCP over the use of that capital.

In addition to the data generated by these interviews, I rely upon a variety of primary and secondary materials as key sources of evidence. These can be divided into three categories. First, economic and financial data collected from collections such as *CEIC China Economic Premium* and the *China Statistical Yearbook* [中国统计年鉴] (economic data at national, provincial, and city level) and the *Almanac of China's Finance and Banking* [中国金融年鉴] (financial sector data). Regulations, policies, and decrees are found in sources such as *A Collection of Financial Regulations and Systems* [金融规章制度选编]. Second, the research is strengthened by consulting Chinese secondary literature as well as media coverage of financial reform. This secondary literature includes a number of internal government journals including *Financial Reference* [金融参考], *Financial Statistics and Analysis* [金融统计与分析], *Financial Research Report* [金融研究报告], *Internal Reference of Reform* [改革内参], and *Leader's Policy-Making Information* [领导决策信息]. Finally the book also draws upon academic journal articles and monographs written by financial elites and policymakers, including records of key thinkers and decision-makers such as Wu Jinglian 吴敬琏, Xue Muqiao 薛暮桥, Chen Jinhua 陈锦华, Zhu Rongji 朱镕基, Dai Xianglong 戴相龙, and Zhou Xiaochuan周小川. These records significantly assist us in tracing the path of reform within the financial sector and connecting ideas and discourses to policies and outcomes.

The book unfolds over seven chapters. Chapter 2 positions the current study of China's evolving capitalism in the broader context of China's historical politico-economic evolution, and the significance of a distinction between a market economy and a capitalist economy for the study of contemporary political economy. Underlying the current debate as to the nature of China's state capitalism both in a comparative and a global context remains the challenge of better understanding the role of socio-political authority in underpinning different modes of economic development. I reassess the concept of rational action and argue that the Eurocentrism that has dominated debates as to why China 'failed' to develop capitalism is the same Eurocentrism that has reified the conceptual state and market as the definitive analytic categories of Western political economy. This connects with the concerns outlined above as to the difficulties of reconciling China's contemporary economic transformation with the fact that its political system remains firmly rooted in what some still view as the pre-modern, as well as retaining lineages of a decidedly modern socialist era. Thus, it is only by way of understanding contemporary capitalism as more than the various configurations of state and market institutions – as the broad literature surrounding varieties of capitalism would reduce it to – that we can begin to make sense of China's otherwise highly paradoxical path of development. More specifically, it opens up the theoretical space for conceptualizing the role of the CCP as an integral element of this evolving capitalist enterprise.

Chapter 3 develops an analytic framework for understanding how the financial system underpins a particular path of politico-economic development. First it examines how the concept of uncertainty and its relationship to financial risk is fundamental to making socio-economic action possible, a process with both economic and political implications. The management of uncertainty not only generates the potential for economic growth, but also contains the mechanisms for structuring that growth in particular ways. The chapter thus embeds the role of the CCP in sociocultural and historical context, reconceptualizing it as the key locus of authority around which this management and exploitation of uncertainty takes place in Chinese capitalism.

Chapters 4 to 6 trace the role of the financial sector in China's broader strategy and path of economic growth and development between 1990 and 2012. Chapter 4 focuses on the period 1990–97. The politico-economic retrenchment following the social protest movement and events in Tiananmen Square that unfolded in June 1989 would lay the basis for economic revitalization, but along lines very different from a liberal free-market ideal. The chapter examines this legacy of neoconservative ascendancy in the aftermath of 1989, combined with Deng Xiaoping's successful reassertion of economic growth and development as the foremost economic, political, and social priority. Together, these laid the basis for a path of reform that combined an effort to increase the commercial effectiveness and rationality of the financial system with the reconsolidation of centralized political authority, and an upgrading of the political and ideological cohesion of the most significant and critical sectors of the political economy at the time; the banks and the state-owned industrial firms. In doing so, the financial foundations were laid for two decades of stable, rapid, yet unsustainable growth.

Chapter 5 examines the process of financial reform and restructuring following the 1997 Asian financial crisis, during the process of accession to the World Trade Organization (WTO), and through to the unfolding of the 2008 financial crisis. As China transitioned from what had been a position of (relative) international isolation to (partial) integration with the global economy, it was necessary to develop a set of financial and macroeconomic policies that would support trade and attract investment. China's leaders therefore sought to construct an internationally oriented modern financial system, which for all appearances was now increasingly geared for competition with foreign banks both at home and eventually abroad. Yet the premise of reform during the 2000s was not to replicate a Western financial system, but to transform the banking system into a more effective tool for achieving the broader politico-economic goals of the CCP. Reform was intensified, not in order to create more independent market forces, but rather to improve the market as a tool for the CCP.

Chapter 6 traces how the 2008–09 financial crisis precipitated further steps towards developing technocratic and rationalized financial regulatory institutions under the auspices of continued overarching CCP authority. The Chinese financial system was faced with the immediate economic imperatives of supporting growth and the discursive discrediting of an Anglo-American regulatory model. These combined in a crisis response that directly tied financial institutions ever closer to the heart of the Chinese political economy rather than seeking to insulate the real economy and public finances from the private financial sector, and the emergence of a shadow banking system that both supported and posed risks to financial stability. At the same time, shadow banking gave rise to new technology-driven financial institutions and channels of credit intermediation, which are now increasingly being brought under CCP control and authority, further deepening the conjoined processes of market development and political consolidation. Counterintuitively, the very forces behind deeper and broader financial liberalization are now also consolidating the CCP's overall legitimacy and ruling capacity.

The concluding chapter considers why, in the study of the intertwined processes of evolution in the global order and China's ongoing socio-economic transformation, it is both useful and necessary to study the role of the financial system in China's economic development, and in turn to study the role of the CCP in China's financial system. It points to some of the ways in which the arguments developed in the book are important to future research into the reshaping of China's political economy and the global political economy in the aftermath of the 2008 financial crisis. Finally, it draws out some of the book's implications for the conceptual, theoretical, and methodological ways in which we approach the 'China question' and the future of authoritarian capitalism in an era of flux and change in the global capitalist order.

Notes

1   See further Hu et al. (2012).
2   Interview 28 November 2012, Beijing – China Investment Corporation.
3   This interpenetration of the political and the economic is addressed admirably by Greta Krippner, who details how 'financialization' in the United States offered a 'solution' to the socio-political crises of the 1970s. Likewise, I seek to understand how a particular mode of economic growth 'solved' the socio-political dilemmas faced by the CCP. Further, and in contrast to a Marxist world-systems theoretical perspective, we both seek to 'scale back the analysis to more manageable proportions where precise mechanisms and specific social actors are more visible' (Krippner 2011, 15).
4   This is apparent even amongst the most notionally 'private' of the joint-stock commercial banks, such as Minsheng Bank (Stent 2017).
5   Often referred to as the *nomenklatura*, having been modelled upon the Soviet methods of Party control over the bureaucracy. Within the 5000-strong core list there exists a more select 1000-strong 'elite within the elite' list known as the Central Cadres List [中央干部目录], as well as a longer list of 39,000 official positions whose appointment must be reported to the Central Committee [向中央备案的干部职务名单].
6   As Hamrin and Zhao (1995, xxxvii) have described it, 'Economic units are afraid of the [NDRC] and all units fear the Organization Department'.
7   Interview, 6 June 2012, Beijing – Ministry of Finance.
8   The 1990 position-list was published on 10 May 1990, particularly as one of the measures to reassert party discipline in the aftermath of 4 June 1989.
9   Interview, 15 April 2014, Beijing – China Banking Regulatory Commission.
10 Interview, 9 August 2013, Beijing – China Construction Bank.
11 Giving rise to such concepts such as a 'partial reform equilibrium' (Hellman 1998) that have underscored studies discussed above such as those by Huang, Shih, and Walter and Howie.

12 These perspectives rely upon the McKinnon-Shaw Hypothesis, which holds that common instances of government intervention in the financial sector, such as interest rate control and directed credit, generated financial repression that constituted a fundamental obstacle to economic growth in developing countries (Li Kui-Wai 1994; Lardy 1998; Xu 1998).

13 This derives from the traditional characterization of China's 'paramount leader' as the core of the CCP, willing to enter into discussions with others, but ultimately wielding the prerogative of final, and sometimes arbitrary, decision-making power. Xi Jinping's entrenchment at the heart of power in Zhongnanhai reveals the enduring importance of centralized authority in Chinese politics and society, and thus economy.

14 As Walter and Howie (2011, 25) state, 'with all aspects of banking under the Party's control, risk is thought to be manageable'.

15 Zheng (2010) points towards the rootedness in Chinese culture of the CCP's functional characteristics.

16 A similar argument is made by Arif Dirlik (1989) with respect to the dialectical interplay of ideology and organization in the formation of the CCP's formation in 1921, following the Russian Revolution of 1917 and the May Fourth Movement of 1919.

2

Ancient markets, modern capitalism: China and the problem of Eurocentrism

[N]one of the standard models of economic and political theory can explain China. ... China still does not have well-specified property rights, town-village enterprises hardly resemble the standard firm of economics, and it remains to this day a communist dictatorship.

Douglass North (2005)

It is merely in the night of our ignorance that all alien shapes take on the same hue.

Perry Anderson (1974)

If, as I argue in this book, it is necessary to reconceptualize the institutional underpinnings of Chinese capitalism around an economic sociology of the CCP, then what purpose is served by historical analysis of China's political economy? First, the problem of Eurocentrism challenges theorists to deconstruct the potentially biased and context-specific foundations of the scientific knowledge with which we seek to make sense of the contemporary world. Secondly, if we are to take seriously the path-dependency of institutional and social change, then it is instructive to ground new concepts and theories (even if inadequately) on as secure a historical foundation as possible. In this chapter I develop both this critique as well as the constructive response, thereby outlining a rationale for the remaining chapters and also beginning to lay their conceptual basis.

Drawing on a Braudelian (1982) distinction between a free-market and a capitalist economy, I highlight the importance of the connection between the nature of the market economy that developed in imperial Qing China and the emergence of China's present-day capitalism. I argue that important lineages of China's political economy have been obscured by the Eurocentrism of mainstream political economy, and that this helps to explain why it remains difficult for Western-trained academic and policymakers to appreciate the highly capitalist yet decidedly non-liberal contemporary role of the CCP. Placing this distinction between a market economy and a capitalist economy in historical and empirical context enables us to see how China's experience and practice of markets was, and remains, different from the Western historical experience, but this by no means demands the conclusion that China's market-based economy during the period of the 'great divergence' (Pomeranz 2000) was not amenable to capitalism. Rather, it was simply not amenable to European-style capitalism.

Neglect of this distinction has led to deficiencies in the integration of China's political economy into existing typologies and conceptual frameworks for the study of institutional development and change in capitalist societies. The result is a regrettable lack of nuanced yet comprehensive analyses of the institutional dynamics within this interpenetration of state and market in China. The comparative historiography of China's and Europe's development compels us to look beyond the well-established insight of state–market variation in the institutional configurations of capitalist societies.[1] Not only may capitalisms vary, but they may also be constructed upon underlying social structures that disrupt existing conceptualizations of the actors, processes, and outcomes within these institutions. Through analysis of China's distinctive experience of pre-capitalist 'economic rationality', we thus begin to approach the socio-institutional underpinnings of China's contemporary development as a positive question of China's own developmental trajectory, rather than a negative one of its failure to emulate the Western experience.

The second section briefly examines how modern political economy embodies a Eurocentric relationship of equals between the state and market, and how its underlying ideal-typical rationality has come to constitute the counterfactual benchmark for a linear process of capitalist modernization. This clears the way for a more positive reconstruction of Chinese political economy in the third section, investigating the respective processes of market and state formation in China and Europe. I home in on the role of the financial system and the management of capital flows through the economy in this distinctive historical experience of market development in China. Just as the European experience of state-building was intertwined with the role of finance in its capitalist development, the relationship between political authority and financial capital in China played an important role in the developmental trajectory of its non-capitalist political economy. But in contrast to the European experience, China developed a sophisticated market economy that was underpinned by a centralized political authority that retained dominance over financial capital. China's construction of a capitalist and globally embedded economy in the post-Mao era continues to evince these historical lineages that have been obscured by political economists' persistent neglect of China's long-standing experience of market economy. The fourth section details the implications of this comparative historiography for the study of China's contemporary political economy, arguing that the longer-run historical contextualization of the role of the CCP is crucial to analysing China's institutional landscape and economic trajectory. The final section paves the way for this economic sociology of the CCP to be mapped out in Chapter 3.

The Eurocentric rationality of political economy

The classic theory of the emergence of Western capitalism is epitomized in the comparative sociology of Sombart and Weber, who argued that

Economic growth and development in the West over the long term has been due to the institutionalized separation of business and household capital, the widespread adoption of rational book-keeping and accounting techniques; the creation of a formally free labor force; ... the development of rational structures of law and administration; of industrial processes and technology; and importantly, of a business orientation that valued the accumulation of capital as an end in itself. (Marshall 1982, 64)

These conclusions led to the corollary development of the theory of the 'failure' of capitalism in China as being centred on the weakness of separation between firms and their owners and thus the lack of institutions to define the relationship between capital and owners, a cultural and spiritual environment resistant to capital accumulation, and the crushing presence of the imperial state. As Blue and Brook (1999, 2) have observed, this question of why China 'failed' has continued to serve both in East and West as 'the basic intellectual horizon for scholarly research and practical planning with regard to Chinese society and China's place in the world'.[2] Nowhere has this become more evident than in the discourse surrounding China's economic reforms, in which the idea of 'the modern' is assumed to comprise a set of institutions underpinning a market-based economic system that over the course of its development eluded China.

In this section I critically review the connections between how the writing of history and the formulation of theory that accompanied 'the great divergence' embodied a pronounced Eurocentrism, and our conceptual and theoretical difficulties in making adequate sense of the relationship between political authority and financial capital in China's contemporary political economy. That is to say, our previous errors in attempting to understand historical divergence are proving a serious limitation in our current efforts to come to terms with contemporary convergence. An exhaustive treatment of this subject is beyond the scope of this book, but my intention is to pave the way for the more positive reconstruction of the historical origins of the relationship between political authority and capital that characterizes contemporary China.

Classical political economy, as practised by Smith, Marx, Durkheim, and Weber, was concerned with understanding not only how processes of economic development transformed society, but also with how certain social and political formations affected the development of capitalism as a mode of production. Max Weber was the first in a line of historical sociologists to make a determined effort to view 'capitalism' in a worldwide context (Goody 2006). Yet his theorization of the rational state and its relationship to modern capitalism as a uniquely European phenomenon drew upon a comparative framework that treated the West and the 'non-West' very differently. Given his ultimate aim of identifying those features of Western civilization and capitalism in particular 'that were responsible for the emergence, in the West alone, of cultural phenomena he thought of as having universal validity' (Blue 1999, 95), the ideal-typical characterizations of Western rationality that emerged from his analyses would therefore, when combined with a linear conception of social progress, come to be regarded as the inevitable and sole manifestation of a capitalist rationality. Weber would ultimately view this process of bureaucratic rationalization in Europe with great pessimism, and yet the shadow of Weber's ideal-typical rationality remains evident throughout attempts to understand the cultures, economies, and politics of the non-West (Wang Hui 2011).

One of the results of this grounding of political economy in the assumed universality of the Western European experience of the allied yet antagonistic relationship between capital and political authority is the conceptualization of the state and market as largely discrete analytic categories. Western developmental economics and political economy became embroiled in the states versus markets debates from the 1970s (Hamilton et al. 2000). It is the Eurocentric legacy of this distinction between state and market in contemporary mainstream political economy at which I take aim here. From its roots in the thought of these classical political economists, who were each sensitive to the socially mediated interplay of the forces of market exchange and bureaucratic hierarchy, the analysis of the relationship between society and the economy became subject to a tendency towards an economistic reductionism, in which social relations and order are functionally derived from the 'laws' of economic activity. The tension between the political and the economic was apparent in the treatment of '"the economy" … as "nature": as an exogenous complex of fixed relations of cause and effect that political actors had to take into account so they could use them to their advantage' (Beckert and Streeck 2008, 10). The gradual yet seemingly inexorable encroachment of the economy and its 'laws' upon the polity beginning in the 1980s rendered this conceptual dichotomy between the ideal-types of the freely competitive market and social and political institutions increasingly doubtful. Political economy reacted by incorporating the analysis of the social as a functionally driven product of economic action.[3] The rational actor models on which both mainstream economics and orthodox political economy are founded proceed thus from conceptions of rationality independent of any actor's cultural interpretation of the relevant situation (Beckert and Streeck 2008).

The limitations of a political economy approach founded on an atomistic methodological individualism prompted a turn in attention towards the study of social institutions, and their effect upon economic growth and social development. North and Thomas (1973) argued that the key to effective development was the establishment of sound institutions that equated the private to the social rate of return, setting in place incentives that would deter rational individuals from taking actions that were privately profitable but socially harmful and encourage them to engage in behaviour that was privately costly but socially beneficial. Nevertheless, in many ways the emphasis upon the formality of institutions and their consequent materiality meant that the 'new institutional economics' came largely to be premised upon methodological principles similar to the neoclassical theories of political economy whose limitations it had originally sought to ameliorate.

The result was that property rights as an efficiency-enhancing condition of economic change became a fundamental conceptual element of the neoclassical economic theory that underpins modern neo-institutional political economy (Weimer 1997). Property rights were therefore closely tied to the relationship between the state and the market – put bluntly, the most important role of the former is to ensure that property rights are protected within the latter. Further, it was the basis for the distinction drawn by classical political economists between the different forms of income: wages for workers, profits for capitalists, and rents for landlords. As Sugihara (2003, 87) has noted, judged by this yardstick East Asia was always going to fare poorly, and as I explore in greater detail in the next section, these boundaries between merchants, families, and elites as different economic and political groupings had simply never operated in the same way as in Europe.

For a variety of reasons, not least the self-orientalizing tendency of both liberal and Marxist scholarship in East Asia (Blue and Brook 1999), our conceptions of political and economic rationality remain largely constrained within the conceptual horizon that was established during this formative period of contemporary political economy and which manifests in important accounts of China's reform-era development. We begin to see the implications of positioning the historiography of European economic development as the root theoretical foundation of the concepts and analytical constructs that operationalize contemporary political economy. In the next section I reconstruct this comparative historiography of market-development and state-formation, exploring how Braudel's distinction between markets and capitalism opens up greater space for a non-Eurocentric view of contemporary Chinese capitalism.

Markets, states, and the variegated origins of capitalism

If we suspend the universalizing assumptions of Eurocentric political economy, then on what basis can we understand the rationalism that was present in China during the late imperial era and of which we find evidence in the political economy of contemporary China?

36

In order to address this question, the following two subsections examine comparative lineages of market-based economic development and state-formation. Three arguments emerge: (1) these two processes constituted a rational and sophisticated economic sociology of market behaviour and economic development; (2) this economic sociology was distinct from that which led to European-style capitalism, but was not necessarily incompatible with it; and (3) accordingly, the construction of a capitalist system in contemporary China – one that is deeply embedded in the competitive dynamics of an integrated global economy – represents potentially the coalescence of logics of politico-economic organization that are as rational as they are qualitatively distinct.

The emergence of markets

There is a wealth of evidence showing that China's imperial economy from at least the Song dynasty (960–1280 CE) established deep and broad market relations in a range of commodities and a wide variety of credit/debt relationships, along with the first national issuance of banknotes and paper money (Arrighi 2008; Pomeranz 2000; Wong 1997). Economic (along with political) integration is not a novel theme in Chinese economic history, as 'national markets and interregional financial links between major commercial centers' were in continual existence and operation for many centuries before the Opium Wars (Rawski 1989, 146). Trade between different provinces took place within a much more unified market structure, and easily eclipsed intra-European trade (Wang 1992; Pomeranz 2000). By the time of the late Ming and early Qing dynasties, China was far less mercantilist than Western Europe was at the same time (Deng 1999).

In China, by the seventeenth century at the latest, a largely unconstrained market existed in land, underpinned by 'recognized rights of private ownership [that] included those of utilization, inheritance and alienability' (Rowe 1990, 242). The concept of real property much more closely resembled that of the modern West than that of any other imperial states, and arguably than that of early modern Europe itself (Pomeranz 2000). Likely no more than 3 per cent of

37

total arable land belonged to the state (Huang 1985), and in any event, its hereditary tenants sold and mortgaged it as if their tenure treated much of this as private property in which their tenure was wholly secure (Pomeranz 2000). As a result there were 'constant, complex, and extremely dynamic' markets for land and labour in order to facilitate evolving production processes and new social relations in the late Ming and early Qing (Wu 2000 [1985], 17). As Bramall and Nolan point out, this 'casts serious doubt on the idea that private property in land was a uniquely European phenomenon which formed the basis of wider concepts of private property, which in turn facilitated capitalist investment and innovation, which in short was responsible for "the rise of the West"' (Bramall and Nolan 2000, xxiii; cf. North and Thomas 1973).

This was not necessarily evidence of capitalism per se. Rather, it was evidence of a sophisticated market economy, in which large-scale production was based on simple division of labour and the unified movement of commodity prices was the result of supply and demand across relatively unified yet localized markets (Wu 2000 [1985]). The state actively promoted the unification of national markets and was engaged in the construction of both institutions and the physical infrastructure necessary for this to take place. This delivered significant benefits for the many peasants who bought and sold goods; however, it did not translate into the concentration of wealth amongst particular actors on the basis of market manipulation. It is here that the importance of Braudel's distinction between a 'Smithian' (Arrighi 2008) mode of market development and the Marxian accumulation of capital that prompted the rise of capitalist financial systems in Europe becomes clear. The unification and highly competitive nature of China's markets were what led Smith himself to praise the Chinese political economy, and what distinguished it from the European configuration of small and politically vulnerable states aligned with large corporate interests, a crucial distinction the significance of which will be highlighted in the next section.

The Chinese financial system played not only a significant role in underpinning the dynamics of this Smithian market economy, but further (and perhaps more importantly) reflected the broader nature of the relationship between people, capital, and the state. Just as was the case in Europe, the initial development of banking in China was the 'progressive centralization of clearance' (Usher 1943, 4), a process in which credit was extended within an increasing geographical area for a greater variety of socio-economic activities and for longer time periods. Although there remain only limited analyses and sources of data on the nature of systems of credit and finance in the late-imperial period, we can nonetheless reach several conclusions. First, the system of credit and finance was well developed, with a variety of different institutions fulfilling different roles. Secondly this system was intimately connected to the real economy, servicing the merchant class and the trade of commodities, with no evidence of the financial accumulation that played such a central role in the emergence of European financial systems (Arrighi 2009 [1994]). By the late imperial period, China's indigenous financial system had come to represent

> a complex and sophisticated adaptation to the requirements of an agrarian economy with substantial and interregional trade. ... China's financial system paralleled that of preindustrial Europe in its complexity and sophistication. There were numerous intermediaries, from local moneychangers and pawnshops to large institutions with far-flung networks of branches or correspondents. (Rawski 1989, 125–6)

These institutions for allocating the investment, fixed, and working capital necessary for carrying out commercial business therefore provided the requisite stability for the smooth functioning of markets in the real economy, but not necessarily for the continuing accumulation of capital that was so essential for the development and survival of European political economies that eventually coalesced around the nation-state. The utilization of capital had sociological foundations that were rooted in the historical experience of constructing the Chinese state, which was itself closely related to the structural features of Chinese society and its economy, and thus hewn out of a very different social setting than that of the modern European state.

The structure of social relations that underpinned the interplay of commerce and capital in imperial China was fluid and complex, but not unsystematic (Pomeranz 1997). There was a logic of capital accumulation and reinvestment that operated through a rational and sophisticated relationship between the personal and commercial components not just of a sole family lineage but also within the broader fabric of elite society. Family firms embedded within these financial structures were able to finance a significant part of the commercial agenda that in the West has been attributed to managerial firms and Western corporate forms linked to independent capital markets.[4] Considerable evidence thus exists that different forms of Chinese partnership allowed entrepreneurs to organize investment capital and reinvest profits for the long term in ways similar to those made possible by Western joint-stock companies (Zelin 1988, Pomeranz 1997).

These lineage-based firms both hired professional managers but also had interlocking arrangements with each other for the raising of investment capital (Chan 1982). Some of them lasted for over 300 years, such as the Ruifuxiang Company, and several in Tianjin that existed from the late seventeenth century into the twentieth (Kwan 1990). In the absence of 'any compelling evidence for the supposed historical necessity of making clear separations between business and household activities' (Gardella 1992, 322), the organizational character of the family in late imperial China was productively and securely able to function as much as an enterprise as a domestic group (Cohen 1991). Through the Ming and the Qing dynasties, this pattern of corporate investment continued to evolve in conjunction with the rise of the *qianzhuang*, which 'held the ganglions of the financial lines of the country' (Tamagna 1942, 47). The *qianzhuang* were financial firms organized around either a single proprietorship or more commonly through a partnership rooted in members of a family, clan, or close circle of friends. They handled deposits, lent capital, and facilitated remittances and the exchange of money, with unlimited financial liability guaranteed by the resources of the proprietor or partnership. The interlocking partnership structures across the family lineages of the urban elite of both urban commercial firms and these native banks therefore facilitated the raising of long-term capital and financing in innovative ways during this period. Rowe (1990, 252) has described this process of development:

> The banking institutions that had developed by the late eighteenth century offered a sophisticated range of credit instruments, and the joint-stock company, with its capacity for growth-oriented refinancing, had appeared even earlier. The technology of mobilizing and managing had also reached an impressively high level. Moreover, China developed systems of agency, brokering, and factoring arguably much more refined than those of the early modern West.

It is important here to stress that this relationship between finance capital and the real market economy within Braudel's middle 'Smithian' stratum of the economy lays the basis for, but does not actually itself constitute, a capitalist dynamic of financial accumulation as a mechanism of pursuing market power. The Chinese case indicates how the emergence of a capitalist economic structure is not the natural and inevitable result of a market economy. Even as Smith's analysis of the growth of European market economies would still stress the importance of agriculture, assume the finite nature of economic growth, and predict real wages to ultimately fall to subsistence levels, China had long been constructing an economy that was similarly advanced in its market dynamics and vibrancy. The distinction that would produce divergence in the European and Chinese trajectories would be found not in the process of market development, but in the process of state formation.

The emergence of capitalism

Whereas Europe's experience of economic and political development produced the modern nation-state, China's did not. As Tilly (1992, 16) sums it up pithily, 'within their own space, Europeans farmed, manufactured, traded and, especially, fought

41

each other. Almost inadvertently, they thereby created national states.' In contrast, the distinctive rationalism underpinning the process of market-formation and state-building in imperial China would translate into a different form of political economy from that which developed as a product of economic development and state-making in Europe. If capitalist transformation in Europe was not a naturally endogenous product of the spread of European markets, then we ought to consider the possibility that it was the emergence in Europe of a particular variety of state that was the source of this transformation. This in turn could either be driven by endogenous or exogenous factors. The endogenous explanation centres on the development of a Weberian bureaucratic rational state that, as noted above, remains the conceptual baseline for much analysis of political economy around the world. Hobson (2004, 283–4) deconstructs the mythical tenets of the Western origins of rationality in political economy. The reification of this Western mode of rationality as universal obscures the possibility that the politico-economic configurations contained within and between European states were not the driver of the path of capitalist development in Western Europe but rather were merely the vehicle – and but one of potentially several – for the mobilization of capital in order to secure the interests of the dominant political forces within Western European society. If such a nation-state was not inevitable, then there must have been some other factor that precipitated its emergence. It is this exogenous explanation that we are concerned with. In this formulation, the Western European nation-state was the effect rather than the cause of the capitalist imperative that arose from the political circumstances and fortunes of the various sociocultural groupings – church, state, and nation – that were vying for supremacy at the time.

Capitalism emerged in Western Europe as a result of the existential conflict that unfolded between these different sociocultural groupings. Interstate competition in early modern Europe became 'literally murderous' (Vries 2002, 76). Financing past, present, and future wars was by far the greatest expenditure of European states (Bonney 1999), a phenomenon that Sombart (1913) argued was the foundation for Europe's wealth. In contrast, there never existed an incentive for the imperial Chinese state to embark upon this form of commercialized accumulation of capital. This was not because China lacked sociocultural or scientific features conducive to capitalist development. Rather, it possessed deep structural conditions for the ongoing development of a Smithian mode of market exchange (Arrighi et al. 2003, 265). The city in imperial China was also located at the nexus of two overlapping hierarchies: as economic centres embedded in a national market, and also as political centres embedded within the imperial regime (Skinner 1977, 275–352). Just as in Europe, there existed all the potential elements for what Skinner refers to as 'macroregions' to form into competitive warring states, by concentrating capital within urban centres and mobilizing resources for waging war and preparation thereto, precipitating the development of attendant social and political institutions that would come to form the modern bureaucratic state. Both Europe and China as continental landmasses each contained the necessary endogenous ingredients for the development of capitalism. However, it was an exogenous factor – existential competition – that spurred European national societies as embryonic states to in turn give birth to capitalism. The absence of such interstate competition for mobile capital therefore goes a long way towards explaining why capitalism did not 'spread like an epidemic' (Arrighi et al. 2003, 280) in East Asia as it did in the European world.[5] Looking at the other side of the coin, Pomeranz (2000, 207) is inclined instead to label Europe a 'fortunate freak' whose capital-intensive, energy-intensive, and land-consuming path of development was a product of projecting the competitive state-making process out into the world – generating a confluence of resource and energy flows, and both the domestic and colonial institutions to take advantage of them.

Again, it is crucial to examine the way in which this process of forming states was linked to the financial underpinnings of economic growth, which would manifest in the various different forms of the relationship between the state and capital. By the sixteenth century China's financial system had developed considerable efficiency in facilitating a long-distance grain trade across the empire (Wong 1999). The guildhalls that arose during the early Qing period were active promoters of a rapidly expanding national market and thus regulated production in order to eliminate competition between their members. Of these, the *huiguan* were region-specific organizations that provided association and networks amongst merchants from a shared hometown or province, whilst the *gongsuo* were industry-oriented and devoted to fostering connections between those involved in the trade of a particular commodity (Fang et al. 2000). In these ways they resembled the medieval guilds of Europe, but with one crucial distinction. They remained always subordinate to the imperial government, for the reason that the cities in which they were based, and which formed the locus of the long-distance trade that expanded rapidly in the eighteenth century, were always first and foremost centres of commerce rather than of politics. European guilds became intimately connected to the political fortunes of the urban centres in which they were embedded: ongoing warfare secured not just property rights writ large, which were also highly secure in imperial China, but 'property in privileges', which extended through the contracting out of tax collection through tax farming ventures, the establishment of highly venal offices, a broad range of state-granted monopolies, and confirmation of guild privileges (Pomeranz 2000, 196). This was an instructive example of capitalist growth emerging not from property rights and free markets, but rather from the effective accumulation and mobilization of resources for market domination and monopoly.

This was in direct contrast to the Chinese situation, with its widespread guilds and regulatory frameworks for merchant activity designed to regulate markets, rather than to raise revenue (Mann 1987; 1992). China was simply more unified and coherent than Europe could ever hope to be. It was not so beholden to the corporate groups and elites, with their own bases of power and authority either urban or rural, that featured so strongly in the

European experience. There was an absence in China of those commercial dynasties that gradually accumulated a stock of capital independent of other loci of power, and which gradually became sufficiently powerful social forces to promote capitalist expansion (Braudel 1977; Chaudhuri 1990: Feuerwerker 1984). Further, the state's commitment to social order was shared by elites, a form of state-making that did not encounter many of the challenges faced by Europe (Wong 1997). The economic sociology of the process by which firms in imperial China raised capital for large-scale commercial activities has implications for how we conceive the relationship between individual firms' behaviour, the broader political economy in which they were embedded, and the institutional foundations for the imperial state.

Land, labour, and capital were treated differently. The former were no less secure in China than in Europe. But the capital of merchant firms remained insecure, attached as it was to the individual. Whereas the concept of private property in land was not restricted either through scale or on the basis of its owner, this was never the case with trading capital, and the merchant and his working stock remained indivisible (Chaudhuri 1985). Other factors of production – land and labour – were socially divisible, as they were openly available on the open market to anyone who possessed sufficient purchasing power. Yet the working capital necessary for trade and industry remained closely tied to mercantile groups (Chaudhuri 1985). This is not to say that merchants were therefore vulnerable and suffered more expropriations than was the case elsewhere (Pomeranz 2000). But they operated within tight constraints that arose out of the contentedness of the state to rely upon fiscal, rather than financial, sources of spending power. Monetary issues were not of central importance in imperial China, since the majority of state revenues were derived from the land tax, rather than through debt or commercial activities (Peng 1994). Consequently, capital was always 'the junior partner, at best, and closely guarded' (Vries 2002, 87), and Chinese society possessed no particular social grouping comparable with the 'capitalists' or the bourgeoisie of Europe.

45

This comparative historiography of China's economic development points to one overarching conclusion. The organization of the factors of production in China was no less rationally effective than those in Europe, but they were organized in different ways and for a different purpose. Whereas the symbiotic relationship between merchant capital and the state in Europe came to be premised on the need to accumulate capital in the hands of the state, thus enabling the waging of war, the relationship between merchant capital and the state in China was premised on the desire to construct a unified national market. Both qualitative innovation in financial organization and the quantitative scale of merchant loans were absent, in the absence of existential threats and thus the financial imperatives that confronted European states between the sixteenth and eighteenth centuries. Competition was greater, prices more responsive, and productivity greater in China than in Europe. However, given the rootedness of both production and trade in landed property rather than working capital, and the corresponding reliance of the imperial state upon direct taxation rather than the raising of capital, the power of merchants remained subordinated to the state. And this subordination has significant implications for how we think about the political relationship between the CCP and financial capital in contemporary China.

Historical lineages of contemporary Chinese capitalism

This economic sociology of a non-capitalist yet market-oriented imperial state is not only historically significant in its own right, but also serves as a 'bridge rather than a barrier' (Gardella 1992, 334) to the modern era of Chinese political economy. Hamilton and Chang (2003, 176) have argued that significant parallels between the imperial-era and modern Chinese economy can only be explained as 'having emerged from similar ... shared understandings of social organization and from similar ... structural conditions confronted by economically active participants, such as relations of power and authority'. The characteristics outlined above of China's pre-1949 experience of market economy, as Brandt et al. (2012, 5) acknowledge, 'continue to exert a powerful influence' on China's contemporary political economic development. Continuity over change in the realm of economic organization is the prevailing scholarly consensus (Bramall 2009). As Strauss (2006, 895) has observed, although the early People's Republic of China (PRC) was forced to confront myriad problems inherited from the Republican era under which it drew a sharp ideological line, it was a revolution that 'quite literally completed the work of the old regime, with "a central authority with powers stricter, wider, and more absolute"'.[6] The basic institutional arrangement of the PRC's SOEs was laid under the auspices of the National Resources Commission during the period of Guomindang control (Kirby 1990). As early as 1940, Mao Zedong (1967, 658) identified continuities that would mark the transition to any future communist state, proclaiming that 'the big banks, big industries, and large commercial establishments' would belong to such a state. Several years later, he would quote the 1924 manifesto of the first Guomindang congress, to the effect that such enterprises 'shall be operated and administered by the state, so that private capital cannot dominate the livelihood of the people' (Mao 1967, 958).

Before proceeding further, two brief digressions are necessary. First, I do not claim that China's contemporary socialism is essentially just the most recent incarnation of the country's age-old tradition of absolutist state power (see Blecher 2003), but argue for the need to adopt a more nuanced approach to the rise of the CCP and the patterns of political authority at the centre of which it has come to exist. That is to say, neither the cultural-philosophical foundations of Confucianism that underpinned imperial rule from 221 BCE (Fairbank and Goldman 2006), nor a transplanted system of Western political thought giving rise to an endogenous organizational dynamic of CCP rule, should be seen as exclusively responsible for the structuring of contemporary Chinese politics.[7]

Secondly, if the emergence of capitalism is symbiotically connected to the emergence of a state in economic competition with other states, then a corollary hypothesis is that a likely driver of capitalist development in reform-era China is that of its having entered into a set of competitive relationships with other major economies of the world. Exploring this theory in depth is beyond the scope of this book, but suffice it to note that there is a direct connection between the weakness of the nineteenth-century Qing response to foreign incursion and the PRC's deep drive for internationally competitive developmentalism, whether it be under the aegis of a socialist or capitalist model (Brandt et al. 2012). Contemporary desires for reclamation of national pride and the absolution of its historical humiliation thus have deeply economic roots (Schell and Delury 2013). The contrast with the absence of competitive transnational pressures facing China during the period of its greatest centrality to the world economy, from the fifteenth century to the eighteenth century, is instructive. But to assert that China has become an internationally competitive capitalist economy is not to say that it was to adopt the same kind of capitalism as arose out of Western Europe and had been developing along its own historical trajectory. Even as it was to become capitalist, it was to do this according to a very different institutional logic, and one that is embedded deeply within and which displays strong continuity with its own historical experience of market-based economic activity.

Conclusion

In this chapter I have argued for a need to reconceptualize our study of China's contemporary political economy on the basis of a deeper appreciation of the historical and cultural context out of which it has developed. I identify some of the problematic consequences of a persistent Eurocentrism in the frameworks of political economy that are dominant in our study of contemporary Chinese capitalism, and point to how a positive reconstruction of China's historical experience of market development assists us in better understanding the trajectory of its capitalism today. In arguing against Eurocentrism, I am not claiming that 'there

are ... no universal social patterns and no universally valid principles by which all societies are held together' (Hamilton and
Zheng 1992, 16). I hope instead to prompt political economists
to move one rung up Sartori's (1970) ladder of abstraction, and
begin to piece together conceptual architectures that decontainer-
ize Chinese economic and political behaviour from the state and
the market.

The above reconstruction of the historical relationship in China
between political authority and financial capital generates a basis for
probing how the structures and logics of market-based economic
exchange that characterized imperial China, having underpinned
the emergence of a large and stable imperial state, would come to
underpin capitalist forms of economic exchange in post-1978 and
particularly post-1989 China. At its heart is a unified central political structure that monopolized influence upon the state's capacity
to collect and utilize financial capital. The state would constitute
the organizational apparatus for interacting and controlling the
market, but the real source of power resided not within the abstract
constitutional rights of an institutionalized bureaucracy, but in the
deep-seated legitimacy and acceptance of a national structure that
itself commanded authority over both the state and the market in
equal measure.

The contemporary economic role of the CCP – in Zheng's
(2010) words, the 'organizational emperor' – thus emerges in a
subtly different light. The networked relationships between the
state, the market, and the CCP extend from the highest echelons
of central Party rule through to the local level at which Party
committees are established and embedded within organizations
across state, society, and market. The resulting analytic relationships are difficult to unpack owing to their complexity and
degree of penetration combined with the difficulty of obtaining
documentary evidence of its core decision-making processes.
This produces a tendency within Western scholarship to treat
Party bodies as somehow irregular and exogenous to the state
bureaucracy. Rather, they 'must be recognized as part of the core
institutions of policy-making and supervision' in China's present

49

political economy (Heilmann 2005, 4). Yet even as the interpenetration of the CCP with the Chinese state is universally recognized, the socioculturally embedded nature of its foundations and its 'sinews of governance' (Yang 2004) has been downplayed as largely epiphenomenal from a Western politico-economic perspective.

Notes

1 A caveat: my intention is not to attempt to enter into the rich and voluminous empirical debate on the nature and causes of state-formation in general. My point of departure within this literature is the prominent fiscal resource mobilization thesis, in which the causes of the great divergence are traced to the unique dynamics of interstate conflict that were present in Western Europe but absent in China (Hoffman 2015; Tilly 1992). Rather, it is to leverage recent advances within comparative economic history to enhance our understanding of the current trajectory of Chinese capitalist development, without assuming that the relationship between political authority and financial power should be expected necessarily to resemble, even in broadest form, that which emerged in the Anglo-American conception of liberal capitalism.

2 This was a symptom of a commitment to modernity, rather than a reflection of the desirability of capitalist development. For a good example of how Marxist scholarship within the PRC internalized this frame of reference, see Fang (2000 [1985]).

3 Exemplifying this approach, Weingast and Wittman (2008, 3) state that 'in our view, political economy is the methodology of economics applied to the analysis of political behavior and institutions'.

4 Although family firms were also core features of early European capitalism, it was their transmutation into capital structures legally independent of other elite social formations that is the important aspect of their distinctly capitalist nature.

5 Snooks (1996, 323) describes it such that 'ultimately, China's misfortune was a lack of serious competition'. The economic dynamism and innovative capacity of the Song dynasty was related to the fact that it was much smaller than the Ming or Qing empires, and only one state amongst several. Accordingly it was compelled to wage numerous wars, taxation was higher than in later eras, and a greater proportion of it was spent by the state on industry. China during this period therefore resembled Europe more than was the case under Ming or Qing. See Vries (2002, 90).

6 Quoting de Tocqueville's (1978) observations on the French Revolution.
7 A similar argument is made by Arif Dirlik (1989) with respect to the dialectical interplay of ideology and organization in the formation of the CCP's formation in 1921, following the Russian Revolution of 1917 and the May Fourth Movement of 1919.

3

CCP authority and the two faces of uncertainty

It is time for us to distinguish the responsibilities of the Party and those of the government and to stop substituting the former for the latter.

Deng Xiaoping (1984)

The special defining characteristic of Chinese socialism is CCP leadership, and without an understanding of the Party one simply cannot deal with China.

Wang Qishan (2015)

Placing Chinese political economy in historical and comparative perspective raises a question about how adequately the extant concepts of state and market – so fundamental to Western political economic theory – serve as lenses through which to identify and analyse 'rational' socio-economic action. Given the extent to which states and markets in contemporary capitalism are understood to interpenetrate one another in iterative and mutually constitutive ways, a rationale emerges for deprioritizing such concepts as the core building blocks of political economy and developing new conceptualizations of how economic and political dynamics interact within contemporary capitalism. China's socialist market economy offers an opportunity for doing so, and this chapter makes the case for analysing these dynamics in Chinese capitalism as revolving around socio-economic uncertainty and its relationship to both political power and economic activity.

Two faces of uncertainty: governance and power

Financial systems in contemporary capitalism are organizational systems that embody mechanisms for growth, stability, and distribution at both the microeconomic and macroeconomic levels. At the microeconomic level, the first role is that of allocating funds to projects with higher or lower rates of return, thus affecting the marginal productivity of capital (King and Levine 1993). Second, financial development can also allocate resources at lower costs, if it causes the financial system to be subject to lower taxation and regulatory burdens (Lardy 1998). Finally, financial systems have an effect upon the rate of private savings (Pagano 1993). At the macroeconomic level, as a set of social institutions that cause certain forms of financial market dynamics such as perpetual crisis (Krippner 2011) or financial bubbles (Akerlof and Shiller 2009), a financial system matters first and foremost either as a force of real economic pro-cyclicality or conversely as a tool for moderating the business cycle.

At the core of the redescription of these financial processes is socio-economic uncertainty. One of the fundamental obstacles confronted by social actors is that of the uncertainty that arises out of an actor's embeddedness within a social environment (Knight 1985 [1921]). For a rational institutionalist such as Douglass North, uncertainty is a product of the complexity of the problems to be solved, the limitations of the problem-solving software possessed by an actor, and incomplete information between social agents (North 1990). In contrast, for an economic sociologist such as Jens Beckert uncertainty must be regarded as qualitatively different from situations of risk, since the problem of risk is commonly understood to be one that is to be measured, evaluated, and responded to on a quantitative basis (Beckert 1996). In situations of risk, 'the distribution of the outcome in a group of instances is known ... while in the case of uncertainty ... it is impossible to form a group of instances because the situation dealt with is to a high degree unique' (Knight 1985 [1921], 229). Uncertainty is thus much more than the probability distribution problem that arises

53

out of the 'complexity' emphasized by rationalist institutional analysis.

As a concept, I develop and use socio-economic uncertainty in a way that denotes two things. Firstly, socio-economic uncertainty is a problem to be solved for financial behaviour to be undertaken on a 'rational' basis. Secondly, it constitutes an opportunity – an epistemic space – that can be exploited for political purposes. There is a tension between these two 'faces of uncertainty'. It is at once a hindrance to economic action, and particularly financial investment, yet it is also an indispensable element in a profit-driven market economy. In the world of perfect information that remains the counterfactual benchmark for modelling economic behaviour, economic decision-making is easy, but profits do not exist. It is this fine tension between the two, and the possibility of action being interpreted as either or both, that constitutes the intersection between finance as a basis for economic prosperity and finance as a mechanism for political authority.

This use of the concept of uncertainty emerges out of the broader sociological literature on action, and economic action in particular. The essential relevant insight of economic sociology is that:

> Although economic action is conditioned by the social contexts in which it takes place, it is not determined by these contexts but rather depends on how they are interpreted by economic actors ... understanding economic action requires that the responses of actors and their assessment of the risks and opportunities inherent in a given situation be explained with reference to the meaning that the situation has for them. (Beckert and Streeck 2008, 17–18)

At a general level, therefore, under conditions of uncertainty social action can be contrasted with the reduction of rationality to an under-socialized conception of an individual's utility-maximizing calculus of either economic wealth or political power. At the same time, such an understanding does not preclude an emphasis upon the intentional agency of the social actor, seeking to avoid an over-socialized view of institutional constraints and macro-structures.

The importance of approaching the issue of risk and uncertainty as a socially mediated factor is borne out through field research. Actors within the Chinese political economy and particularly the financial sector refer frequently to 'expectations' [预期 or 期待] in how they deal with not only government and Party officials but also, if they are bankers, with their clients and creditors. The basis of these expectations is rooted in their interpretation of a broad variety of factors and variables stretching across the directly political (elite Party politics as well as localized political dynamics), the sociocultural (shifting patterns of demand and consumption and the evolution of social values), and the directly economic (production efficiency, earnings records, and investment prospectuses). In this way, financial elites refer to 'structures of expectation' in their decision-making processes, and the manner in which they do so then reinforces certain patterns of expectation and intersubjective acceptance such that they also emerge as social rigidities capable of structuring individual agency.

Uncertainty is socio-economically significant because equilibrium within complex systems – including modern economies – is a contingent, entropic, and thus consistently elusive condition (Beckert 1996). Decision-making under conditions of uncertainty demands that a variety of complex and interrelated social conditions be interpreted and then managed in order for any form of agency to be exercised in a coherent manner. These dilemmas can only be resolved via a system of more or less stable reciprocal expectations on the part of actors that enable them to manage the uncertainty and risk that arise not just within market-settings, but which also obstruct agency within the political economy more broadly. These expectations are 'fictional' in nature (Beckert 2013) and buttressed by both rational means-end calculations and social macrostructures, although the decision-making process is ultimately reducible to neither. A distinctive feature of contemporary capitalist societies that differentiates them from other historical modes of political economy is that both economic growth and political stability are intimately connected to the construction of 'stable reciprocal expectations' (Beckert 2009, 245), which are capable of reducing financial uncertainty for both political and economic actors. Accordingly, rather than beginning with the assumption of static institutional equilibria that are disrupted by bouts of institutional change, we must first assume that the landscape of social institutions is constantly in flux and that it is through the contingent and highly contested construction of institutions that some inherently limited and temporary degree of social order is achieved.

Examining the sociological role of the financial system in economic growth demands addressing not only the way in which the financial system allocates capital according to economic and political interests, but also the way in which discourses and ideas about the financial system itself affect the path of economic growth. First, it will affect the internal structure and dynamics of the financial system, but it will also affect the way in which non-financial markets and broader economic systems come to structure themselves vis-à-vis the financial system. The deployment of financial capital and its investment into production thus stimulating employment, economic activity, and the resulting accumulation of greater capital is a process that demands intersubjectively shared understandings amongst a wide variety of actors throughout the political economy. The flow of capital throughout the real economy as financial capital rests upon sociological foundations, and it is thus socio-economic features that both require and are reflective of capitalism's systemic dynamism and individual innovativeness.

This emphasis upon uncertainty builds upon and extends recent advances (e.g. Braun 2016) at the nexus of economic sociology and political economy. Beginning with the contributions of Knorr Cetina and Bruegger (2002), and Mackenzie and Millo (2003), which built upon Callon's (1998) initial performativity thesis, social studies of finance have made significant advances in understanding exactly what kind of socially constructed environments financial systems are embedded in. The question of why this embeddedness matters in macro-distributive terms has generally been more the preserve of constructivist political economy, pioneered in such studies as those edited by Hall (1989) and Blyth (2002). The two fields, however, have struggled to engage fruitfully with one another, and the ideational underpinnings of economic processes and their political outcomes remain largely separate areas of inquiry. The dialectical interplay between the two faces of uncertainty is an important point of articulation between the microfoundations of actors' decision-making processes and the broader contexts in which this decision-making takes place. A constructivist analysis of how financial actors across the state-market divide, manage, and exploit uncertainty provides a concrete basis for integrating the micro- and macro-levels of action. It also prompts a much deeper connection between economic sociology with its emphasis on actors and micro-level agency, and political economy, with its emphasis on structures and macro-level consequences.

Seen from this perspective, China's transition has involved much more than the introduction of markets as mechanisms for price setting and resource allocation. The underlying rationale for the nature of financial reform has been to preserve the macroeconomic stability of a dynamic real economy, whilst stimulating headline economic growth and ensuring that this growth remained under the political control of the CCP. Each of these outcomes – stability, growth, and political control – depends on the management of expectations within a deeply uncertain socio-economic environment. The structures of expectation that mitigate uncertainty are therefore sources of social power and authority, thus becoming laden not just with neutral 'steering capacity', but also with the potential for realizing profoundly normative visions and agendas for the nature of social action. These 'two faces of uncertainty' are crucial to understanding how, in China, the point of intersection between state and market resides with the CCP and its simultaneous construction of mechanisms of governance and mechanisms for the extension of power.

Conceiving directly of the financial system itself as a broader tool of socio-economic governance and not just a system of microeconomic intermediation with macroeconomic implications opens up scope for reinterpreting the institutional foundations of the connection between the financial system, the real economy, and the political system. Notwithstanding the specific combination of state or market actors within the institutional dynamics of a financial system, its capacity to intermediate capital effectively is dependent upon systems of trust, expectations, and the investor confidence thus generated. Providing a financial risk-minimal environment is thus critical for both economic growth and stability, a policy challenge otherwise generally known as financial governance. This risk can be managed within the financial system, for example through financial market securitization, or through the use of implicit or explicit guarantees. The use of government guarantees of loans and credit is an effective method of stimulating economic growth when financial market freedom either fails or is not permitted. This model of risk management has underpinned growth in China to the extent that one banker summarized it pithily thus: 'moral hazard is state policy'.[1]

Yet such techniques of financial regulation and policy, whilst necessary, are clearly insufficient to secure the broader stability of a system of financial intermediation. The belated recognition of the myth of the self-regulating financial market is opening up greater scope for understanding and parsing the social foundations of financial governance. The management of socio-economic uncertainty should be distinguished from the more specific task of attending to financial risk itself, either at the micro-level of individual financial transactions or institutions, or at the systemic level of macroprudential regulation.[2] Rather, the management of socio-economic uncertainty is a broader social project; one that the technocratic exercise of risk assessment and management itself is both dependent upon and deeply embedded in. This is a problem that is further accentuated when financial markets themselves lack adequate mechanisms for signalling the appropriate price of capital. In such circumstances, the management of financial uncertainty within a complex economic system becomes much more than the deductive application of principles of financial regulation. This has the result that

> Motivating the decisions of actors by shaping their expectations, including the shaping of the social and political structures underlying these expectations, becomes one of the main tasks of political regulators and a major goal of speech acts uttered in the field of the economy. (Beckert 2013, 326)

The management of uncertainty in this way articulates the relationship between financial markets and substantive economic conditions. It is clearly apparent in the evolving central banking practice of 'forward guidance' (Braun 2015; Abolafia 2010). Yet whilst central banks might be the single institution most closely linked to coordinating this relationship, it is by no means the only factor involved in the process of constructing economic narratives, setting financial expectations, and injecting meaning into otherwise disconnected data points. The management of socio-economic uncertainty, then, is clearly the responsibility and priority (even if one assumed unknowingly) by a broad and deep array of actors throughout the political economy.

This role of a financial system as a tool for economic governance dovetails with its role as a tool for exercising political authority. To take seriously the status of financial systems – and the risk environments within which they operate – as social systems further involves recognizing that the economic outcomes produced by a risk environment will have socio-political implications that are the product of power relations. Socio-economic action relies upon the reduction of uncertainty by way of structures of expectations that are generated through cognitive frames, social institutions, and relational networks. Power emerges from these frames, institutions, and networks; the intersubjective understandings that reduce socio-economic uncertainty and thus enable a fundamental capacity for action – generating social agency – necessarily do so in a variegated and differentiated manner. Structures of expectation are thus laden not just with neutral 'steering capacity' as a result of functional imperatives, but also with the potential for realizing profoundly normative visions and agendas for the nature of social action. Accordingly, these structures of expectations are manipulable by actors in order to achieve particular objectives and interests.

Scholars in political economy and economic sociology have increasingly turned their attention to theorizing the connections between ideas, institutions, and power (Carstensen and Schmidt 2016). Financial uncertainty constitutes a particular kind of social space in which ideational power can be exercised. The power of ideas, when combined with concrete agents, and the social institutions and networks through which it is exercised, is crucial to understanding the structure, operation, and consequences of financial systems. Developing ideas about the role of risk and return in credit and finance have implications for the wielding of social power, as creditors can leverage their expectations so as to compel a debtor to act in confidence-preserving ways (Beckert 2013). The outcome of appealing to economic interests in the use of investment capital is that the necessity of maintaining such confidence, and thus loyalty, 'gives to the capitalists a powerful indirect control over government policy: everything which may shake the state of confidence must be carefully avoided because it would cause economic crisis' (Kalecki 1943, 139). And yet this confidence and game of expectations remains a mutual one. The establishment of market-oriented institutions was necessary not just for the purpose of being rational and efficient, but also for being rational and efficient for specific political purposes.

The process of managing uncertainty in order to achieve both economic growth and stability therefore also has distributional consequences. Yet the social agency behind this power-infused management of uncertainty is opaque, and often deliberately so; the use of ambiguity and uncertainty is a well-established mechanism for the extension of political authority. Heilmann and Perry (2011, 8) have argued that one of the central elements of the style of 'adaptive governance' practised by the CCP is that of 'guerilla-style policymaking' in which secrecy, versatility, speed, and surprise enable the CCP and its leaders to 'embrace uncertainty in order to benefit from it'. Although Heilmann and Perry limit themselves to assessing the mechanisms by which individual elites and policymakers 'push and seize' policy innovations, this deliberate embrace of ambiguity and uncertainty generates a broader phenomenon of 'multivocality' as a distinctive mechanism of control and authority. The multivocality of interpretation is 'the fact that single actions can be interpreted coherently from multiple perspectives simultaneously, the fact that single actions can be moves in many games at once, and the fact that public and private motivations cannot be parsed' (Padgett and Ansell 1993). In their illuminating study of Florentine state-building in the fifteenth century, Padgett and Ansell argue that this was key to how the 'sphinxlike character' of Cosimo de Medici was capable of founding a dynasty that dominated Florence for three centuries, paradoxically even as he appeared to possess no formal institutional authority within the city. Both in maintaining a high degree of opacity in its own institutional workings and dynamics, and conscientiously cultivating a legal culture that preserves ambiguity and encourages the exercise of discretion according to interpretations of political priorities, the CCP ensures that it remains at the indispensable centre of Chinese politics, society, and economy. The significance of the CCP lies in its role in confronting uncertainty, a necessary but insufficient condition for China's economic and political development.

This focus upon the role of the CCP does not exclude the roles played by other factors, but rather highlights the central and distinctive nature of that role, and its implications for how we conceptualize development as a product of socially embedded action capable of being undertaken by a variety of actors independently of their preconceived role within either bureaucratic or market structures. This conception of the CCP is therefore not one to explain the behaviour of 'the market' under conditions of economic uncertainty, nor to explaining bureaucratic decision-making or policy development. Rather, it is dedicated to comprehending the evolution and behaviour of particular agents and institutions arising from a context of social embeddedness in which they not only constitute the political sphere, but also simultaneously determine the parameters and shape of the market. That is to say, it operationalizes the political implications of economic activity and the economic implications of political activity, without relying upon the operation of the state vis-à-vis the market or vice versa. By extension, it therefore represents a means of understanding the political and economic significance of the CCP within a single analytical framework.

Embeddedness and Chinese social structure

This begs the question of what – if neither exclusively a black-boxed political economy of state regulation nor an economic sociology of market competition – *does* determine how uncertainty is managed and why the CCP is central to this process. Mechanisms for confronting uncertainty render it more or less rational for actors to undertake certain economic activities. They do so in historically and culturally mediated configurations of social structures, bridging an actor's micro-social circumstances and actual social outcomes by detailing the social theoretic dimensions across which logics of action will play out so as to produce particular outcomes. Such mechanisms of some form or another underpin all socio-economic activity by generating an array of intersubjectively generated capacities to act within an inherently uncertain social environment. In any given historical circumstance, they will assume a particular institutional configuration that permits and encourages a particular form of economic growth and development. Shifts in this institutional configuration will produce corresponding change in the nature of economic growth and political development. The exercise of power within this social space is what enables actors to engage in sense-making of the social world, to develop interests and preferences, and to coordinate meaningful social action. The recognition that mechanisms for confronting uncertainty are socially constructed and preconditional for economic activity allows us to turn one of the central questions of political economy on its head. Rather than asking how effectively an environment enables one to manage uncertainty, we may ask how the effective management of uncertainty itself has been defined via the construction of a particular politico-economic environment. To answer this question it is necessary to turn to how these mechanisms are embedded in historically contingent and culturally mediated social structures.

A number of prominent Chinese intellectuals have taken steps to attempt to construct a Chinese social science that is 'both informed by Western social science and at the same time critical of mainstream Western thinking' (Fewsmith 2008, 129). Central amongst these are Wang Hui and Cui Zhiyuan, who have argued that China should avoid the single-minded pursuit of the Western neoliberal economic model, not only because the validity of that model has been rendered highly doubtful in recent decades and years, but also because China has the intellectual resources and legacies that will enable it to avoid some of the problems that afflict the West (Cui 1997; Wang 2003 [1998]; Wang 2009). The arguments developed by such intellectuals during the reform era and their influence will come into play in later chapters. However, their thought functions most effectively as a method of critique and for framing the theoretical endeavour at hand, rather than as the basis for a positive conception of social order in modern China. For the purposes of developing such an analytical framework the most useful figure to turn toward is that of Fei Xiaotong, who in *From The Soil* (2006 [1948]) was the first Chinese sociologist to attempt to develop an indigenous theory of Chinese society that was intelligible through the conceptual and linguistic idioms of Western social science, and which thus enabled a comparative reference (Yang 2001).

Fei's sociology assists in developing a framework for analysing a structure that does not abide by traditional categories of institutional design dominated by the state/market dichotomy. The culture question is not one that should be resolved here through epistemological debate. Rather, it can and should be approached empirically as a relevant and influential factor in the process of social evolution; a 'practical sociology' (Sun 2012) that, in its due attentiveness to the practice of socio-economic evolution and transformation, embeds its theory and analysis in the social reality undergirding and surrounding this process. Fei's theory draws clear conceptual distinctions between the social structures of Western (the Anglo-Saxon western world) and Chinese society. He argues that whereas Western society is characterized by an 'organizational mode of association' (*tuantigeju* 团体格局), Chinese society is characterized by a 'differential mode of association' (*chaxugeju* 差序格局). Fei's conception of the Western mode of association as a distinct social formation is thus described:

> Western societies are somewhat like the way we collect rice straw to use to cook our food. After harvest, the rice straw is bound into bundles; several bundles are bound into larger bundles; and these are then stacked together so that they can be carried on shoulder poles. Each piece of straw belongs in a small bundle, which in turn belongs in a larger bundle, which in turn makes up a stack. The separate straws, the separate bundles, and finally the separate stacks all fit together to make up the whole haystack. In this way, the separately bound bundles can be stacked in an orderly way. (Fei 2006 [1948], 61)

According to Fei, in Western society these separate units are *organizations*, each with its own boundaries clearly defining membership, and with a priori rules establishing any distinctions or hierarchy amongst these members:

> My purpose in making the analogy [...] is to help us see more concretely the pattern of personal relationships in social life, what I will henceforth call the 'organizational mode of association'. (Fei 2006 [1948], 61–2)

In contrast to the organizational mode, the concept of *chaxugeju* represents an attempt to describe analytically the patterning of Chinese society through non-equivalent ranked categories of social relationships. These social relationships have four key features. First, networks are discontinuous, in that they centre on individuals and are composed differently for each person. This means that egocentrism and an a priori social embeddedness can coexist. They are egocentric since everyone is at the centre of their own social network (Feuchtwang 2009). Yet simultaneously the Chinese mode of association presupposes multiple linkages of self with others and a categorization of those linkages in sets of 'consanguineous coordinates' such as the 'socialized space' of geography, close family, or broader lineages (Fei 2006 [1948], 121). Secondly, each link in a Chinese person's network is defined in terms of *guanxi*. Each social tie is simultaneously both normatively defined and strictly personal.[3] They are normative in the sense that they consist of an explicit category of social relationship that demands specific, prescribed 'ritual' [礼] behaviour (see Hamilton 2010); personal in the sense that the specific prescribed actions necessary to maintain the link are rooted in norms of reciprocity and are defined as personal obligations on the part of each individual, particularly the subordinate in the dyadic relationship: obligations of the child to the parent, the wife to the husband, the official to the ruler, and the younger to the older. Thirdly, networks have no explicit boundaries, since they are not created on a jurisdictional basis – 'signed up for' – as is the case for Western organizational forms, but rather are preset. Whether someone in fact conforms to the obligations and expectations of the relationships, and thus is 'moral and upright', is another matter. Although the relationship pre-exists, a person is called upon to 'achieve' the relationship by rising to the normative standard demanded by that specific tie. A society thus comprised contains no sharp boundary lines, but only ambiguous zones of more or less dense and more or less institutionalized network configurations that impose normative demands upon the individuals within them. Finally, the normative content of behaviour in society is context-specific. Embedded in a world of differentially categorized social relationships, people evaluate ongoing action by considering the specific relations among actors. What is considered moral behaviour depends on the situation and social categories of the actors, rather than on abstract standards pertaining to autonomous individuals.

In sum, it is a profoundly personal, relational, normative, and egocentric system of social networks linking people together in multiple ways and placing different, though clear-cut, moral demands on each person in each specific context. The Confucian state was seen by its members as an enormous, but nevertheless united group, whilst the Western version is doctrinally at least an abstraction, a universal or absolute idea. It is not too far a stretch that the CCP conceives of its role as the patriarch of the 'super-family of Chinese people' (Redding 1990, 44). Yet it is not that Chinese society is group-oriented; the popular notion of Chinese society as oriented towards the 'collective' and thus disinclined to prioritize self-interest is a fallacy. Rather, Chinese society is indeed centred on the individual, but as the basis of social egoism, not social individualism. Social structure emerges from networks created through relational ties linking the self with discrete categories of other individuals. It is a society in which considerations of order, not laws, predominate. In this context, social order rests not upon the adherence of individuals to norms whose universal legitimacy is defined procedurally and thus in the abstract, but rather on the ability of individuals to uphold the normative obligations inherent in their network of concentrically expanding social relations. Fei's conception of this social egoism identifies clearly the paradox of Confucian normative theory: how Confucius himself was never capable of identifying a universal definition of 'benevolence' [仁], always relying upon discrete examples to identify what would not be 'benevolent' in the context of a particular dyadic tie or personal relationship (Zhao 2007). That Confucian political philosophy remains rooted in practical circumstances – in simple terms lacking a universal theory of justice – is intimately related to how it both emerged from and shaped fundamental characteristics of Chinese social structure itself.[4]

The organizational mode of Chinese commerce thus stands in contradistinction to the Western model of economic organization that revolved around those who controlled access to economic sectors and had jurisdiction over economic institutions. It was with the development of constitutional government that citizens emerged with the right to unfettered access to the economy, where their profit-making was unrestricted, and only the law limited control. Rather, in the Chinese mode of economic organization, the emphasis has always been upon harmony, upon a relational order that solicits obedience to the relationships that will ostensibly generate that harmony. As Needham (1956, 582) states,

> The Chinese notion of order positively excluded the [Western] notion of law ... The Chinese world-view depended on a totally different line of thought [from the law-based world-view developed in the West]. The harmonious cooperation of all beings arose, not from the orders of a superior authority external to themselves, but from the fact that [the Chinese] were all parts in a hierarchy of wholes forming a cosmic pattern, and what they obeyed were the internal dictates of their own natures.

This Chinese emphasis upon ordered relationships and on the achievement of harmony in those relationships profoundly influenced the establishment of social and political institutions (Hamilton 1996). That influence is still profoundly apparent in the mechanisms through which contemporary Chinese governance structures both manage and exploit socio-economic uncertainty.

Confronting uncertainty: frames and institutions

Fei's ideal-typical analysis provides a basis for integrating substantive features of Chinese social structure and relations into a model of how socio-economic uncertainty is confronted in China. Making the conceptual link from the nature of socio-economic embeddedness to socio-economic outcomes involves identifying the mechanisms by which social actors are both conditioned by and elect to shape that embeddedness. From the cognate fields of constructivist political economy and economic sociology, two key analytical concepts form the basis for this theory: cognitive frames and social institutions. Together they generate analytical space for understanding cross-societal variation in how institutions are constructed and assembled so as to confront uncertainty, without devolving into a state–market binary dichotomy. Cognitive frames and social institutions serve as mechanisms for reducing the uncertainty that would otherwise inhibit the development of a coherent basis for social action. In doing so, they do not simply function as 'neutral' devices to resolve coordination problems, but shape patterns of competition, mediate the exercise of power, and thus make a deep contribution to socio-economic stratification. A focus on how frames and institutions both reconfigure and reinforce the social world is therefore not to deny the role and significance of interests, but rather to emphasize the extent to which these interests are shaped and modulated by a pervasive and multidimensional social embeddedness. This emphasis permits the development of a dynamic model of the role of ideas in cognitively framing the process of institutional change and the production of socio-economic outcomes that in turn precipitate the renegotiation of dominant ideas and thus new cognitive frames.

Cognitive frames are essential for managing Knightian socio-economic uncertainty. Frames are 'schemata of interpretation' (Goffman 1986, 21), comprising 'narratives that guide both analysis and action in practical situations' (Rein and Schon 1996, 89). The development, contestation, and agreement of such frames enable actors to coalesce around shared interpretations and understandings of social reality. They function heuristically, contributing to the normative and mental organization of a social environment, and thereby establishing foundations for confronting uncertainty. Working with the related vocabulary of economic ideas, Blyth (2002, 37) argues that 'economic ideas make it possible for agents to reduce uncertainty by acting as interpretive frameworks that describe and systematically account for the workings of the economy by defining its constitutive elements and providing a general understanding of their "proper" (and therefore improper) interrelations'.

Given the uncertainty of outcomes that afflicts all social action, such frames assist in reducing uncertainty and generating stability in two ways: first, as lenses through which interpretations of institutions and social networks are refracted,[5] and secondly as social structures in their own right that both catalyse the formation and legitimize the perpetuation of such institutions and networks (Beckert 2010, 610). Such shared understandings are essential to the skill of actors in interpreting their situations, constructing viable courses of action, and innovating upon existing routines and practices (Béland and Cox 2011; Bourdieu and Wacquant 1992). Just as the economy is embedded in economic ideas (Callon 1998), economic ideas are embedded in broader society as an inflection of deeply rooted lineages of cultural heritage and historical trajectories of politico-economic development. As Beckert and Streeck (2008, 13) state emphatically,

> Economic action, like social action in general, takes place and is bound to take place within collectively constituted social macro-structures of social order, and it depends on their integrity. The interests that economic actors pursue and the rules that they follow must be culturally sanctioned; not being naturally given, they are also in need of discursive reflection whenever they become problematic.

It is therefore appropriate to view the cultural resources of Chinese society as important for understanding socio-economic action in the context of contemporary China. Within such framings, decision-making will never take place out of the context of concrete social circumstances, as officials, executives, and entrepreneurs will absorb information immediately at hand and use their intuition to process it, rather than looking for abstract theoretical explanations removed from the complex social context in which such decisions are always embedded (Redding 1990, 77). Understanding frames in this light draws attention to the multivocality of CCP authority in China, in which the ambiguity surrounding the nature of CCP rule is at once a producer of socio-economic uncertainty within broader society, as well as a solution for coping with that uncertainty. Nonetheless, the underlying sociocultural basis for the CCP's paradoxical embrace of uncertainty is not solely to be derived from Mao's revolutionary experiences, as Heilmann and Perry (2011) argue, but derives also from more fundamental structures of Chinese social relations, many of which came to be embodied in the CCP itself through the revolutionary period. Yet as I argued in Chapter 2, the cultural-historic rootedness of Chinese social relations is by no means incompatible with processes of institutionalization, rationalization, and systematization of social structures and decision-making mechanisms. The distinctive intersubjectivity of these social relations raises the issue of institutions and the role that they play in the rational organization of social order.

Institutions and the norms underpinning them create mutual expectations for interactions and limit the choice set of actors.[6] They reduce contingency in action situations by generating sanctions for norm transgression and providing credibility to decision-making processes (Beckert 2002; Hodgson 2006). Yet at the same time what is distinctive about social institutions is their need to be legitimated within a given social order and thus integrated into a specific social, political, and cultural context (Beckert 2002). Further, how an institution, and the rules and norms underpinning it, is mentally perceived and self-represented by an individual is constitutive of that institution (Searle 1995; 2005), for in their peculiarly social nature institutions are dependent for their existence upon the supporting beliefs and mental attitudes of those individuals that both 'make' and 'take' the relevant rules and norms (see Streeck 2009; 2010).

The implications of Fei's conception of the differential mode of association for institutions of social order are profound. The logic and actual unit of control differ between Chinese society (the relationship between individuals) and Western society (the individual). In the West, individuals are presumed to be autonomous, and thus subject to the rule of law as individuals. Individual rights, as identified and secured through a constitution, specify the basis for individual autonomy. Laws itemize those actions that would unduly infringe upon these rights. In China, society is regulated and order generated more through rituals, which means that order depends upon people's obedience to their social obligations. Accordingly, the obligations for each relationship must be identified, people must learn those obligations, and be corrected when they fail to fulfil them. The entire network of people joined through a set of relationships is implicated when one person fails to perform appropriately (Hamilton and Zheng 1992).

Significant differences begin to emerge between the West and China in terms of conceptualizing the nature and role of institutionalized norms and rules in society, and therefore the nature of state authority. The state is the highest organization in Western society. As Nettl (1968, 559) once classically stated with reference to the state, 'the thing exists and no amount of conceptual restructuring can dissolve it'. It has historically been extremely difficult for the Chinese state to maintain order and rule by jurisdiction, since ruling elites were inevitably faced with a disparity between their direct and formal tools of power, and the scale and diversity of the country (Wright 1962). In such circumstances it was role compliance, rather than formal legal structures that protected social order (Redding 1990), and this was thus a social order that 'could operate by itself, with the minimum of assistance from the formal political structure' (Yang 1959, 164). Given the nature of Chinese society, such a formal political structure, with the rigidity and constitutionalizing nature of 'rationalized' laws and codified norms, was fundamentally impractical and undesirable. In this sense, Chinese social structure developed on the basis that 'reasonableness' is superior to 'reason' (Lin 1941, 86).

This formed the basis for the distinctly social role of the state as it has existed historically in China. The CCP was already twenty-eight years old when it forged the Chinese state and thus, 'to the revolutionaries, a state constitution surely did not mean something like a contract that a democratic government makes with society or an agreement on how political power should be divided and shared' (Zheng 1997, 47). It is the CCP that provides coherence and consistency across a fragmented and decentralized state, as its institutional presence extends across all branches and levels of the bureaucracy (Florini et al. 2012). The fundamental nexus of authority and control is not a jurisdictional top-down system that controls the actions of every individual through the imposition of legal rules through a transparent bureaucratic state structure. Rather, the means of control is located in the institutionalized networks of relationships, and power holders' authority derives from their 'educational' function. Conceiving the role of the CCP in this manner casts in a different light the well-known aphorism that 'heaven is high and the emperor is far away'. This means that officialdom is removed from local society, and whilst it is in principle responsible for managing the whole, it does not intervene in the parts. It is only when disorder arises that it must ensure that all involved in the network work within their own successive circles of relationships to ensure that order is restored. The logic is that if everyone is attentive to the normative expectations of his or her close relations, then the whole world is at peace and the people can prosper (Hamilton and Zheng 1992).

Understanding the nature and role of cognitive frames and social institutions in this way allows us to begin to make sense of the politico-economic roles that the financial system and the CCP have played in the course of China's development since 1978, and also gain a social-theoretic understanding of why certain features of these roles have displayed resilience at the same time as others have undergone radical transformation. Frames concerning the relationship between 'socialist' ideology and the market economy gave rise to cognitive frames that guided debates within the CCP over institutional design, providing the motivation and generating the normative resources for certain actors to stabilize particular institutional forms and to delegitimize others. The cognitive frames that have underpinned Chinese political economy both in the modern and pre-modern eras generated the ideational basis for the CCP to act simultaneously as the guarantor of economic control and of economic growth. They generate a means of controlling uncertainty by way of embracing uncertainty. Institutional design thus reflects the shared understandings of how frames are to be interpreted, as actors draw upon them as resources and tools for catalysing institutional change. The resulting evolution of legal-bureaucratic and market institutions reconfigured the relative positions of individuals and groups within the political economy and enabled certain actors to reinforce their position within a stratified political economy, even as others' positions were weakened and subordinated through newly emergent institutions of reform and development. In the realm of financial and monetary policy, this change involves regulating and modulating the flow of capital. An array of institutions embodies particular conceptions of how to manage the social relations that constitute financial networks, including those that affect the quantity and value of capital (central banking), the allocation of capital (financial intermediaries), and the dynamics of financial markets (financial regulation). The resulting changes in the real economy and the ever-present prospects of financial crisis have continually catalysed these processes of social change. The consequence of this distinctive set of ideational and institutional mechanisms for confronting uncertainty has been an unbalanced stability in China's economic developmental trajectory.

Consequences of uncertainty: unbalanced stability

This allows us to begin to make greater sense of the politico-economic roles that the financial system and the CCP have played in the course of China's development since 1978, but also gain a deeper insight into the dynamics of stability and change in these roles. Ideas concerning the relationship between 'socialist' ideology and the market economy gave rise to cognitive frames that guided debates within the CCP over institutional design, providing the motivation and generating the normative resources for actors to stabilize certain institutional forms and to delegitimize others. Having embraced the idea that stable economic growth was essential above all else for securing the social and political goals of the CCP, China's policymakers and financial elites sought to orient the banking system and the allocation of capital towards this particular set of economic goals and priorities in the absence of sophisticated financial market mechanisms and in the face of increasing market dynamics in the real economy. Fulfilling these goals involved approaching the financial system as a set of socio-political resources – a tool of macroeconomic and political policy. The resulting evolution of legal-bureaucratic and market institutions reconfigured the relative positions of key individuals and groups underpinning the CCP and its relation to the real economy, and enabled certain actors to reinforce their position within a stratified political economy, even as others' positions were weakened and subordinated through newly emergent institutions of reform and development. These distributive consequences in the real economy and the ever-present prospects of financial crisis continually catalysed further processes of ideational and institutional change. In this light, it becomes both possible and necessary to base an analysis of the foundations of economic growth on a sociological analysis of the financial system as constitutively embedded within the broader economy.

Within this conceptualization, these economic goals can also be thought of in terms of a variety of dichotomies that flow from the 'two faces of uncertainty' – its management and its exploitation. As China's political economy has become increasingly rationalized, but rationalized around the power of the CCP, both the management and exploitation of socio-economic uncertainty have been integral and central to the path of market-led economic reform under the authoritative control and guidance of the CCP. Crucially, though, they can be both at the same time, as this environment incentivizes a constant straddling of a fine tension between conditions necessary for economic growth as well as those that imperil growth. As one prominent academic stated in relation to China's financial development,

> There is a serious inequality in the distribution of wealth and capital resources. ... This is directly connected to the way in which interest rates and financial markets must be managed in order keep China's economy on an even footing as it speeds forward like a high-speed train from Shanghai to Beijing and back again.[7]

The result is to make it easier and cheaper for one set of actors in the economy to access capital than others (Johansson 2012). In China's case, assets are highly concentrated within the banking system and associated financial institutions. This 'deep but narrow' financial profile is reflected in the observation that 'China is an extremely credit-dependent economy. Without the role of credit finance, the China growth story would not have been possible.'[8] The implication is that credit intermediated through banks has played an integral role in influencing not only the rate but also the nature of economic growth.

This takes place by mediating financial capital through the shaping of actors' expectations of the consequences of particular pathways of action. For example, cognitive frames emerged that fundamentally disrupted expectations for the extension of credit. Expectations for the use of capital shifted from underpinning egalitarian social policies through the all-encompassing firms of a command economy to a mechanism for capital accumulation.[9] Yet the ways in which this capital would be accumulated, however, was to remain firmly within the control of the CCP. Implementing this notion of development would thus lead to an institutional framework that fostered growth and retrenched control at the same time:

> On the one end, the financial framework has arranged a forced marriage between the deposits of the masses and state-owned commercial banks. On the other end, the illegal fundraising law has served as a means to keep public deposits from running away from their arranged marriage. This in effect serves as an official announcement that financial independence is forbidden. (Wang 2013)

Understanding the function of the financial system in these terms sheds further light on China's financial development. Conventional wisdom holds that financial liberalization and economic growth are positively correlated (McKinnon 1973; Shaw 1973; Roubini and Sala-i-Martin 1992; Levine 2005). There is a growing literature on how repressive financial policies foster a number of specific politico-economic imbalances, including inequality (Johansson and Wang 2012b), sectoral transformation (Johansson and Wang 2011), and an economy's external position (Johansson and Wang 2012a). However, China's experience has also led many to question this line of argument and re-examine the role of financial repression in development. Arguments have therefore also been made in favour of the need for developing countries to manage money supply and financial stability through repressive domestic financial policies (Stiglitz 1994; Hellmann et al. 1997), and limits upon the extent and pace of external liberalization (Stiglitz 2000; Prasad et al. 2003).

The relationship between financial repression and growth, however, is not linear (Johansson 2012), and thus these two views are not necessarily incompatible. Huang and Wang have argued that financial repression was beneficial to China's overall economic growth during the 1980s and 1990s, however, after 2000 it had a negative impact upon headline GDP growth (Huang and Wang 2011; Huang and Wang 2017). Of all of these measures of financial repression, the one form that did not have a negative impact upon growth was that of the share of state-owned banks in total bank loans. The hypothesis is that the capital allocation of the state banks is not significantly different from that of the other banks (Huang and Wang 2011). The implication is that under certain conditions financially repressive policies of interest rate regulation and directed-credit allocation may be beneficial for economic growth. Such repression can generate an 'adaptive efficiency' at the expense of 'allocative efficiency' (Li 2001; Maswana 2011), by carving out the policy space for fostering rapid development in the real economy through a state-led growth strategy (Hausmann and Rodrik 2003). Financial repression may thus be beneficial for economic growth under certain conditions, but it will nonetheless generate economic dynamics that threaten the balanced nature of that growth.

These distributive consequences of stratification have the potential to disturb the intellectual coherency of cognitive frames, generating an impetus to challenge and reconfigure existing institutions. Whether or not the actual social outcomes produced by this process – in terms of stability, aggregate material wealth, social equality, and so forth – coincide with the still salient cognitive premises upon which institutions constructed have an effect upon the evaluative interpretation of those cognitive frames as fundamentally normative socio-economic discourses. Exogenously, shocks and events further have the potential to disturb the coherency of cognitive frames, as new interpretations and understandings disrupt the continuity and harmony between still salient cognitive framings and actual socio-economic outcomes. These endogenous and exogenous trends and disruptions thus in turn produce 'cognitive evolution', as this diffusion reconfigures interpretations of actual social outcomes and reflects back upon the salience or acceptability of the original cognitive frames.

Conclusion

The distinctive position of the CCP – deeply embedded in China's distinctive patterns of social structure – reflects a specific and inherently normative vision of political economy as an unequal relationship between political authority and financial capital. The uncertainty of socio-economic action has enabled the CCP to maintain control, even when circumstances undermine its legitimacy. Entrenched and resilient CCP control has arisen out of the CCP's ability to exploit the functional imperative of managing uncertainty, such that the capacity to manage uncertainty becomes concentrated within the CCP as a particular social grouping. This need for cognitive and institutional mechanisms for reducing uncertainty and mediating (and thus translating) the social world into a comprehensible environment for action has historically been conceived of as being satisfied either by the structures of state governance or market exchange. In constructing a capitalist political economy, the role of the CCP disturbs these traditional categories of state and market, not because the functional characteristics of hierarchical control or contractual exchange as a means of organizing socio-economic reproduction have been modified, but rather because the imperatives of capitalism find clear expression in how the CCP seeks to orient financial activity towards economic growth whilst also satisfying the priorities of social stability and order.

Existing accounts of the expansion of markets throughout different economic sectors in China too often neglect the implications of how particular markets are constructed in particular ways. The construction of a capitalist economy is not a matter simply of guaranteeing market exchange, but rather one of accounting for the assumption of risk and the distribution of the profits of that market exchange. This reflects Braudel's characterization of the system of capitalist exchange as distinguished by the existence of a layer of systematic appropriation of profit, an activity that presupposes but is not necessarily directly attached to a lower stratum of participants in trade and exchange whose rewards are more or less proportionate to the costs and risks involved in such activities (Braudel 1981). For Braudel, market economies can exist wherever buyers and sellers convene to exchange goods at prices considered sensible by both parties. In historical comparative context, as we saw above, the construction by the CCP of particular markets for capital in China has not been neutral, but rather been directed towards a particular vision of national growth and development.

Notes

1 Interview 20 November 2012, Beijing – Minsheng Bank.
2 For more on embedding financial regulation within broader social practices and objectives, see Lothian (2012).
3 For an interpretation and update of Fei's concepts of *chaxugeju* and *tuantigeju* see Chang (2010).
4 The extent to which Confucian philosophy merely reflected or itself played a performative role in this social structure is a complex debate which shall be left alone here.
5 At a fundamental level, modes of cognition shape social reality. For example, one particular aspect of Chinese language is significant in this regard. The creation of a graphical language as opposed to a phonetic one relies upon the medium of the senses, the notion of a tangibility that permits it in some way to be 'seen'. This requirement thus hinders the emergence of purely abstract and non-tangible notions and concepts, and goes some way in further explaining the emphasis placed upon developing both social philosophy and political practice through practical and tangible examples, rather than as a deductively abstract exercise. See Redding (1990, 75).
6 An institution is any collectively accepted system of rules (procedures, practices) that enable us to create institutional facts. These rules typically have the form *X counts as Y in C*, where an object, persona, or state of affairs X is assigned a

special status, the Y status, such that the new status enables the person or object to perform functions that it could not perform solely in virtue of its physical structure, but requires as a necessary condition the assignment of the status. See Searle (2005).

7 Interview, 24 November 2012, Beijing – Tsinghua University.

8 Interview, 14 December 2012, Beijing – Bank of China.

9 As Deng Xiaoping stated at the crucial Central Work Conference of 1978, in a speech that would become official policy of the Communist Party in December 1978,

> We should allow some areas, enterprises, and workers and farmers to earn more and live a better life earlier than others through diligence and hard work. When some people become better off ahead of others, they are bound to have a tremendous demonstrative impact on their neighbors and will prompt them to follow their examples. In this way, the national economy as a whole will keep advancing wave upon wave, enabling people of all ethnic backgrounds throughout the country to become rich at a relatively faster rate. (Li 2009, 69)

4

From Tiananmen onwards: constructing capitalism in the 1990s

国家负亏，银行负债，老板负赢
The nation takes care of losses, the bank takes care of debt, and the boss takes care of profits.

Satirical aphorism from the 1990s[1]

Looking at today's financial chaos, I cannot help but admire Comrade Zhu Rongji's wise foresight.

Lou Jiwei (2018)

Although reform and opening commenced in the late 1970s, the Party line that has undergirded economic policymaking in the reform era emerged with the conceptual and ideological development of the socialist market economy [社会主义市场经济] in 1992. What has been labelled the 'neoconservative legacy' (Eaton 2016, 2) was a catalyst for the reassessment of the path of reform that had been adopted during the 1980s prior to the 1989 Tiananmen Square protests. During the 1990s, rather than the CCP becoming detached from administrative hierarchies and institutions of state, the Party was even more tightly integrated into other chains of command. The hierarchical relationships in the government and CCP were 'more clearly specified, monitored more effectively, and tied more closely to material rewards' (Naughton and Yang 2004, 8). It was thus in the period 1991–97 that the duality of the financial system began to emerge clearly as a critical feature of China's political economy, reflecting the two faces of uncertainty. It was the product of a commitment to the active construction of a capitalist political economy under the continued authoritarian rule of the CCP, and thus constituted the roots of a discourse and logic of economic growth as the means by which the goals of governance by the CCP could be achieved (Gruin 2016). The financial system's utility in the commercialization of real economic sectors began to be better understood and appreciated. At the same time, however, the financial sector remained closely bound to the administrative and political demands of restructuring centre–local relations, thus enabling a hybrid political economy of centralized political control and localized economic dynamism (Brown 2016).

In this chapter I trace the reinvigoration of the discourse of economic growth and its manifestation in the drive to establish a distinctly 'modern' financial system that satisfied the increasingly commercial imperatives of economic development, the evolution of a rationalized bureaucratic structure, and the need to retain authority over capital within the existing CCP-dominated political structure. The banking sector lay at the heart of this rationalization and reconsolidation of the CCP's role within the economy. From the point of his elevation to the Politburo Standing Committee (PSC), Zhu Rongji was determined to assert macroeconomic control, and consolidated personal and Party control over the financial system in order to restrain lending and reduce inflation whilst taking steps to elevate savings and provide a source of capital. This was achieved through institutional reform, but in no way did this actually create market competition within the financial system, but rather simply a more effective system of Party control. He developed and pushed through SOE reform, but the savings that accumulated at the same time as he worked to deflate the monetary base were channelled not into making sure that laid off workers were supported, but that large SOEs were bolstered and were given further growth opportunities. CCP mechanisms of control were essential to the duality of the financial system, even as it began to assume a modern institutional form.

The fallout from Tiananmen: doubling down on development

In the aftermath of Tiananmen, neoconservative concepts came to take a powerful hold on politico-economic thought. This was not simply a matter of reform-averse conservatives holding sway over liberal-minded reformers. Rather, the neoconservative vision was as much characterized by a drive for reform as the liberal vision, but insisted upon maintaining a concerted and realistic appraisal of what development-oriented reform necessitated in a new environment where it was clear that China's future lay equally with global integration and economic development, but also with CCP-led authoritarianism. For many intellectuals, Tiananmen came to be seen 'not so much as a case of repression as another instance of romantic radicalism bringing about its own defeat' (Fewsmith 2008, 102). What goes more unnoticed is the extent to which the events of June 1989, as much a product of economic instability and loss of price control as concerned with direct political liberalization, came to place the CCP leadership in a position whereby not only was its political legitimacy increasingly dependent upon its managerial capacity, but its margin for error in terms of economic governance was increasingly thin. The CCP needed to produce rapid economic growth, and it needed to make sure that this growth was stable and under control at all times. It is this feature of the path of reform in the early 1990s that sets it apart from that of the 1980s. In contrast to the loss of macroeconomic control during the 1980s and the austerity drive of 1989–90 (see Central Committee of the CCP 1990) that catalysed a sharp decrease in growth, the bid to control inflation in 1993 through Party discipline and financial repression was achieved without a corresponding drop in growth. The soft landing following the macroeconomic instability of the mid-1990s was so effectively achieved because the financial repression that was necessary in order to reconcile economic and political priorities in the post-1989 environment involved the strengthening of control over the financial system even as it was subjected to increasing commercialization and rationalization.

In the post-Tiananmen period, the Chinese Party leadership was confronted with a pressing need to reconstruct its interpretation and understanding of 'reform'. The validity and appropriateness of Deng Xiaoping's vision of China's reform path – particularly as it had manifested in Zhao Ziyang's leadership of the Party – was contested by conservatives as it rendered the CCP vulnerable to a diminishment of control over a process of socio-economic change that was clearly in motion throughout China (Fewsmith 2008). The issue was as deep as having to determine whether the socialist orientation itself would be upheld (Central Committee of the CCP 1998). These questions would be intensely debated and contested for the next two years, revolving around the fundamental issue of whether a market economy was fundamentally capitalist in nature or if it could potentially exist in a socialist economy [市场姓社还是姓资]. The process of renegotiation of the ideological and politico-economic foundations of China's now suddenly uncertain development trajectory necessarily addressed two forms of challenge: the political challenge of defining the foundation for the Party's ruling legitimacy, and the economic challenge of shaping policies and institutions that would enable this foundation to be consolidated and built upon. The financial system resided at the core of both of these issues, as loss of control over the money supply was regarded as one of the greatest risks for social stability,[2] whilst the provision of bank credit constituted a crucial component of fuelling the necessary high-speed growth. Following the blow to the CCP's socialist legitimacy dealt by 1989, the issue of how to engineer the growth necessary for political survival came to be in direct tension with the need to maintain economic stability as a matter of political survival.

The search for legitimacy in the post-Tiananmen era thus produced a reconsolidation of economic growth and development as the new raison d'être for the CCP. The interregnum in reform and opening following 1989 gave rise to a fierce debate over the future direction of Chinese economic development. 'Anti-reform' conservatism was seemingly entrenched in Beijing, as conservatives led by Chen Yun took a series of steps to charge Deng's rapid economic reform efforts with having precipitated the inflationary pressures of the late 1980s. This manifested in two ways: first that a reconsolidation of central planning capacity was necessary for the ongoing sustainability of China's economic growth,[3] and secondly that Party discipline had to be re-established on the traditional terms of Marxist thought.[4] It was imperative, therefore, in 1991 and 1992 that Deng Xiaoping should take drastic measures before the Fourteenth Party Congress. Deng's offensive was a critical point in the ideological reorientation of Chinese society (Hu et al. 2012). Whilst engaged in the Southern tour, Deng's first priority was thus to end the prolonged ideological and policy debate that had constrained his efforts to accelerate economic growth and development (Zhao 1993). However, this resolution derived from fundamentally different sources from those underlying the liberalizing reforms of the 1980s, and sought to separate the economic from the political in a way that had been anathema to Hu Yaobang and Zhao Ziyang. In targeting the 'leftist' tendency to hold fast to orthodox Marxist ideology, he argued that 'describing reform and opening as the importation and development of capitalism and viewing the main danger of "peaceful evolution" as coming from the economic field are leftist manifestations' (Hu et al. 2012).[5] He further emphasized the Party line of 'one centre and two basic points' [一中心 两基点] (Tang 1998). The centre was that economic growth and development of the forces of production was the central task of the Chinese state, whilst the two basic points were the means by which this was to be achieved: (1) centralized political control and the upholding of the 'Four Cardinal Principles',[6] and (2) insisting upon reform and openness to the outside world.[7]

The repercussions to Deng's pre-emptive attack in the south indicate that no side had decisively won the struggle before the Fourteenth Party Congress in October 1992. However by the close of the conference it was evident that Dengist policy circles had thoroughly marginalized the voices of intellectuals from across the political spectrum, insisting that GDP growth was the fundamental means of ameliorating the potential risk of social discontent (Qin 2008). This reflected the demise of what remained of a true

84

egalitarian streak within the leadership, as central planners such as Chen Yun who believed rapid economic growth was inherently destabilizing lost influence, and the younger conservatives including Li Peng and Yao Yilin adopted an 'indicative planning' perspective, rooted in the experience of Japan and the newly industrializing economies of East Asia (Heilmann and Shih 2012; see also Xue 1996). As Jiang Zemin gradually sought to establish himself as the 'core' of the third generation of leadership, he sought to articulate a coherent vision of socio-economic development, one which would come to revolve around strengthening CCP authority on three bases: development, stability, and national unity (Zheng 2001). Zhu Rongji was elevated to the Standing Committee of the Politburo in 1992 by Deng Xiaoping with the implicit support of Chen Yun, and tasked with the responsibility of bringing his technocratic style to bear on macroeconomic management (Shih 2008). Each of these leaders recognized the imperative of economic growth, and the fact that the CCP's political future was inextricably tied to it.

The political turmoil of 1989 had now given way to a renewed emphasis upon economic growth, and the economic dimensions of the challenge confronting the CCP in the early 1990s were numerous and varied in nature. Under the conditions of pervasive uncertainty that faced CCP policymakers, financial elites, entrepreneurs, and the managers of SOEs, it was virtually impossible for any of these actors to accurately gauge the potential risks of financial decisions. Rather, it was necessary to draw upon existing social resources and structures in order to manage this uncertainty during the process of reconstructing social order in the aftermath of an existential crisis in 1989. The ideational and institutional change that unfolded in the early 1990s profoundly influenced the path of socio-economic development, underpinning the duality of the banking and financial system as a means of generating economic growth without endangering political authority. This duality of the role of the financial system enabled these tensions to be resolved, reconciling the compromises demanded between the adoption of economic policies for purely economic purposes, and the adoption of economic policies for extra-economic purposes. What emerges

85

is a clear sense of demarcation between these two realms, and the manner in which their reconciliation was a fundamental necessity for maintaining the social foundations not only of economic activity, but also for maintaining the coherence and integrity of the broader social compact that has characterized social, political, and economic relations in China since 1989.

Frames: rectifying the market economy [正名市场经济]

The pressures confronting the CCP during the years following 1989 precipitated a deep-seated reconsideration of the bases for the Party's legitimacy and policymaking mandate. The attitudes, principles, and ideas that would guide financial reform in the years following did not emerge from an ideological and intellectual vacuum. The 'rectification' of the market economy was a process that generated the space for developing positive plans for subsequent reform;[8] it lay at the basis of the socialist market economy, and thus as a conceptual heuristic it provided the cognitive frame that would enable actors to reorient their behaviour and action within the political economy towards a different conception of the relationship between the state and the market. It was the CCP that would guide and engineer the evolution of this relationship, by taking this cognitive frame of a socialist market economy and diffusing it through the Party organizations that spanned both market and state. It was not simply a matter that institutions such as universities, think tanks, or professional associations had an effect upon the socialization of discourse and actors within new and evolving cognitive frameworks. Rather, the very foundational institutions of the economy and the socio-economic outcomes that these had produced (economic instability and the imperilling of the CCP's political and ideological legitimacy) served to motivate a shift in the framing of potential reform trajectories, but also firmly anchored and stabilized cognitive frames and their associated normative orientations.

The entrenchment of the discourse of economic development in the post-Tiananmen era had particular ramifications for the financial system. Doubling down on development also meant doubling down on capital, and it meant that the CCP was compelled to begin to confront the question of how to construct a modern financial system that would not disembed itself from either the real economy or society, and especially not the CCP itself that mediated between the two. The real dimensions of the conundrum facing the Party in the ideological and theoretical debates of the early 1990s is apparent in the following statement by a retired official:

> You [the author] ask about the question 'does the market have a socialist or capitalist surname?' [市场姓社还是姓资], but I think that in those days, the question was not just about the market. The market was already a reality for China.[9] The question for me at the time [the mid-1990s] was really 'does capital itself have to be capitalist?' [是否资本一定要属于资本主义]. Deng Xiaoping seemed to believe that the answer was no, and Zhu Rongji seemed to agree with him.[10]

Deng Xiaoping identified the purpose of reform as being to maintain and strengthen, rather than weaken and relax, CCP leadership (Wang Qinghua 2011, 94). In this way, the consequence of Deng's successful drive to embed the CCP's legitimacy within its capacity to generate economic development was to generate a need for transformation of the financial system. Furthermore, it became necessary to do this in a way that ensured that not only the market but also capital itself retained an allegiance to socialist ideology.

Socialism and the market [社会主义市场经济]

The foundation for this was the theoretical development of the socialist market economy. The State Commission on Economic System Reform [国家体改委] had been established in 1982 as a top-level body under the State Council to lead thinking on economic reform. From 1990 until 1993 it was headed by Chen Jinhua, who brought forth the line of reasoning that was to find favour amongst Deng Xiaoping and the highest leadership of the CCP at the Fourteenth Party Congress. Chen argued that combining the 'visible hand' with the 'invisible hand' had begun to become

87

a universal trend for managing and optimizing the global economic system. If capitalist countries were to draw upon planning mechanisms to overcome the drawbacks of the market, it only stood to reason that socialism could also utilize markets in order to raise efficiency and overcome the deficiencies of planning (Chen 2005). It was a matter of embedding the market within a socio-cultural context that would retain its socialist ideological values, notwithstanding the new-found significance of monetary exchange relations. During his 1992 Southern tour, Deng (1993, 382–3) had declared that

> Setbacks have befallen socialism in some countries and regions, and may appear a diminishing force. However, the experiences we gain and the lessons learnt will propel the development of socialism in more healthy directions. Therefore do not panic, thinking Marxism is going to disappear, become redundant, or is destined for failure. It is no such thing!

Stripping away the ideological hyperbole, this meant that, 'in Deng's grand game plan, the predicate "socialist" in China's "socialist market economy" remained largely a strategic capability to be carefully preserved under the continued rule of the communist Party' (Gore 2001, 202). As one retired academic said,

> In today's China the idea of 'socialism' is not taken very seriously, but in the 1990s when Deng Xiaoping was in charge, there was still a commitment to the socialist identity. Of course, this meant the Party, but isn't this what socialism has always been about?

He characterized the implications of the idea of the socialist market economy for economic thinking at the time in the following terms:

> Yes, of course there were lots of politics involved; Deng Xiaoping was fighting for his legacy. But it was also something more. It was recognition that both the market and the Party were essential for China's future. The challenge was to make them fit together.[11]

88

In November 1993 at the third plenum of the Fourteenth Party Congress, the Central Committee adopted the fifty-point 'Decision on Some Issues Concerning the Establishment of a Socialist Market Economic System' (Central Committee of the CCP 1993a). This decision would come to have profound effects upon the understandings of institutional change in the financial sector.

After Deng had 'rectified' understandings of what a market economy was and was not for, the next task was to determine how the concept that underpinned the necessary regulation of such a market economy was to be understood, interpreted, and implemented in the context of the newly developed concept of the socialist market economy itself. In his promulgation and support for Deng's formulation of the socialist market economy Zhu Rongji was profoundly antithetical to the ideological debates surrounding the role of the market. As a task-oriented problem-solver, Zhu interpreted Deng's southern talks not in terms of the ideological status of the market, but rather purely as a call to 'seize the moment . . . and not let it slip by' (Zhu 2013a, 54). Zhu has been accurately portrayed as a centralizing figure in the course of economic reform, a reformist technocrat who dominated financial policymaking from when Document No. 6 was promulgated in 1993 until the end of his tenure as Premier in 2003.[12] Yet this is not to imply that he was in any way apolitical. As a member of the Standing Committee, he not only unsurprisingly played a role in the deal-making and power dynamics that characterize Chinese elite politics, but he was firmly committed to a political vision that conceived of economic growth as both the product and the guarantor of financial stability and social order. As a senior banking executive described it,

> Zhu Rongji's financial and commercial knowledge meant that he understood how signals worked in the financial system. He saw how Deng Xiaoping's Southern tour was interpreted as a sign that it was now politically acceptable again to embrace the market, but he also saw how that led to inflation and a loss of economic control. But he knew the solution to this was not to return to central

89

planning like some wanted. For him the solution was to signal that markets were good, but that they needed rules and he would be the one setting and enforcing the rules.[13]

Zhu Rongji's personal and political style was reflected throughout his tenure. His authority over the government apparatus was characterized by a significant personalization and deinstitutionalization of the policy development process (Naughton 2002).

Jiang Zemin's interpretation of the socialist market economy was that macroeconomic tools, rather than administrative means, should be the main instruments of control; the plan should be confined to 'strategic targets'; and the state should endeavour to remove local barriers to an 'integrated national economy' (People's Daily 1993). However, where Zhu Rongji was the technocratic reformer, Jiang Zemin was the consummate politician. Following the 1994 fourth plenum, Jiang Zemin begin to firmly consolidate his position as the 'core' of the Party and instigated a movement away from the position held by Deng that economics was to constitute the politics of reform-era China, towards an increasing emphasis upon the ideological requirements of reform and governance. He asserted that the 'unification of understanding' between all cadres was essential, above and beyond economic development, and pointedly criticized those cadres who would 'bury their heads in the sands of economic reform and ignore the work of ideological education' (Jiang 1996). However, as Wu Guoguang has highlighted, the fundamental cause of the return of ideology in the mid-1990s was rooted in the absence of institutional rebuilding in the political domain that would reflect and be in accordance with China's socio-economic evolution (Wu 2001). Thus, rather than viewing the re-ideologization of the Chinese political system and broader society in general as conflicting with Deng's previous emphasis upon matters of practice rather than ideology, the dedication to Party work and strengthening in the post-Deng era should be seen as the entrenchment and reinforcement of Deng's maxim that the prioritization of the economic should be foremost for the CCP. Further, in this way it constituted a reorientation of CCP ideology itself towards the economic, and an exhortation to carve out moral precepts and norms with which to guide the CCP's pursuit of economic development. This reflected not only a morally charged approach to the establishment and regulation of markets, but one that began to catalyse and in fact itself constitute 'the cultural and technical work necessary to produce, to sustain, or – conversely – to constrain the market' (Fourcade and Healy 2007, 305). For Jiang, the socialism underlying the establishment of a 'socialist market economy' was thus about 'public ownership' (CCP Research Department 2002, 45), and public ownership was about control and Party leadership (see Dai 2010).

Commercialized control [宏观调控]

The two main policy priorities in 1992 and 1993 were 'rectification' [整顿] and 'reform' [改革]. Zhu Rongji conceived of these as separate but mutually reiterative: 'The first thing is to rectify and the second is to reform. We use reform as a means to rectify and to speed up reforms on the foundation of rectification' (Zhu 2011 [1993], 298). Addressing the weaknesses that had emerged in the fiscal and tax systems was part of this effort, building upon the influential arguments of Wang Shaoguang and Hu Angang, who argued that the decline in the central government's 'financial extractive capacity' since the beginning of the reform era was a substantial cause of China's macroeconomic instability (Wang and Hu 1993). In late June 1993, when the debate concerning the assertion of macroeconomic control over the overheated economy was at its fiercest, Hu Angang and Wang Shaoguang met the Minister of Finance and were informed that 'the line of thought relating to the reform of the fiscal system that you propose in the report comes very close to the way of thinking on the part of the central leaders' (Hu 1998, 17). This extended not only to Zhu Rongji, who was the lead architect of the fiscal and financial reforms in the early 1990s, but was 'entirely in line with General Secretary Jiang Zemin's line of thinking' (Official in the Central Policy Research Office, cited in Hu 1998, 18). Wang and Hu's arguments for the strengthening of the state's financial capacity formed the basis for the 1994 reforms towards a unified taxation system.

Zhu Rongji had the same desire to consolidate control over and resurrect the financial system as an effective tool for macroeconomic stability.[14] In contrast to the fiscal reform that was a 'way to dig the government out of [its] hole', the financial reforms were 'a way of advancing reform through the whole economy and generating future growth'.[15] Concomitant with the decline in the central government's fiscal capacity, monetary policy arose as the necessary basis for macroeconomic control. As Naughton observed,

> Previously, only fiscal policy was important; since reform, fiscal policy has been rendered impotent. By contrast, whereas monetary policy used to be fairly trivial, today only monetary policy can really matter for macroeconomic stability. (Naughton 1996, 125)

The loss of monetary control in 1993 precipitated the drive for configuring systems of economic control that preserved the political compromises and understandings that existed as between society and Party (Wu 2012b). This was one of the primary motivations of Zhu Rongji's drive to establish the central bank as a credible institution that could both implement decisive monetary policy as well as control the banks.

In 1993, despite the fervour of a reignited emphasis on economic development and growth, Zhu Rongji highlighted the numerous problems associated with ill-discipline within the banking system and the volatility of credit growth. As he announced in a March speech,

> [M]ost provinces and municipalities don't have the money, they have red-ink finances, and when they have shortfalls they borrow from the banks. Last year, just to make up for losses in edible grains, they borrowed almost RMB 30 billion from the banks, and in the first quarter of this year they added another RMB 3 billion in loans. That's why 'do it big and do it fast' relies on nothing but an expansion of bank credit, on printing more money. (Zhu 1992, 66)

This exemplifies the shift in policymaking priorities. 'Do it big, and do it fast' was originally a positive slogan popularized in the 1980s to exhort officials and entrepreneurs to maximize every possible opportunity to undertake new business and public projects. However, Zhu came to associate it with carelessness in economic decision-making that endangered the sustainability of economic growth and reform of the enterprise structure and financial system (Zhu 1992). Although structural reform of the SOE sector was a pressing challenge facing the CCP in 1992, the immediate concern was to rein in those projects and activities that were fuelling the demand for working capital loans from the banking system. The level of triangular debt swelled to RMB 380 billion by 1991.[16] It is common to assign cause for this build-up to competition with the newly emerging township–village enterprises, high interest rates, and their own inherent inefficiency (Fewsmith 2008). Zhu's conclusion in 1991, however, was that these might have been exacerbating factors, but the primary cause of the triangular debt was that departments, local governments, and enterprises were blindly starting up projects in pursuit of production value and speed (Zhu 1991).

In late 1992, the Party Central Committee sought to consolidate control over the loss of macroeconomic control by issuing 'Document No. 8' (PRC State Council 1992a). This emphasized four macroeconomic control measures. First, it placed priority on strengthening control over the scale of fixed-asset investment, whilst also strengthening the management of social fundraising for such investment. All forms of securities were to be issued in accordance with the national plan, whilst it was forbidden to raise money outside the plan by arbitrarily issuing bonds and stocks, or forcing enterprises to pay mandatory contributions. Secondly, control over credit quotas was to be strengthened. As Zhu Rongji stressed in October 1992, Document No. 8 was strict in stipulating that 'if any bank exceeds [its proportion of the overall RMB 350 billion in credit to be issued nationally], it will be held responsible; if any region exceeds [such a limit], the principal leaders of that region's Party committee and people's government will be held responsible' (Zhu Rongji 1993, 119–20). Thirdly, it was considered necessary to actively organize the 'recapture' of money and the placement of funds by strictly enforcing a system of responsibility for government agencies at all levels. Fourthly, increasing the level of forex reserves was regarded as a priority; maintaining reserves at no less than USD 20 billion was seen as a minimum benchmark. The document focused on administrative measures, rather than market-based measures secured through economic principles, in part because the problems of lax macroeconomic controls were largely a product of government maladministration, but more importantly because there was a belief that a socialist market economy was always necessarily to retain a strong element of administrative planning and government control over macroeconomic trends and dynamics (Zhu Rongji 1993, 121).

The extent of overheating in the financial sector by mid-1993 resulted in the Party Central Committee and State Council issuing the 'Proposal on the Current Economic Situation and on Strengthening Macro-Economic Control' ('Document No. 6') [国务院关于当前经济情况和加强宏观调控的意见] (Central Committee of the CCP 1993b). Its implementation was the most pressing issue confronting the leadership at the time (Chen 2005). Zhu emphasized three principles that were essential for cadres to heed in approaching the implementation of Document No. 6. The first and most important was to 'unify thinking':

> We must align our thinking and see the entire country as a single chessboard. Because they're not in the same place, localities may feel differently from the central government, and feelings may differ from one locality to another, or between the coastal areas and the interior. But no matter how you feel, we must all align our thinking; otherwise we won't be able to solve the present problems. (Zhu 2013 [1993], 134–5)

Secondly, Zhu called for measures 'not to manage and rectify but to further deepen the reforms. . . . We must turn the resolution of the most pressing current programs into a force for accelerating the reforms and for building a socialist market economy' (Zhu 2013 [1993], 135). Thirdly, he argued,

> Without powerful organizational tools, without steely disciplinary tools, and without impartial legal tools to complement them, it will be hard even for correct economic tools to be effective. It's very harmful to view all of these as administrative tools. (Zhu 2013 [1993], 136)

In order to effectively deploy market forces as a mechanism for economic growth and development, it was necessary to develop guidance on the nature of a concept that resided at the core of the debate around the appropriate relationship between the plan and the market, and socialism and capitalism: 'macro-level control and adjustment' [宏观调控], reflected in Zhu Rongji's assertion that

> As a socialist country, only with reliable macroeconomic control is it possible for China to effectively guide the direction of a market economy, and to realize the superiority of a socialist system. Accordingly, the construction and development of a socialist market economy must rely upon macroeconomic control; the spontaneous development of the market economy is not capable of bringing about a socialist market economy. (Liu et al. 1997, 2)

In the post-Tiananmen reassessment of China's path of socio-economic development, there was one constant: the CCP would remain at the heart of the political system. In order to generate the economic development that now more than ever constituted the Party's basis for socio-political legitimacy, commercialized control and guidance under the leadership of the CCP would come to be regarded as the key to the realization of a socialist market economy and thus the reinvigoration of China's development. This concept of the socialist market economy was not simply the oxymoronic manifestation of the ideological desperation of China's political elite, but rather came to serve as a subtle yet crucial cognitive frame that takes the necessarily authoritarian basis for CCP rule and combines it with the belief that the market is a tool for realizing

95

economic aims, rather than a politically significant institution that constitutes a normative end in and of itself.

Institution-building: (in)formalizing ambiguity

The reforms of the 1980s maintained an 'administrative regulatory system that imposed state supervision over virtually all economic transactions' (Potter 2001, 250), a characteristic of economic relations that was evident nowhere more clearly than in the financial system. This changed following the reinvigoration of reform in 1992. Establishing the institutions of a 'modern' financial system was recognized as an essential component in the construction of a socialist market economy, yet many of the specifics of the necessary reform were not spelled out within the broader ideological debate concerning the market and plan that was unfolding at the time (Wu 2012a). Institutional development in the financial sector in the early and mid-1990s unfolded within two broader trends: first a process of economic growth in which the financial sector played an important role, and secondly a process of reconsolidation of CCP control and authority over the political economy.

The development of the financially repressive urban-biased path of development was a reflection of how the implementation of the concept of macroeconomic control and adjustment was a response to the twin political and economic exigencies of the post-Tiananmen neoconservative era. The banking system channelled savings from the household to the enterprise sector. Between late 1989 and mid-1993 the overall economic policy priority of the leadership evolved from one of controlling inflation to reigniting growth. By the early 1990s, however, the strategy of 'growing out of the plan' via dual-track price reform and the transformation of rural enterprise had reached its logical conclusion (Naughton 1995). This meant that the preferential credit policies for state firms, originally designed to shield SOEs from the austerity imposed between 1989 and 1991, quickly turned into conduits for channelling large amounts of bank credit to state firms. In contrast to the 1980s, during which the immediate efficiency gains of price reform had propelled growth, China's rapid economic growth in the 1990s was based on the rapid accumulation of capital, and particularly physical investment.[17] Rapid capital accumulation was the critical component of China's economic growth, and was the result of 'economic reform policies making and keeping enterprise investment highly profitable, and of powerful incentives for households, enterprises, and government to save; and that the extremely inefficient financial system did not prove to be a serious obstacle' (Knight and Ding 2012, 124). The rate of return on capital was high throughout the decade, and despite the rapid rate of capital accumulation, expected profitability was sufficiently high to induce high investment levels. Entrepreneurial expectations of rapid economic growth were crucial for this high investment rate.

Mechanisms of Party control and commercialization emerged and developed in tandem across the institutions necessary for supporting economic activity. China's policymakers were seeking to accommodate the needs of an increasingly market-oriented and internationally integrated production system by commercializing the financial system. The development of a legal and institutional framework for banking and finance in the early 1990s was thus integral to the national effort to transform and commercialize the financial system. However, neither in conception nor in practice was it part of a strategy to promote the development of financial relationships that would rely upon either a legal and rational state bureaucracy or a secular market in order to maintain their integrity. In other words, financial relationships were placed on a more commercial footing, yet the efficacy of this commercialism remained highly dependent upon the role and utility of the CCP itself.

Through this process, institutional ambiguity constituted the means by which the CCP exercised instrumental control through multivocality, but at the same time this was incompatible with an internally contradictory normative framework. Achieving some degree of ideational (and thus ideological) coherency in this template for action was therefore a necessary prerequisite for preserving an intersubjective faith and confidence in the 'vision' of the CCP. The cognitive frames that emerged out of the intense struggle over the meaning of the market [姓社还是姓资] generated this latent basis for reducing uncertainty. Whilst the 'guerilla policy style' (Heilmann and Perry 2011, 12–13) certainly provided a crucial underlying basis for the resilience and policymaking versatility of the leadership during this period, just as the revolutionary CCP was itself founded upon the shared ideological foundations of socialist struggle as the path towards rejuvenation of the Chinese nation, China's capacity to construct a market-led economy came to be underpinned by an ongoing transformation of the shared ideological basis for an ambiguous but essential role for CCP leadership in the flow and management of capital.

Developing a guiding line on financial policy

Institutional change in the central financial policymaking apparatus was built upon the ideas that framed policy debates during and following the 1992 decision to establish a socialist market economy. Both Jiang Zemin and Zhu Rongji (although for different reasons) recognized that a centralization of political power was necessary in order to realize this objective. The interpenetration of Party and state functions and organizations was reinforced through the relationships between think tank researchers and policymakers. As Zhu Xufeng (2013b, 40) has argued, 'because of China's special administrative system, its think tanks have relationships that Western think tanks lack, namely, the institutionalized networks attached to the Chinese administrative system'. The position-list system serves not only as an institutionalized mechanism of Party control, but also embodies sets of informal networks that diffuse ideas generated through government think tanks such as the Chinese Academy of Social Sciences (CASS) and the Development Research Center of the State Council. Accordingly, this enables us to view the CCP's organizational presence across the financial system not as extra-institutional or supplementary, but as a set of integral social structures that integrate the formal institutions of governance with processes of socio-economic reproduction.

In the aftermath of Tiananmen, reconfigured networks of intellectuals and scholar-officials emerged who drew upon Western
academic theories as well as their direct experiences of the West
in order to advocate for a rational and systematic approach to the
reform and liberalization of the economy. This reconfiguration of
intellectual and Party networks involved two trends that would
guide policymaking. First, they became more closely integrated
with the formal policymaking process, and although in practice
this meant seeking an audience with and persuading Zhu Rongji,
this was increasingly taking place within the institutional structures
of the Party-state. Secondly, the ideological divisions in these networks became less acute, as there was a greater coalescence around
the intellectual challenge of conceptualizing and advocating market
reforms. The areas of institutional reforms seen as necessary in the
early 1990s concerned the financial, enterprise, and fiscal systems.
The 'comprehensive reform group' [整体改革派], led by Wu
Jinglian, had argued that the intertwining of all these broad areas
meant that it was necessary to undertake reforms concurrently
rather than seeking problems in the different areas sequentially
(Wu et al. 1995). This group included young officials such as Zhou
Xiaochuan, Guo Shuqing, and Lou Jiwei. They would come to
represent a network of economic thinkers who would later rise
to prominence in leading government positions.[18] Wu Jinglian
had already been an influential advisor to Zhao Ziyang during the
1980s, but nonetheless his views have always been highly mindful
of the destabilizing and regressive effects of inflation (Xiao 1999).

Another influential voice was that of Chen Yuan, the son of
Party elder Chen Yun. The younger Chen had become a vice-
governor of the PBOC in 1988, and would later take over the
helm of China Development Bank (CDB) in 1998. In 1991 he published an article that emphatically argued for the strengthening of
macroeconomic control over the economy (Chen 1991). Despite
emphasizing the fundamental prerequisite nature of applying
market pressure for the reform of the enterprise system, he differentiated such market pressure at a basic level from the principles
and institutions of macro-economic control, which constituted a

market-active paradigm but one that prevented any separation of growth imperatives from social imperatives. Warning against the 'hollowing out' [掏空] of Party control over the economy, Chen advocated the consolidation of market forces under political control and the adoption of a 'new centralization' (Chen 1991, 19). This would involve harnessing the power of the state, even as markets were permitted to break through local protectionism and micro-level distortions of enterprise efficiency. A year later Chen (1992) published another article, in which he assessed the thought of both John Maynard Keynes and Milton Friedman. Regarding the former, he approved of the role of government in achieving quantitative macroeconomic regulation and control [宏观调控], but rejected the methods of expansionary fiscal policy in order to achieve it. He also rejected Friedman's laissez-faire philosophy but approved of setting monetary policy goals. From such writings, it is clear that he was disinclined to develop an ideological preference for emphasizing either government or market, but rather was insistent that 'western economics can be turned to serve our socialist revolution' (Chen 1992, 32).

These intellectual networks, however, were dually enmeshed; in addition to advancing their own ideas through intellectual debates, they were deeply embedded in the Party networks that not only secured their careers and provided them with a policy audience, but impressed upon them also the significance of the conditions in which China, and the CCP, found itself increasingly alone in the post-Soviet liberal global order of the 1990s (Wang and Hu 1993). As Bell and Feng (2013, 126) have observed, the 'vagueness in interpreting the incentives and preferences of senior bureaucrats is also due to their dual identities as government officials as well as Party cadres'. As these intellectuals-cum-officials-cum-cadres rose to leadership positions in the late 1990s and 2000s, the contradictions between their Western-informed economic training and the demands of CCP authority and control would become increasingly apparent. However, in the early 1990s, their role within the policymaking process was to encourage the increasing expertise and concomitant rationalization of economic thinking, coalescing around the idea of 'macroeconomic control' [宏观调控] as the fundamental basis upon which to realize a 'socialist market economy'. At the same time, since Zhu Rongji was emerging as the lynchpin of economic policy, the process of financial restructuring became increasingly dependent upon the personalization of the policy process, and the concomitant personalization of policy credibility.[19]

One institutional lynchpin that re-emerged for linking financial and economic policy to the political imperatives of the CCP was the Central Finance and Economics Leading Group (CFELG) [中央财经领导小组]. The CFELG is an extra-constitutional policymaking body that links together the highest echelons of the CCP and the formal state bureaucracy. As a leading small group, it possesses tremendous influence (Yang 2000), and moves 'back and forth between government and Party depending on which leader is taking charge of economic work' (Shirk 1993, 61–2). However, all members are Party cadres and one of its primary functions, as with other leading small groups, is to provide a mechanism for the CCP General Secretary to reassert authority over economic policymaking whenever it is deemed necessary. The Staff Office of the CFELG is a crucial source of intellectual policy proposals, as it works directly for the highest leadership and draws upon a flexible and wide-ranging network of officials and researchers for 'document-drafting groups' [起草组] that frame financial and economic policy (Wu Guoguang 1995).

During the 1980s Zhao Ziyang relied upon the CFELG heavily as a means of resisting the pressure for centralization mounted by the State Planning Commission. Following 4 June 1989 and Zhao's downfall, the CFELG became practically dormant. It existed merely as a shadowy advisory organ and had no role in day-to-day policymaking until 1993 (Party source, cited in Lam 1995b). Jiang often deferred to Zhu Rongji on financial policymaking, and Zhu's guiding hand would be highly evident in this area until 2003. Under Jiang's stewardship, however, the CFELG underwent major expansion and was transformed into a policy-setting and in many ways a policy-implementing and supervisory body.[20] This was emblematic of the way in which Jiang Zemin expanded the functions of a number of the leading groups within the Central Committee in the early 1990s. This was a series of moves that ran counter to the principle of increasing separation of the Party and government, and a streamlining of the Party bureaucracy (Lam 1999).

Reshaping the PBOC: centralization without independence

In December 1993 the State Council promulgated the Decision on Reform of the Financial System, identifying the following objectives of financial reform (PRC State Council 1993):

1. Establishment of an independent macroeconomic control mechanism by the PBOC (independent from local governments, but under the control of the State Council);
2. Establishment of policy banks;
3. Transformation of SOCBs into commercial banks;
4. Establishment of unified, open, well-ordered, competitive, and well-managed financial markets,
5. Reform of foreign exchange controls, by unifying rates and moving towards current account convertibility;
6. Issuance of guidance for the development of non-bank financial institutions (NBFIs);
7. Development of a financial services infrastructure and modern financial management system.

The decision on financial reform was intended to transform the system, providing the basis for substantive and far-reaching changes in the institutional structure of the financial sector. The document emerged out of the State Commission on Economic System Reform in the context of the debates of 1993 surrounding the centralization of macroeconomic control (Chen 2005). It reflected a recognition that market-oriented reforms were necessary, yet preserved the ambiguity of implementation of process that has remained a hallmark characteristic of the financial system ever since in several key aspects: lines of regulatory authority and control, delineation of property and ownership rights, and the allocation of both risk and return (Wu 2005). Nevertheless, it marked the beginnings of systemic 'modernization' of the financial system as one that would successfully support capital accumulation. The most important component of the round of reform that arose out of the 1993 decision was the establishment of the PBOC as a fully functioning central bank at the heart of a modern central banking system (Wu 2012b). Establishing the goal of central banking as that of ensuring price stability for growth was an essential element in creating expectations of a favourable investment climate. High inflation depresses savings as the real interest rate decreases, and interest rate repression was necessary in order to ensure a flow of cheap capital and spur investment. SOEs were growth-oriented rather than profit-oriented per se, which is what Zhu Rongji desired. Given the necessity and success of price reform, he knew that the CCP needed market forces to drive the real economy, and that it needed to establish a modern central bank in order to allow it to do so.[21]

The most striking feature of the reforms of the central banking system was centralization without independence. Zhu Rongji (2011, 25) argued that his governorship of the PBOC was irrelevant:

> It doesn't matter whether I'm the governor of the Central Bank. I'm already responsible for finance and for the banking sector. [. . .] In the case of China, no matter how independent the Central Bank is, it can't be independent of the State Council. The independence of the China's central bank refers to its independence from local governments and other ministries and commissions under the State Council.

This reflects the fact the PBOC 'is not a puppet agency, nor is it independent of the central state leadership' (Bell and Feng 2013, 11). Its establishment was a deliberate rationalization of central banking but a rationalization according to the logic of financial and monetary policy serving a development strategy rather than being committed to a deductive application of market principles.

A relationship of mutual dependency evolved between the PBOC and the Party-state following 1993.[22] Zhu Rongji replaced Li Guixian as governor of the PBOC in July 1993 in the context of a significant decline in bank deposits in early 1993. His efforts thereafter to reverse that decline were made because he was determined to launch a capital-intensive growth strategy based on the intermediation of household savings through the banking sector.[23]

The focus of analysis has often been on the capacity of central authorities to maintain macroeconomic stability and achieve a soft landing after the overheated economy and inflation spike of the mid-1990s. Yet during the 1980s the PBOC developed another fundamental function and practice, that of re-lending [再贷款], a role that was contradictory to that of providing macroeconomic stability. Re-lending was a practice by which the central bank redistributed financial resources through the imposition of high reserve ratio requirements. Those funds that were deposited with the central bank could then be re-lent as earmarked policy loans (World Bank 1995). Under the credit plan this practice continued to constitute a primary basis for the ongoing viability of the specialized banks, as they were enfolded within Zhu's strategy for resolving triangular debt, managing inflationary pressures, and maintaining contributions to SOE working capital needs (Lardy 1998).

On 18 March 1995, the Law of the People's Republic of China on the People's Bank of China (*Central Bank Law*) was passed by the National People's Congress (National People's Congress of the People's Republic of China 1995). One senior official has stated:

> The law was passed so that everyone knew that the drive to commercialize was serious. Zhu Rongji had become governor of the PBOC already, but what were people to make of that other than that he was becoming more powerful? The inflation and economic instability of the early 1990s meant that there was no other option but to create a real central bank.[24]

Legally the central bank formulates an 'independent monetary policy' under the leadership of the State Council (Dai 2001, 4).

Article 2 of the *Central Bank Law* explicitly places the identification of policy objectives and goals under the purview of the State Council (National People's Congress of the People's Republic of China 1995). The law formally confirmed the PBOC's status as a central bank, and mandated that it 'formulate and implement' monetary policy. This remit was defined in Article 3 as: 'the aim of monetary policies is to maintain the stability of the value of the currency and thereby promote economic growth' (Article 3, National People's Congress of the People's Republic of China 1995). Although the article's phrasing indicates that price stability is viewed as a necessary if insufficient condition for economic growth, there is an inherent ambiguity as to the extent to which economic growth is the ultimate objective of central bank policy (He 1998; Wu 2012b). In reality, the PBOC was expected to pursue a comprehensive policy objective, 'aiming to balance inflation, employment, growth, and balance of payments concerns' (Bell and Feng 2013, 141). Although, as Bell and Feng argue, the consensus view within the PBOC is that price stability remains the bank's core contribution to the pursuit of economic growth, its leaders acknowledge the institutional realities that arise out of the tension between the PBOC's formal status and the reality of its role in China's political economy. First, they understand the difficulty of pursuing multiple goals simultaneously. Secondly, they accept the extent to which their responsibilities are embedded within a wider set of political and economic priorities, and that their performance is assessed not by reference to fulfilling a formal mandate but by how well they negotiate these priorities.[25]

Building 'real banks': specialized, commercialized, policy, or what?

There was little indication within the pre-1992 banking system that it had undergone significant change from the pre-1978 centrally planned model in terms of how the process of credit allocation was to relate to the broader sphere of production. It remained institutionally incapable of performing the ideal liberal role of financial intermediation in an increasingly market-oriented economy

(Dipchand et al. 1994; Tam 1995; Lardy 1998). Yet China's overall growth rate averaged 11.5 per cent between 1991 and 1997. As recent studies of the impact of China's financial repression have argued, whilst it is possible that deeper reform and a more liberalized financial sector would have increased this growth rate, it is improbable (Huang and Wang 2011). This militates against a deductive focus upon the banking system's allocative efficiency. Neither was it purely because of the banking system's unreformed and developmental nature that growth was so high. The ability of an institutionally underdeveloped banking system to underpin these rates of growth was less the product of a developmental technocratic leadership led by far-sighted pragmatists, but rather emerged as an ad hoc and internally inconsistent product of the conflicting imperatives to secure economic growth at the same time as guaranteeing the primacy of CCP political authority.

The December 1993 'Decision on Reform of the Financial System' (PRC State Council 1993) provided the basis for the transformation of the specialized banks [专业银行] into commercial banks [商业银行]. The reforms in the institutional structure and role of the banking system over the next several years were substantive, yet they did not have the effect that market-oriented liberal reformists would have desired. Rather, they effected an enhancement and realignment of the existing role that the banks had played in the reform process thus far; there was recognition that reform was necessary in order to support a rapidly developing market economy, but this was not necessarily commensurate with reform that would improve commercial allocative efficiency. Rather, the path of reform was consistent with the construction of a commercial environment that prioritized growth and stability over efficiency, in circumstances where both of these priorities were dependent upon satisfying both investors (household depositors) and consumers (enterprise borrowers) that the institutional structure of financial intermediation remained intact and viable.

The process of banking reform therefore cannot be understood except in the context of reform of both the fiscal system and the situation confronting SOEs at the time. Furthermore, even though, as Naughton (1995) admits, it is easier (if not impermissible) to identify ex-post coherence to the reform process, it is necessary to assess the path of reform as part of the broader and significantly contiguous development of the economic and industrial capacity of the Chinese economy since the post-1989 interregnum. In the early 1990s Premier Li Peng was in the midst of implementing the 'Large Enterprise Strategy' [大企业集团战略], which arose out of a deep concern on the part of the central government at the time that the decrease in the state's share of industrial production to 59 per cent was 'not only an economic but a major political problem' (Lam 1995a, 55). The 'grasping the large and letting go of the small' [抓大放小] policy of consolidating and rationalizing state ownership was at the same time being developed by Zhu Rongji and was first presented at the 1993 third plenum of the Fourteenth Central Committee, before being adopted officially in 1995 at the fifth plenum (Lin 2008). This programme built up the capital of large SOEs at the expense of those loss-making SOEs that were privatized (Institute for Industrial Economics 1998).

The premise of these strategies for reform of SOEs was not to seek to improve enterprise efficiency, but rather to strengthen them as pillars of China's national industrial capacity. The legacy of this line of thought that took shape in the post-1989 period has been clearly discernible in the evolution of central government policy ever since (Eaton 2016). This reflected the fact that the incentives facing enterprise managers at the time were oriented towards growth, rather than towards profitability (Steinfeld 1998; Knight and Ding 2012). The consolidation of the state-owned sector was underpinned by a commensurate centralization in financial control and repression. The pattern of bank lending was structured around this industrial policy, rather than as a matter of transferring funds to those SOEs and regions which had the largest number of workers made vulnerable as a consequence of the drive towards SOE privatization (cf. Lardy 1998; Shih 2008). A similar logic was evident in Zhu's solution to the SOE's triangular debt crisis. He compelled the banks to disburse loans of RMB 80 billion to the most heavily indebted enterprises who were in turn ordered to resolve their outstanding debts to other SOEs. This had the effect of eliminating RMB 380 billion in interfirm debt, but simultaneously created a further raft of bad debt on the balance sheets of the SOCBs (Shih 2008).

The institutional evolution of the state-banking sector also involved the establishment of three policy banks in 1993 to take up the policy-directed lending activities of the state commercial banks. These were the CDB,[26] the Export-Import Bank of China (EIBC), and the Agricultural Development Bank of China (ADBC). Each of these policy banks were intended to serve a particular function within a financial landscape that was being reconfigured in accordance with the new-found commitment to a 'socialist market economy'.[27] The CDB is ostensibly responsible for the financing of major infrastructural projects; the EIBC is to promote foreign trade; and the ADBC finances agricultural and rural development projects. The rationale for their establishment was that economic areas existed in which the commercial banks were either unwilling or unable to extend finance (Chen 2008). Upon establishing the CDB the bank was therefore immediately authorized to issue financial guarantee construction bonds [财政担保建设债券] (PRC State Council 1994).

In the debate surrounding the establishment of the policy banks, it was widely recognized that they would only work if the core functions of the banking system were transformed (Huang 1992). Zhu Mingchun argued at the time that once policy banks were established, the government would be able to desist from having to assume complete responsibility for enterprise and industry (Zhu Mingchun 1993). This would have necessitated the transfer of significant quantities of policy loans from the specialized banks to the policy banks. The decision to retain these non-performing loans (NPLs) on the balance sheets of the existing banks was made on the basis of the absence of a sound plan for recapitalization of the still not yet 'commercial' banks.[28] This was the case prior to the acceptance of the socialist market economy at the third plenum of the Fourteenth Party Congress, and it was argued that unless the government was prepared to solely utilize interest rates, re-lending, and open market operations to regulate commercial banks, it made little sense to establish separate policy banks (Huang 1992). Following the acceptance and diffusion of the frame of a socialist market economy, attitudes towards policy banks shifted (Zhu Mingchun 1993). One central regulator described it in the following terms:

> The banking system was such a mess at the time, because there was no real banking system. The idea of the 'specialized' banks was one that didn't make much sense, especially to reformers such as Wu Jinglian. But he would have been disappointed I think, because the policy banks clearly fit into the strategy of industrial development, but left the other banks behind with a lot of problems.[29]

Following the establishment of the policy banks, there was little indication that SOCBs began operating on commercial terms. The conventional view of the commercialization of the big four banks in this period was that it was a crucial but partial and failed series of steps on the way to the establishment of a 'modern enterprise system' [现代企业制度] (Leng 2009, 2). As Kwong has observed, the role of the big four as government policy agents to finance state projects and SOEs involved processes of capital allocation 'on the basis of social and political consideration instead of profitability and business criteria' (Kwong 2011, 164). Throughout the process of financial reform during the 1980s and well into the 1990s, policy lending remained a defining characteristic of the Chinese banking system. One-third of total loans outstanding in 1985 were policy loans, and one-fifth in 1995 (Lardy 1998).

In 1995 the *Law of the People's Republic of China on Commercial Banking* (*Commercial Banking Law*) officially reclassified the existing big four banks as commercial banks, in an effort to increase their independence from the state. Notwithstanding the formal change in naming the SOCBs, the law made it clear that lending behaviour was not to be guided purely by commercial considerations of profit. Article 34 of the *Commercial Banking Law* stated that 'A commercial bank shall conduct its loan business in accordance with the need for the development of the national economy and social progress and under the guidance of state industrial policy.' Further, Article 41 continues, 'A commercial bank owned solely by the state should provide loans for special projects approved by the state council.' This closely reflects the process – paradoxical from a Western perspective – of legal rationalization around the prerogatives of national development as they are determined contextually by the CCP. One member of a central government think tank provided the following frank opinion:

> Some say that there needs to be responsiveness to 'market needs'. In corporate governance this means transparency and clear lines of loyalty. But since 1993 the banks are at the center of China's economic development, and if there is a conflict between what the government needs from the banks, and what the market wants from the banks, why should the market always be right?[30]

The law stipulated that the banks' business operations were to be governed by principles of efficiency, safety, and liquidity, and they were to make their own decisions regarding business operations, take responsibility for their own risks, profits, and losses, and exercise appropriate self-restraint in their operations. The banks took a number of immediate steps to reform their organizational structures and behaviour, including the establishment of asset/liability management committees, credit committees, closure of loss-incurring branches, major investments in information technology, and staff training. However as one former SOCB manager turned regulator stated, 'these things were basically "window-dressing" [装装门面的] that did not change the basic facts of the banks' existences'.[31] Yet the drive to commercialize and rationalize the banks between 1993 and 1996 did have an effect upon the banks; as the same interviewee somewhat later observed, 'it seemed like the changes to the banks made them more effective at what they were doing'.

Notwithstanding the shifting legal status of the banks following the passage of the Commercial Bank Law, credit remained controlled almost exclusively through the state credit plan [信用计划], under which the PBOC set credit limits on the state commercial banks, thereby controlling the volume of fresh credit. This was gradually phased out and abolished in January 1998, as credit ceilings on financial institutions other than the specialized state-owned banks were eliminated and replaced with regulations regarding assets and liability and risk management. Whilst the credit plan was still in operation, the central bank had, until 1994, permitted local PBOC branches to adjust their credit ceiling by 7 per cent on either side of this limit. This flexibility in setting credit ceilings was removed in 1994, although local branches were still able to determine the distribution of credit quotas. Although these policies provided the central government with significant and close control over the amount of credit in circulation, local governments and the SOEs associated with them for the purposes of taxation and revenue came to accumulate debt that had very little likelihood of being repaid in full. Acceptance of this situation by the banks generated a self-replicating system, deriving from the ongoing lack of commercial experience on the part of the commercial banks and the familiarity of local government officials with state-planned credit.

NBFIs played an important and often under-appreciated role in the financial landscape of post-Tiananmen China (Table 4.1). Rural credit cooperatives (RCCs) had existed as deposit-taking institutions since the pre-reform era, and continued to be the largest set of NBFIs during the 1990s. RCCs were always conceived of as independent financial institutions that operated according to principles of democratic collective management (China Finance and Banking Society 1991). However, they have historically possessed very little operational autonomy but rather have been run as the lowest rung of the state financial administration, executing much of state policy across rural areas and sectors (Tam 1988). The close connection between RCCs and the state financial system meant that government officials considered their loans to be 'from the public, to the public' (Zhu and Jiang 1997). The non-bank financial sector evolved to split in two directions during the 1990s, with RCCs playing a crucial role in the broader intermediation

Table 4.1. Assets, loans, and deposits, by financial institution in 1997 (%)

Type of Institution	Assets	Loans	Deposits
Banks	84.6	80.7	76.5
State-owned banks	82.1	77.5	72.3
Other banks	2.5	3.2	4.2
Non-banks	15.4	19.3	23.5
Urban credit cooperatives	3.2	4.0	5.8
Rural credit cooperatives	8.2	10.4	12.8
Trust and finance companies	3.0	3.9	4.9
Total	100	100	100
(RMB billions)	7,697.1	6,115.3	6,857.1

Source: Almanac of China's Finance and Banking 1997

system, whilst trust and investment companies (TICs) were engaged in highly speculative and risky investments with a low level of allocative efficiency (Laurenceson and Chai 2003). After having had their activities curtailed dramatically in the late 1980s, during the early 1990s as the central government's fiscal capacity declined, and when restrictions upon SOCB lending were implemented through the credit plan, TICs again proliferated until in 1997 there were more than 600 in existence. During the 1980s TICs were largely established by SOCBs in order to promote a greater horizontal flow of funds between financial institutions even though local governments possessed a high degree of direct and indirect control, whereas in the 1990s TICs became very closely associated with local governments and their development objectives (Dipchand et al. 1994).

Generating space for reform: repressed money markets

From the beginning of reform, the question of interest rate adjustment as a mechanism for the efficient allocation of capital was present. Prior to 1978, the PBOC had directly controlled and targeted more than 100 different rates. The prevailing view had been that maintaining these controls would allow the PBOC to control and reduce any potential volatility in interest rates and thus liquidity during the price-setting experiments of the 1980s.[32] The administrative regulation and management of interest rates was a critical institutional foundation for stable investment-led growth. Financial repression was the basis for guaranteeing a cheap and stable source of capital for the fixed-capital investment that was the primary contributor to aggregate output growth between 1990 and 1998.[33] This degree of investment was feasible only with a commensurately high level of savings, and as the World Bank (1996, 13) noted, China's growth-engendering capital accumulation 'was supported by an extraordinarily high savings rate that has come to depend increasingly on China's thrifty households'. The importance of financial repression raised the question of how faith in the banking system was to be maintained so as to avoid large-scale deposit withdrawals. In contrast to other transition economies in which households hold most of their hard currency in cash, China's households were willing to retain vast sums of hard currency in state banks (Lardy 1998).

This issue of how to prevent disintermediation of capital in periods of high inflationary pressures had been faced in the late 1980s and arose again in late 1992 and 1993 when inflation peaked again at 24.3 per cent. The interest rates on sight deposits had been fixed at 2.88 per cent since the mid-1980s, and were raised only to a maximum of 3.15 per cent in July 1993 when inflationary pressure was at its highest (China Finance and Banking Society 1994). The real deposit rate was thus significantly negative. In order to stem deposit leakage from the banking system, when Zhu Rongji assumed the governorship of the PBOC in 1993 he indexed long-term interest rates to inflation, encouraging the public to hold more illiquid savings deposits (Table 4.2).

These moves had the effect at least of stemming the withdrawal in 1992 and 1993 of capital from the banks in the face of inflationary pressures. However, interest rates on sight deposits remained highly negative during the years of high inflation between 1993 and 1995, with real interest rates averaging approximately −16 per cent across these three years. The need to maintain liquidity meant that households continued to hold as much as 35 per cent of their savings in sight deposits, such that the proceeds of this de facto tax on liquidity provided an implicit subsidy to borrowers who

Table 4.2. Long-term interest rates, 1994–95

	March 1994	March 1995	September 1995
Indexed deposit rate			
Three-year	13.43	24.11	24.88
Five-year	16.13	26.81	27.58
Eight-year	18.83	29.51	30.28
Loan rate for fixed-asset investment			
Three- to five-year	13.86	14.58	15.12
Five- to ten-year	14.04	14.78	15.30

Source: Wei (1999)

benefited from interest rate repression. Nevertheless, despite this financial repression, by 1997, bank deposits had exceeded GDP, overwhelmingly underpinned by household savings (Figure 4.1).

The efforts by the central government to prevent disintermediation of both household and enterprise savings were underpinned by controlling interest rates. This remained a form of control that mediated between the needs of households and enterprises by subjecting the banking system to significant financial pressure. It was

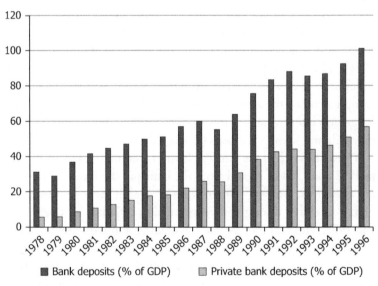

Figure 4.1: Savings levels, 1978–96
Source: Almanac of China's Finance and Banking 1996

114

only by entrenching the relationship of mutual dependency between the PBOC and the banks that it was possible to avoid both a banking crisis and a ratcheting up of pressure upon financially fragile SOEs, without producing further inflationary pressure. What liberals had hailed as a milestone in 1993 for financial reform was at the same time being actively undermined by the utilization of the banking system as a system for the PBOC to implement monetary policy as well as retain control over industrial policy and financial inter-mediation.[34] The underlying dynamics of the relationship between households, enterprises and China's rapid industrial development were thus established, with the banking system residing at its core.

New sources of capital: equity markets

Since the commencement of reform, the fundamental channel for the flow of capital throughout the Chinese economy has remained one of bank credit (Wu 2012b). It was nevertheless inevitable that the prospect of establishing financial exchanges as mechanisms for the allocation of capital was one that would have to be grappled with, as the CCP sought to reduce the degree of direct political intervention in the financial system. Deng Xiaoping had resolutely answered the question of the relationship between the market economy and socialism. Financial markets embody acutely its logical extension, 'does capital itself have to be capitalist?'.[35] During his Southern Tour, Deng (1993, 373) had the following to say on the topic of financial markets:

> Securities, stock markets, are they good or evil? Are they dangerous or safe? Are they unique to capitalism or also suitable to socialism? Let's try and see. Let's try for one or two years; if it goes well we can relax controls, and if it goes badly we can correct or close it. Even if we have to close it, we may do it quickly, or slowly, or partly. What are we afraid of? If we maintain this attitude, then we will not make big mistakes.

The Shanghai (SHSE) and the Shenzhen (SZSE) Stock Exchanges were established in December 1990. By the end of the 1991, the

SHSE had eight listed stocks and twenty-five members, whilst the SZSE had six listed stocks and fifteen members (CSRC 2008, 159). Following the 'August 10 incident' in 1992, the central government recognized the need to bring the emerging capital markets under a systematic framework of control.[36] The CSRC was established in October 1992. This further led to the State Council in December 1992 promulgating the first set of comprehensive regulations for capital markets (PRC State Council 1992b). One of the architects of the CSRC was Gao Xiqing, who has described himself (Duke Law School 2005, 22) as a 'Lei Feng type – a small cog in a huge Party machine, and wherever they put me I'm happily there'.[37] When drafting the initial regulations for the capital markets, Gao says that

[my colleagues and I] tried to copy [the American securities system] in many ways, we also borrowed rules from the British, Taiwanese, Japanese, and German systems, because the American rules of laissez faire just wouldn't work in China. People wouldn't agree to it. Even after all these years, we have a system that looks on the surface like others, but when you talk about the enforcement level, and the actual details of the laws, it's very different. (Duke Law School 2005, 23)

Although the CSRC would emerge during the 1997 National Financial Work Conference as the pre-eminent regulator over the financial markets, the State Council Securities Commission [国务院证券委员会] was established at the same time in October 1992 in order to provide overall macroeconomic management of the emerging securities markets. Further, the Securities Supervision Office of the PBOC had been established in May 1992 (CSRC 2008).

The scope for the development of capital markets that operated according to the ideals of Western principles was limited owing to the weaknesses of the banking system, and the fact that unfettered competition for the banking system was not a prospect that the CCP was willing to countenance (Xie 1994). The fate of the capital markets remained intimately connected to that of the SOCBs. However, this was not of material concern for those policymakers who had provided the original impetus and sanction for the formalization of these markets to begin with, as the objective of establishing and formalizing capital markets was to facilitate the raising of capital, rather than to achieve more efficient financial intermediation and risk management. As one government report phrased it at the time, 'the purpose of the share system is the share system and not to issue shares to the public' (Gao and Ye 1990, 81). Some accounts portray the emergence of stock markets as a product of the economic liberalism of the 1980s, an embrace of the concept of private ownership, and an increasing preference for free market thinking (Walter and Howie 2003). Yet notwithstanding the entrepreneurial spirit pervading Shenzhen throughout the decade, the efforts of the 'comprehensive reform group' along with other well-connected princelings such as Wang Qishan to advocate for the establishment of stock exchanges crystallized in Yao Yilin's support of experimenting with such markets as new channels for the raising of capital for SOEs (Li Kehua 2000). Zhu Rongji, at the time Mayor of Shanghai, also viewed the establishment of formal stock exchanges as a useful means of retaining control and majority ownership whilst alleviating the financing burden upon the central government to maintain the investment and working capital of SOEs.

As conceived in the early 1990s, the premise of financial commercialization was to achieve a greater concordance between the flow of capital and the needs of economic development, and one mechanism with which to achieve this was competition. The experimentation with futures markets in 1993 further embodied the difficult trajectory of market development in the nascent stages of China's acceptance of markets for capital. The extent to which policymakers were concerned with the impact of such markets upon 'stability' is well known, yet the contours of how this tension played out through the reform process remain obscure. The experiments with shareholding reform of medium-size SOEs in the 1980s had prompted the nascent but rapid emergence of a market for equity shares. Yet market-led competitive rationalization was not to be the premise for growth-supporting rationalization. Rather, it was the ambiguity and uncertainty embodied within the CCP itself in terms of its role in underpinning competitive economic activity that enabled it not only to remain at the centre of the financial system, but also to remain indispensable. Speaking of the relationship between capital markets and the CCP, one academic stated:

> Adam Smith wrote about the invisible hand, and Americans all treat this as the most fundamental part of capitalism. But the CCP does not want an invisible hand. The CCP wants to be the invisible hand itself.[38]

This was reflected in the identification of the state's priorities for commercialization and the role of capital markets:

> Because the government controls the development of China's stock markets, the guiding ideology is very important. I want to emphasize that up until today the guiding ideology in developing the stock markets is still to 'help state enterprises resolve their problems'. (Zhang Weiying, quoted in Wang An 2000, 364–5)

It was thus in the early 1990s that the initial dynamics of the relationship between the banking system and financial markets were established. This was one of the instrumental establishment and utilization of interbank, bond, equity, and foreign exchange markets, all of which were not only minor in quantitative terms relative to the banking system, but also subordinated in role and function to the major financial institutions.

Growth and the origins of the investment binge

Changes in the institutional framework underpinning the relationship between the banking sector and the real economy precipitated a change in the structure of networks that influenced lending decisions in the 1990s. These institutional developments structured the incentives and reconfigured the structural positions of creditors, intermediaries, and debtors within the political economy so as to produce a system of allocation of capital that heavily prioritized the urban over the rural, the coastal over the interior, and produced significant intra-regional income inequality. As savers were incentivized to provide the banking system with a large supply of cheap capital, these funds were channelled across the industrial landscape in such a way as to preserve the twin compacts that existed between the CCP leadership and its major constituencies. Not only the networks of political support that pervaded the basic functional components of the political economy, but also the broader population needed to be reassured that the path of development generated an environment in which continued economic growth was sustainable.

Although the passage of the *Commercial Banking Law* in 1995 and the establishment of the policy banks was a clear indication to banking cadres that changes were afoot in the role of the newly created 'commercial' banks, this was by no means interpreted as commensurate with a wholesale transformation of the relationship between the state-owned industrial sector and the state-owned banking sector.[39] Rather, there was a shift towards commercialization, with loan officers beginning to favour lending to more profitable SOEs over less-productive ones (Cull and Xu 2000; 2003).[40] During the 1990s, Chinese SOCBs discriminated positively in favour of SOEs, such that those cities with higher SOE shares in total output enjoyed greater access to bank loans. In 1997, privately owned companies received only 5.7 per cent of total loans from SOCBs, notwithstanding their contribution of over 20 per cent to overall industrial output (Wei and Wang 1997).

These lending patterns were heavily concentrated through political networks that permeated all levels of the CCP. It is widely documented that in the mid-1990s it was still the case that commercial banks were disbursing loans based purely on political considerations, with no prerogative to act on the basis of commercial considerations in 90 per cent of loan decisions (PBOC 1996, 34). A variety of problematic loan relationships

119

remained common. 'Hatted loans' [带帽下贷], 'designated loans' [点贷], and 'special project loans' [专项贷款] were all means by which Party officials were able to secure finance for projects both beyond the original credit plan and in order to satisfy growth targets (Li Tao 1994). This would have an adverse impact upon the credibility and viability of the credit plan, but the abolition of the credit plan was a development that was acceptable to cadres both within the bureaucracy and industry as long as they retained confidence in the underlying support of the central government and their ability to obtain the necessary finance.[41] It was growth rather than profit that remained the underlying rationale for industrial policy.

This hinged upon maintaining the expectations of a large number of bureaucrats, loan officers, and managers. Just because there was a shift to the market away from central planning did not mean that the bureaucratic apparatus of the old system would simply disappear. As one veteran banker stated,

> This was highly problematic of course, but at the same time it was just one of many problems. Zhu Rongji was trying to deal with inflation and inefficiency without destroying growth. But this is not easy.[42]

It was not easy because the only way to control inflation without destroying growth was to rely upon the existing and highly inefficient networks of lending and borrowing, rather than compelling banks to forge genuinely new and effective networks of credit flow to more commercially viable and efficient enterprises. The goals of simultaneously preserving macroeconomic stability and growth at the same time were prioritized over increasing efficiency, even as the commercialization and rationalization of the political economy were proceeding apace.[43]

The divergence began to emerge between the ideal of the envisaged allocation of resources [理想资源配置] and the reality of the socialist market economy as the effects of reform began to take hold. The reforms of the 1980s had left much of the urban economic structure virtually untouched. China's labour structure was thus shifting from an emphasis upon entrepreneurs to one upon labourers as capital-intensive growth came to rapidly increase in significance and prominence. In contrast to the rural reforms of the 1980s, in which local markets and rural entrepreneurship flourished, paid employment came increasingly to be the predominant option for transitioning out of agricultural production.[44] Whilst GDP growth remained high during the 1990s, it was unsustainable, concentrated upon heavy urban development, and reliant upon foreign direct investment (FDI) and the extraction of resources from rural areas, rather than indigenously sourced finance and capital. According to Huang, Chinese development in the 1980s was a rags-to-riches growth story, whilst the growth of the 1990s led to sharp income inequalities, a reduction of social opportunities available to the working population, slower income growth, and an investment-heavy growth pattern (Huang 2008). The consequence of reliance upon Party-dominated networks for financial intermediation was to generate modes of exclusion from economic and financial opportunity. In contrast to the reforms of the 1980s, in which 'rationalizing reforms had consistently failed' (Naughton 1995, 307), China supposedly demonstrated in the early and mid-1990s that it would 'not be perpetually stuck in a phase of half-reformed institutions and coexisting incompatible instruments of plan and market' (Naughton 1995, 307). Naughton was correct that fundamentally significant reform was achieved during this period, but the rationalization of the institutions and networks of economic activity that emerged through these reforms did not unfold in the manner for which he was expectantly hoping. Rather they were rationalized so as to consolidate the effectiveness of the state-owned networks of capital within an increasingly market-driven economic environment. Direct planning was replaced by indirect control, and the formal diktats of a Leninist command system were replaced by the networked edicts of an organization capable of binding together the institutions of state and market in order to generate the immediate incentives underpinning both political order and economic dynamism.

Conclusion

In this chapter I have traced how the concept of a socialist market economy provided a broad contextual frame for the development of a macroeconomic and financial policy revolving around the accumulation and investment of capital as a means of securing economic growth, without the CCP being compelled to endanger its control over these sources of growth and development. This precipitated institutional redesign in order to both stimulate and control economic growth. The institutions to emerge out of and around these policies were central to the stabilizing of expectations, but given their deliberate non-independence from the CCP, the networks between industry, finance, and Party evolved as the foundation of economic growth in the 1990s, even as the institutional framework increasingly resembled a modern financial structure. The combination of framing China's path of development in terms of realizing a socialist market economy, and the reform and establishment of institutions that emerged as a product of this cognitive orientation, produced a financial environment that structurally produced both high rates of growth and high degrees of inefficiency, but preserved the locus of socio-political control with the CCP. The institutional transformation of the financial sector under Zhu Rongji made possible the financial repression that assured macroeconomic stability as well as a source of capital for industrial restructuring and an investment-biased growth strategy.

It is for this reason that the 'comprehensive reform' strategy championed by Wu Jinglian was not realized in the way that models and expectations of liberal market-oriented reform would have expected. Reviewing the turning points of 1993 in the process of reform, it is possible to identify a number of areas in which the 'new era of comprehensive reform' [政体改革的新阶段] had arrived, yet financial reform was conspicuous in its absence from this list (Wu 2012a).[45] The imperative to maintain control over the flow of capital reflected the limits of the notion that a market economy understood through the lens of liberal Western economic theory was compatible with the continued existence of an authoritarian political system. Minxin Pei has argued that the reforms of the mid-1990s were characterized by a strong and negative influence of the political system: 'as long as the state remains the owner of China's largest banks, political decision-making will unavoidably prevail over commercial considerations' (Pei 1998, 349). However when examined in the broader context of the challenges created by risk and uncertainty facing the CCP coming out of the post-1989 interregnum, and the institutional and socio-economic tools available to the CCP's leaders, the course of reform more clearly indicates that it was not so much the case that political decision-making was unavoidable, but rather that it was essential and deliberate.

Yet this is not to assert that this consolidation of control over capital effectively rendered it a neutral force for economic and social development. The approach to the role of the market that Deng Xiaoping had framed through the concept of the socialist market economy can be understood as one in which the underlying socio-political foundations of modern Chinese society (i.e. a socialism embodied within CCP authority and rule) would be able to absorb, integrate, and utilize the market without being fundamentally threatened. The premise of Deng's socialist market economy was that markets are neutral economic tools, capable of being deployed and manipulated in order to advance broader social goals under the direction of an ideologically cohesive Party apparatus. The separation of state and market was only ever conceived of as possible in circumstances where the Party was capable of mediating between administrative and market mechanisms of politico-economic control. However, the cognitive frames that emerged in the aftermath of Tiananmen were not limited to 'how-to' rules, but also had profound implications on distributional outcomes and 'orders of worth' (Boltanski and Thévenot 2006). What Deng Xiaoping failed to appreciate, however, was the way in which markets are 'explicitly moral projects, saturated with normativity' (Fourcade and Healy 2007, 299–300). As Beckert notes, 'ideological innovations might also have unintended side effects that prevent the control of their consequences even by powerful actors' (Beckert 2010, 617).

The path of reform set in motion during the post-Tiananmen neo-conservative interregnum was successful in neutralizing the volatility of capital, but it served merely to ameliorate rather than eliminate the pressures that accrued from the concentration of profit-making (i.e. rent-seeking) opportunities within a network of firms and individuals that was simultaneously indispensable for securing the stability of the system. [46] This would come to manifest in two primary ways in 1997. The scale and severity of the issue of non-performing domestic loans to SOEs became increasingly apparent in 1997, and the quantity of toxic debt weighing upon their balance sheets was perceived as hindering their prospects of being able to attract capital and compete with foreign banks both domestically and internationally following China's anticipated accession to the WTO in 2001. Also among the developments that would usher in a new wave of reform in 1998 was the build-up of unsustainable foreign debt. The collapse and aftermath of the Guangdong International Trust and Investment Company (GITIC), and the onset of the Asian financial crisis would have profound impacts upon the future evolution of the financial system's role in China's path of development through the late 1990s and 2000s.

China's leadership was beginning to grapple with the inevitable challenge of integrating China's financial institutions into the global financial order. Having built what appeared to be an institutionally complete and thus 'modern' financial system, its potential to raise and then allocate capital for China's ongoing CCP-led growth strategy was to become increasingly reliant upon new stakeholders. As Chapter 5 details, they would increasingly recognize that along with the reliance upon capital holders, and especially foreign capital holders, would come an ever-more acute need to manage expectations and maintain broad faith and confidence. The path of reform would involve the increasing commercialization of financial institutions and the rationalization of state administrative functions. Yet the ongoing pursuit and acceleration of economic growth was possible only through a concomitant deepening of the central role of the CCP in managing uncertainty, even as it exploited that uncertainty to preserve political and economic control.

124

Notes

1 Interview, 29 November 2012, Beijing – Deutsche Bank Greater China.

2 As Zhu Rongji (Zhu 2011 [1994], 128) unambiguously stated it in 1994 in an address to a symposium of central bank branch presidents in 1994: 'if prices aren't stable, people's hearts won't be stable, and we won't be politically stable'.

3 This produced the notably unsuccessful period of austerity of late 1989 and 1990. See Naughton (1995, 273–83).

4 In the aftermath of 1989, Song Ping, along with Yao Yilin one of the most conservative members of the PSC, promulgated a set of criteria for the career advancement of CCP cadres that stressed ideological purity, contending that 'in assessing the performance of officials, Marxist morality should come before ability . . . cadres should have both ability and political integrity with [the latter] being more important]'. Political integrity was further defined by Song (1991) as a cadre's behaviour during the 'political disturbance of 1989'.

5 'Peaceful evolution' was regarded as a process by which subversive elements of bourgeois liberalization and capitalism would gradually and innocuously permeate society, politics, and the economy.

6 The four cardinal principles [四项基本原则] are (1) the principle of upholding the socialist path; (2) the principle of upholding the people's democratic dictatorship; (3) the principle of upholding the leadership of the Communist Party of China; and (4) the principle of upholding Mao Zedong thought and Marxism-Leninism. Twenty years on from Tiananmen, these four principles remain at the heart of CCP orthodoxy for the country's political direction (China's Future Direction Editorial Group 2009).

7 Deng (1989, 200–1) had first announced this signature epithet in June 1989, only five days after having cleared Tiananmen Square.

8 正名 [zhengming – the rectification of names] is a concept deployed in Confucian philosophy, rooted in the principle that order, harmony, and justice in the world are contingent upon social and physical objects being labelled and designated correctly, such that they exist and function in their normatively appropriate position. For example, Xunzi, a later Confucian scholar, exemplified its application to the political realm, arguing for the importance of the maxim 'Let the ruler be ruler, the subject subject; let the father be father, and the son son'. See Staal (1979, 8).

9 This dovetails with Wu Jinglian's observations at the 1990 conference on economic issues convened by the central party leadership on 5 July, where he argued that 'the slogan 'planned economy should be merged together with the market' was inappropriate, and rather what should be promoted is the concept of the 12th 3rd plenum 'socialist commodity economy', which in reality is the same thing as a 'socialist market economy'. See (Wu 2012a, 120–1)

10 Interview 7 April 2013, Beijing – retired party committee member, SOCB.

11 Interview 13 July 2013, Beijing – CASS.

12 A seminal decision of the CCP dedicated to bringing under control the macroeconomic instability that had developed in the aftermath of Deng's Southern tour and the Fourteenth Party Congress. See Central Committee of the Communist Party of China (1993b).

13 Interview 8 June 2012, Beijing – China Construction Bank.

14 Interview 14 April 2014, Beijing – Tsinghua University.

15 Interview 14 May 2012, Beijing – Development Research Centre of the State Council.

16 Triangular debt was interfirm indebtedness within the SOE sector and a consequent reliance upon extensive working capital loans from the banking sector in order to overcome constant cash and liquidity shortages.

17 One comprehensive study of China's growth also examines the contribution of the accumulation of human capital, which arose out of the liberalization of the labour market. See Knight and Ding (2012).

18 Just these three officials would count between them leading positions at the CBRC, CSRC, BOC, CCB, PBOC, MOF, SAFE, NDRC, CIC, and the Shandong Provincial Government, amongst a plethora of other party-related positions.

19 Interview 27 May 2012, Beijing – Chinese Academy of Social Sciences; Interview 12 December 2012, Beijing – Development Research Centre of the State Council.

20 Departments for macroeconomic analysis, industry, and agriculture were added to the CFELG in the mid-1990s, and Jiang further installed a large number of Shanghai Clique-associated protégés within key leadership positions, such as Zeng Peiyan and Hua Jianmin.

21 Interview 14 April 2014, Beijing – Chinese Academy of Social Sciences.

22 This arose out of Zhu's consolidation of control over the central economic bureaucracy, reflected in the appointment of his protégés Dai Xianglong in 1995 and then Zhou Xiaochuan in 2003 to the position of PBOC Governor.

23 Interview 21 October 2012, Beijing – People's Bank of China.

24 Interview 21 October 2012, Beijing – People's Bank of China.

25 Interview 10 October 2012, Beijing – People's Bank of China.

26 As a matter of translation, the official name of the bank should be rendered in English as the National Development Bank, but since the CDB itself adopts 'China' rather than 'National', I do the same.

27 The initial first governor of the CDB was Yao Zhenyen, who was entirely unconcerned with the source of funds of CDB projects. Interview 30 May 2012, Beijing – Beijing Normal University.

28 Interview 21 October 2012, Beijing – People's Bank of China.

29 Interview 7 April 2013, Beijing – China Banking Regulatory Commission.

30 Interview 5 June 2012, Beijing – Chinese Academy of Social Sciences.

31 Interview 10 June 2012, Beijing – Chinese Securities Regulatory Commission.

32 Interview 10 October 2012, Beijing – People's Bank of China. The first sign of interest rates becoming more directly responsive to market conditions was the *Provisional Regulation on Strengthening Interest Rate Administration*, a planning document issued by the PBOC in 1988. However, the basis for this responsiveness was a strengthening of the authority and mediating capacity of the central bank, rather than any relinquishing of authority or influence over the determination of specific interest rates (PBOC 1988).

33 Of the 9.5 per cent total output growth over this period, capital accumulation accounted for 6.4 per cent, labour force growth accounted for 0.5 per cent, and total factor productivity growth accounted for 2.6 per cent (Heytens and Zebregs 2003).

34 Interview 15 April 2014, Beijing – China Banking Regulatory Commission.

35 Interview 7 April 2013, Beijing – China Banking Regulatory Commission.

36 On 10 August 1992, upwards of half a million individuals waited for a share subscription that was to be issued by the Shenzhen branch of the People's Bank of China. When the number of subscription forms distributed was obviously less than had been promised, enraged prospective investors rioted in the streets.

37 Lei Feng (1940–62) was a soldier of the People's Liberation Army, who was characterized by the CCP and China's leaders as a selfless model citizen devoted to the CCP, Mao Zedong, and the people of China. Following his accidental death he became the subject of a posthumous national propaganda campaign 'Follow the example of Comrade Lei Feng' [向雷锋同志学习]. Gao Xiqing's remarks are further interesting for the fact that as one of the early 'returnees' [海龟] he is one of the more 'Westernized' financial policymakers and regulators.

38 Interview 4 June 2012, Beijing – National School of Development, Peking University.

39 Interview 14 June 2012, Beijing – Baoshang Bank; Interview 10 October 2012, Beijing – People's Bank of China.

40 Interview 10 October 2012, Beijing – People's Bank of China.

41 Interview 24 November 2012, Beijing – Tsinghua University.

42 Interview 15 April 2014, Beijing – Agricultural Bank of China.

43 Interview 20 June 2012, Beijing – Institute of Finance and Banking, Chinese Academy of Social Sciences; Interview 15 April 2014, Beijing – Agricultural Bank of China.

44 The drive for capital-intensive growth thus precipitated a profound transformation in the income sources and profiles of rural residents.

45 Interview 12 December 2012, Beijing – Development Research Center of the State Council.
46 As Riedel et al. (2007, 73) have argued, 'repairing a repressed financial system necessarily involves more than changing financial policy. It requires nothing less than a fundamental reorientation of development strategy, which inevitably entails heavy economic, political, and social costs.'

5

Entering the world: consolidating capitalism in the 2000s

> Foreigners wanted it both ways. They wanted the Chinese market to develop, but they wanted the Chinese state to step in to make it safe too. Why should the Party do this? Foreigners are not the concern of the Party.
>
> Retired financial cadre, Beijing[1]

The period 1998–2007 saw China entering the WTO and deeply embedding itself within the global economy, even as it came to grapple with the international discrediting of the East Asian growth model following the Asian financial crisis and the debt burdens brought about by its own unbalanced growth trajectory that had emerged over the preceding seven years. By the eve of the 2008 financial crisis, it was clear that China's financial sector had experienced sweeping institutional change over the preceding ten years. Now spearheaded by publicly listed banking titans and a central bank with an emerging international reputation for effective and technocratic macroeconomic management, the financial system appeared to have served effectively as a lynchpin of China's years of heady rates of economic growth that peaked at 14.2 per cent in 2007. Yet, despite the extent of financial reform between 1998 and 2008, it is also clear that the reorganization of state and market within the financial sector had resulted in the predominance of neither. As would become clear in the final months of 2008, when China's economic stimulus package came into effect, the banking system that had been such an area of concerted focus by both Zhu Rongji and Wen Jiabao in only very limited ways bore a functional resemblance to the liberal financial systems that had supposedly been the model for China's own path of financial reform, but which were now themselves embroiled in existential crisis.

From a standard liberal perspective, this process of financial reform was thus a failure; the market-based elements of the system were immature according to the standards of orthodox financial theory, and the financial sector remained a long way from playing the fully fledged 'mature' role of financial systems in more 'advanced' economies. Although a broad sweep of changes took place within the financial sector during Zhu Rongji's tenure as Premier, as Shih has observed,

> It is evident that the financial sector was little more market-oriented than when he had first taken office. Although some of his efforts furthered market allocation of capital, other policies pulled China back to the planned economy. Thus, explanations that rely on his reform orientation, the capability of technocrats, or the diffusion of market-oriented ideas cannot satisfactorily account for the lack of significant financial sector reform during his administration; those conditions were all present at the beginning of his administration. (Shih 2008, 162)

This is only paradoxical if it is assumed that the ultimate objective of financial reform was in fact to institute a fully market-oriented and liberalized financial sector. The corollary of this assumption is that along with the rationalization and downsizing of the Chinese state in the process of economic reform, so too would the role of the Party be diminished and even eliminated, presumably even more rapidly and deeply than the state itself. This chapter demonstrates how this misplaced assumption obstructs an accurate assessment of how state and Party interacted during this period. It argues that the key to explaining these developments is to focus upon the way in which the CCP was able to reduce the uncertainty inherent in this path of reform, but also to reduce it in a particular way, such that trajectories of growth and development, even whilst highly rapid and stable, were simultaneously unbalanced and unsustainable. Unless we account for the role that the management of uncertainty played as a key driver in the evolution of the financial sector during this era, it becomes difficult to plausibly make sense of why both the market and the CCP enhanced their ability to influence not only the rate but also the structure of economic growth.

As China developed from what had been a position of (relative) international isolation to (partial) integration with the global economy, it was necessary to develop a set of financial and macroeconomic policies that would support trade and attract investment. China's leaders sought to construct an internationally oriented modern financial system, which to all appearances was now geared towards competition with foreign banks both at home and eventually abroad. This process of institutional rationalization within the financial system was not a chimera; policymakers, banks, and regulators each conceived of their roles within the financial system in terms substantively different from those of the mid-1990s. Yet, as would become apparent when financial crisis emanated from the USA in 2008, the premise of reform during the 2000s had not been to replicate a Western financial system, but to transform the banking system into a more effective tool for achieving the broader politico-economic goals of the CCP.

Rather than the path of reform being one of failure or of settling into a partial reform equilibrium as a result of bureaucratic or elite politics, the ways in which the CCP was negotiating a number of risks and uncertainties by way of instituting its own distinctive mode of economic development meant that reform was less about pursuing market-led liberalization or state-led planning, but rather about maintaining capital-led economic growth and accumulation. The duality of the financial sector's role that emerged during the process of reform in the mid-1990s continued to be reflected in the frames, institutions, and networks that evolved between 1998 and 2007. It was only by retaining the foundational role of the financial sector as a centrally controlled lynchpin of an increasingly marketized and globally integrated economy that the CCP was capable of achieving economic growth whilst guarding against the destabilizing implications of relinquishing control over capital flows.

Mounting pressures, international and domestic

As Zhu Rongji ascended to the pinnacle of economic leadership of the CCP in late 1997, the potential for 'crisis' was supposedly pervasive. Although in 1997–98 the economy was in a relatively healthy condition as a result of Zhu's fiscal recentralization, and contractionary monetary policy from 1994 to 1996 (Bramall 2009), this balancing act also heightened policymakers' sensitivity to possible threats to economic growth and stability. At the macro-economic level, economic growth slid downwards, dipping below 8 per cent in 1998–99, whilst China experienced deflation for the first time in the reform era. The drivers of financial policymaking in this period reflected a number of both domestic and international concerns. China experienced its first modern era failures of financial firms, each of which had connections to international sources of capital, and the AFC represented a salutary warning of the possible effects upon domestic monetary policy and currency stability of any wide-scale relaxation of control over transnational capital flows.

The reforms of the 1990s provided a path of navigation through the uncertainty of the immediate post-1989 political economy by framing the financial system in terms of a combination of CCP authority over an expanding market economy. Yet these reforms had themselves given rise to new financial risks, which were now further entwined with China's deepening international integration. Not merely unquantifiable in purely economic and financial terms, these risks and the uncertainty whence they emerged were deeply embroiled in a continuing set of debates as to how China's society and politics were going to confront a critical new phase in the country's contemporary development. This uncertainty surrounded the fundamental questions of who or what was responsible for maintaining the integrity of the financial system, and how they were going to achieve this as China's domestic economy and its position within the global economy continued to evolve. Accordingly, there were two broad interrelated strands of uncertainty that needed to be addressed. First was the concern that the banking system was unable to maintain its own internal integrity, and that at some point existing domestic stakeholders in the banking system – ordinary household and corporate depositors – would lose confidence in the financial system. Secondly, it was clear that the financial system was precariously exposed to destabilizing external competition, and that WTO entry and China's need to attract foreign capital would potentially catalyse financial instability and crisis.

Crisis and the domestic

Although the AFC influenced China in real economic terms, its real significance was normative. It had a deep impact upon perceptions of and attitudes towards the dynamics of the global financial system, and the interpretation of specific aspects of China's integration into this system. This would have tangible effects on how debates unfolded and discourses emerged around the challenges of pursuing financial reform, the cognitive frames that emerged out of those debates, and the actual policy measures that eventuated. In immediate terms, however, the crisis gave rise to two potential risks within the Chinese economy: first a currency crisis, resulting from balance of payment problems or heavy capital outflows, and secondly, a banking crisis caused by loss of depositor confidence and banks' insolvency. However, the AFC was not immediately viewed as a threat with existential ramifications by the Chinese leadership.[2] As Yu Yongding observed at the time,

> For many years, observers have criticized China's slowness in developing financial markets and liberalizing its capital account. The Chinese government itself was also worried by the slow progress. Rather theatrically, the disadvantage has turned into advantage. Owing to capital controls and the underdevelopment of financial markets and the lack of sophisticated financial instruments, such as stock futures and foreign exchange forwards, RMB escaped the attack by international speculators. (Yu 1999, 15)

However, the AFC nonetheless revealed the depth of a potential conflict between the risks posed by China's economic opening and the ability of the financial system to contain and manage those risks.

Immediately following the Fifteenth Party Congress in September 1997, Jiang Zemin stressed the importance of drawing the correct lessons from the AFC and ensuring that the risk of financial instability was comprehensively managed by the CCP (Zhu 1998b). He drew the link explicitly between the financial system and broader social stability, stating that 'if the financial system is unstable, then it will also affect economic and social stability' (Jiang 2006 [1997], 422). The financial sector had to prove capable of withstanding integration with foreign capital, but it had to do so in a way that would safeguard the stability of the financial system as had clearly been lacking in other East Asian economies. Capital controls and a tightly regulated financial sector had prevented the transnational flow of destabilizing capital. From the earliest days of reform, FDI had played a central role in the Chinese growth story, and despite the experience of the AFC there was widespread recognition amongst the leadership of the increasing indispensability of FDI to China's future economic growth (Chang 1998).[3] In practice, financial reform and internationalization following the AFC would therefore maintain a sharp distinction between speculative portfolio and fixed investment capital.

Against this backdrop of the crisis, between 17 and 19 November 1997 the Central Committee of the CCP and the State Council convened an emergency National Financial Work Conference in Beijing.[4] It called for the establishment of a financial system compatible with the socialist market economy and for the strengthening of the risk management capacity of financial institutions over the next three years (Historical Research Unit of the Central Committee of the CCP 1999). Zhu Rongji saw the AFC as demanding a redoubling of efforts to deepen financial reform, stating that it 'has caused us to be determined to solve these problems at the most fundamental level – we can hesitate no longer' (Zhu 2000 [1997], 322). The AFC precipitated a vigorous discussion amongst economic policymakers and researchers as to the nature of these problems. The views about the causes of the crisis fell into two broad camps, one stressing the destructive power of international speculative capital (Pang 1998), the other emphasizing the weaknesses of the financial systems in those countries most heavily affected by the crisis (Ding and Li 1998, Zhu 1998a). Yet insofar as the ultimate direction of post-crisis policy development was influenced by these debates, it was to adopt both messages as mutually compatible. Foreign and transnational capital *was* a potentially destructive and destabilizing force for China, and the financial foundations of a number of the countries *were* weak. However, they were weak not because they departed from the strictures of the so-called Washington Consensus, but because of the weakness of mechanisms in place for managing both the domestic and international financial demands of economic development.

It was in this context that China was progressing steadily towards WTO accession. Accession and the consequent opening up of financial services under the General Agreement on Trade in Services (GATS) was considered an important step in the overall reform process, principally in terms of gaining greater exposure to foreign expertise, but also for its potential to foster greater commercial discipline upon the sector (Allen et al. 2005; Leigh and Podpiera 2006). The idea that the CCP has used global economic integration in order to apply pressure for domestic economic and financial reform is not new. Nevertheless, the course of financial reform in the years 1998–2007 demonstrate the extent to which global economic integration precipitated a particular kind of reform, one which utilized significant elements of 'modern finance' but utilized them in substantively very different ways. Although the circumstances in which the Chinese economy was operating were no longer the same as those of the early 1990s, the risk environment remained functionally highly similar. The banking and financial system was still fundamentally there to provide certainty for domestic financial actors, a function that continued to be reflected in the course of its reform.

In the face of inevitable globalization, a number of questions were being asked of the Chinese economy and financial system in 1998. What was the appropriate relationship between domestic and foreign capital? How did the political implications of international as opposed to domestic financial liberalization differ? What did it mean for the socialist market economy, or for socialism with Chinese characteristics itself? The AFC was an exogenous juncture that, whilst not exposing any direct link between China's path of reform thus far in the 1990s and the potential for financial crisis, certainly both reflected on the frames that had guided financial reform earlier in the decade, and in doing so provoked further reflection amongst the Chinese policymaking elite as to the future path of reform. It reinforced two messages: first, that the East Asian developmental state was by no means immune to financial crisis precipitated by external actors and factors, and secondly, that devising ways in which to generate economic growth whilst maintaining those institutions and characteristics that preserved China's financial stability was therefore crucial to China's management of the 'inevitable' fact of economic integration and globalization. These challenges were intimately bound up with the condition of domestic financial institutions, and as circumstances simultaneously evolved within this domestic sector, the extent to which the realms of foreign and domestic capital were in fact intertwined became increasingly apparent.

Debt and the international

After having 'tamed' inflation through 1995–96 by coupling financial restructuring to a financially repressive and investment-oriented growth strategy, the domestic financial challenges that emerged in the late 1990s were significant. Prominent amongst these was the accumulation of debt relationships that linked together financial institutions of three kinds: state-owned commercial banks, China's international trust and investment companies (ITICs), and the foreign creditors of those ITICs. Amidst the macroeconomic slowdown, a number of financial institutions experienced distress and failure.[5] Principal amongst these was GITIC which, after having accumulated over USD 3.7 billion in liabilities to foreign financial institutions, in October 1998 became subject to a central government inquiry headed by Wang Qishan and entered bankruptcy in January 1999 (Landler 1999). Trust and investment companies, both domestic and international, had always occupied an ambiguous position within the financial eco-system, thereby being subjected to a constantly changing regu-latory environment. The industry had experienced a number of 'rectifications' [整顿] since the beginning of the reform period in 1978, the latest of which had begun in 1995 and was still unfolding throughout 1996.

These internationally exposed financial failures were themselves an indirect product of Zhu Rongji's recentralization of fiscal rela-tions, as provincial governments found themselves deprived of funds that they had come to take for granted after years of pro-gressive decentralization. Instead they turned to foreign financial institutions in order to source capital for development-oriented investment. Foreign investors were assuaged by the presence of implicit guarantees from provincial governments, and such 'com-fort letters' predictably undermined the rigour and strictness of credit risk analysis undertaken by foreign financial institutions in their purchase of ITIC-issued corporate debt (Chang 1999). Following the AFC, these foreign sources of capital had begun to dry up because of concerns both about the integrity of China's financial institutions themselves and the prospects for economic growth amidst a difficult international economic environment. Foreign lending to China's financial system had already in fact declined prior to the GITIC bankruptcy, registering declines in the second and third quarters of 1998,[6] in a sharp reversal of a USD 5.2 billion increase in 1997 (BIS 1999).

The international reaction to the GITIC closure was 'swift and unforgiving' (Chang 1999). Following the episode, a number of banks suffered ratings downgrades (Harding 1999; Moody's Investor Service 1999). Both Moody's and Standard & Poors had assumed that the creditworthiness of both GITIC and the China International Trust and Investment Corporation was synon-ymous with that of the central government, and assigned them both investment grade ratings (Lardy 1995). The PBOC governor Dai Xianglong attempted to reassure investors and creditors in the aftermath of the GITIC collapse (China Securities Bulletin 1998). One of the legal counsel assisting in the drafting of the 1986 bankruptcy law itself believed that the handling of GITIC heralded far-reaching advances in the Chinese business environment:

> In the long term, China has established clearly that it will not fall into the moral hazard trap of rescuing badly run companies just because they are too big to fail. In the future, Chinese companies will no longer be able to obtain easy credit on the basis of opaque financial statements, personal connections (*guanxi*) and vague comfort letters from their parent governmental authorities. (Chang 1999, 43)

The crisis prompted Zhu Rongji to state rather truculently that contrary to the beliefs of international financial investors that 'China is already in the midst of a financial crisis and does not have the capacity to support its payments and is not creditworthy, . . . we are completely able to repay our debt' (Li and Zeng 2007, 474). For Zhu the question was one of moral hazard: 'The issue is whether or not the government should repay this kind of debt' (Li and Zeng 2007, 474). Yet Zhu's distinction between central and local government is crucial, and points to how the GITIC episode represented very different things for foreigners than it did for domestic financial elites. The crucial element of his statement was that

> This affair sends a message to the world: the Chinese government shall not repay the debt of any particular financial sector, if responsibility for those debts is not accepted by every level of government. This is to say, if foreign banks and financial institutions wish to invest in these financial industries, then they should undertake risk analysis and 'steer a careful course'. (Li and Zeng 2007, 475)

Through such comments, Zhu was making the point to foreign capital holders that the central government was willing to assume the role of guarantor where it saw fit. This was in contrast to the message sent to creditors within the domestic system, which was that there would be political consequences if they failed to generate greater financial profit through their activities. A marked cleavage therefore opened up between how domestic and foreign creditors conceived of the role of the market in underpinning financial stability. The experience of GITIC led policymakers to a greater appreciation of the need to find more effective ways to mediate the relationship between domestic and foreign capital:

> They [central policymakers] realized that the [trust and] invest-ment companies were a clumsy and difficult to manage way of accessing foreign capital. Zhu Rongji was outraged that the local cadres in Guangdong had been so foolish to make these kinds of guarantees. If they wanted foreign capital and foreign investors, then they would have to do it the proper correct way.[7]

Following GITIC, the nature of the relationship between state-owned financial institutions and the funding needs of both local governments and SOEs in this management of the relationship between domestic and foreign capital would increasingly come to depend on central government attitudes towards debt and the threat that it posed to broader financial stability. The failures of government- and bank-owned TICs were closely linked to the emergence of large numbers of NPLs in the Chinese banking system following the rapid investment-led growth of the early 1990s. The scale of these NPLs was significant, with most Chinese analysts calculating it at between 20 and 40 per cent (Yi Gang 1996; Li Xinning 1998). Zhu Rongji's administration was therefore caught between the real economic needs for capital to maintain an investment-led trajectory of growth, and the imperatives of maintaining the integrity of the financial system as these sources of capital became increasingly internationalized. The policy basis for addressing these challenges would be laid by constructing cognitive frames that emphasized both the rationalization of the state and the enhancement of distinc-tively Chinese structures of authority and power that would anchor and stabilize this process of reform and rationalization.

Frames: becoming big, becoming strong [做大做强]

The increasing diversity of actors and the interests that they had in the ongoing evolution of the Chinese financial sector meant that the process of managing uncertainty therefore became significantly more complex than it had been during the earlier years of reform. The international economic environment and the domestic pressures of growth and reform precipitated a deepening of reform guided by a set of frames that served to maintain stability as well as enable growth without derogating from CCP power. These cognitive frames were not just convenient rhetoric, nor were they purely instrumental tools to be deployed within a broader game of bureaucratic power plays. The frames that emerged were not just significant in providing guidance to policymakers and CCP leaders in determining the path of institutional change. They were also central to the process of interpreting institutional change, thus generating expectations of how China's political economy was to further evolve and develop in the following years. They accordingly played a deeper and more fundamental role in generating the stable reciprocal expectations that were essential for three purposes. First, they underpinned the political process of reshaping the institutional landscape of China's political economy by shaping the policy parameters of institutional change. Secondly, they served a microeconomic function by enabling the continued intermediation of investment capital throughout the economy by providing the reference point for investors, shareholders, and corporate decision-makers to construct mutual understandings of the politicized and hierarchical power over risk management. Finally, they acted as mechanisms for broader macroeconomic stability within the financial system by anchoring expectations of policy and regulation in the underlying political objectives of the CCP.

The overarching frame that guided the leadership was that of economic growth. Yet such growth narratives were themselves further conditional upon particular discourses that rendered them feasible. These underlying discourses revolved around the preservation of the socio-political structures of the CCP in parallel with the construction of new market and state structures. In this context a broader discourse of economic growth resolved into two frames concerning two interrelated imperatives in the process of reform and opening; that of confronting globalization, and that of

140

transforming and rationalizing the state-market relationship itself. These frames operated at different levels, but each revolved around the central role of the CCP as a means of managing uncertainty, in the process opening up opportunities for the simultaneous exploitation of that uncertainty. The first focused attention on the need to retain authority over the power of capital within China, whilst the second homed in on the consequent need to preserve the locus of that authority within the CCP itself. In this way they respectively focused on the capacity to capitalize upon foreign openings and thus foreign capital, and domestic wealth, without ceding control over the institutions and networks of growth. They were clearly intertwined. The potential challenges posed by 'entering the world' [入世] could only be met through the transformation of the state. In order to confront the challenge of globalization, the state was to be transformed into an internationally palatable as well as functionally effective set of institutions, but power was to remain firmly embedded within the CCP. The distinct yet interdependent roles of state, market, and Party were thus central to achieving these equally interdependent economic and political objectives.

In broader context, the role of the CCP as a functional bedrock of society was not withering in the face of the increased commercialization of economy and society of the 1990s, but rather evolved naturally and was actively enhanced through the eras of Jiang Zemin and Hu Jintao (Jia 2004). Following Deng Xiaoping's death in 1997, there was a brief interlude in which Jiang looked to be emerging from Deng's shadow and embracing a more liberal political and economic perspective (Fewsmith 2008). The discursive demolition of the 'East Asian Miracle' (World Bank 1993) in the aftermath of the AFC, and what appeared as ominous signs of the potential ramifications of allowing 'crony capitalism' to spread in the absence of democratic checks and balances (Li Zhenzhi 1998), led many intellectuals to anticipate further liberal movement. Following lengthy debate, Jiang proclaimed in 2000 that the CCP should open itself to private entrepreneurs and permit them membership (Jiang 2001). Yet at the same time he instituted the 'Three Emphases' or 'Three Talks' [三讲] movement at the beginning of 1999, which deepened and hardened the conservative elements of Jiang's authority.[8] As Gore (2001, 197) has put it, it seemed to many as if the 'forces of the communist polity and forces of the capitalist economy were pulling the country in opposing directions'. But this was to misperceive the way in which the economic fortunes of China's expanding private sector and the 'shadow' finance that fuelled it were not only compatible with the political fortunes of the CCP, but also in many ways were entirely dependent on them.[9] Not so much the exposure of an entrenched political system to liberal currents of thought, let alone the potential transformation of existing institutional structures of one-party rule, Jiang's steps in opening the Party were in hindsight a concerted attempt to ensure that the development of the private sector and the forces of commercial enterprise remained under the close authority of the CCP (Dickson 2003; Tsai 2007).

The ideologically infused frames and policies that emerged in this period of great uncertainty provide indications of how the political and the economic were thus to be reconciled. Those who advocated reform, liberalization, and receptiveness to globalization did so more on the basis of their perceived utility as rational tools for pursuing national economic strength than any committed fundamental belief in the freedom of the market or the value of liberal individualism (Wang 1998; Chen 2000; Zhang 2004). The detachment of these two aspects of political economy provided scope for developing and implementing novel and sometimes inadvertently innovative conceptions of the market as well as conceptions of the state. And this novelty can be traced back to the distinctive position of the CCP at the nexus of this state/market complex, a position that had profound influence upon the path and nature of China's socio-economic development.

Confronting globalization 中体西用

China's deepening integration within the global economy and the experience of the AFC brought positive economic benefits and also awareness of the attendant risks of diminishing economic sovereignty. The challenge of managing this process had a profound

142

effect upon the orientation towards economic and political reform. The lesson drawn by the CCP from this period of financial instability was not that China had to make its financial system more like those of Western countries. Rather, it should appropriate those aspects of Western financial institutional form and practice that would aid it in its pursuit of broader national objectives. These ideas provided the reference points towards which actors straddling both the market and the state could orient themselves. In so doing they further lay at the heart of the construction of an increasingly capitalist political economy whose integrity continued to centre on the CCP's control and authority over capital.

China's leaders thus began to articulate more determinedly how the increasingly inevitable process of coalescence with the global economy might be reconciled with domestic challenges and priorities at the time. On 10 March 1998, Jiang Zemin stated that

> The Asian financial crisis has proven to be both a revelation and a lesson for a number of Asian countries. We have to recognize and treat properly the issue of economic 'globalization'. Economic globalization is an objective trend of world economic development, from which no one can escape and in which everyone has to participate. The key point is to see 'globalization' dialectically; i.e., to see both its positive aspects and its negative aspects. This issue is particularly important for developing countries. We must therefore have both the courage and the virtue to participate in this process of globalization by both cooperating and competing. (People's Daily, 10 March 1998)

The AFC in particular gave rise to a vigorous debate within the Chinese intellectual community as to the nature of globalization in the late 1990s and what it meant for China. As will be explored below, in the process of institutional change within the financial sector this dialecticism would come to manifest in a more fluid perspective of 'Chinese learning for its essence, Western learning for its utility' [中学为体，西学为用]. Zhu Rongji saw the reform of the economy in 'the same way that the self-strengtheners of the previous century had – as selectively borrowing Western methods and techniques in pursuit of wealth and power but on Chinese terms' (Schell and Delury 2013, 348–9).

In the midst of a series of episodes during the 1990s through which many Chinese intellectuals felt as if China was being increasingly ostracized and discriminated against by Western countries,[10] many Chinese intellectuals, especially those who had been educated in the West, began to believe that those in the 1980s who advocated the potential universality of liberal ideals had been at best naïve and at worst had themselves been partially responsible for deepening China's social and ideological fissures.[11] However, it was in the economic realm especially that signs of the discrediting of the 'Western liberal model' were even more apparent, and more specific than the rise of popular nationalism. In the aftermath of Deng's Southern Tour, Lin Yifu had co-proposed a free market theory of comparative advantage (Lin et al. 1994), and this acted as a lightning rod for a strong critical backlash from prominent 'New Left' intellectuals (Hu 1995; Cheng 1994). As Gao Debu (1997, 44) emphasized,

> It is impossible to think sensibly about how to open to the global economy without paying attention to how we protect our national economy. It is a basic principle to develop our national economy, and in doing so we can ensure that the globalization has positive benefits for us.

More importantly, it precipitated new thinking about the institutional development of China's socialist market economy in an era of globalization. In 1997 Cui Zhiyuan (1997) published his theory of the 'second thought liberation', which sought to break down the false dichotomies of the market and the state that saw the former as the embodiment of justice through individual liberty and the latter as the guardian of a socialist egalitarianism. Rather, he argued that 'institutional innovation' was dependent upon strengthening both the market and the state, and on doing so under the 'guiding principle of economic and political democracy' (Cui 1997, 13). Modern capitalism from this perspective was regarded as both liberating and oppressive, the challenge being to unpack its complexity and cut through reified institutions and ideologies. According to Cui, none of the received categories of 'Western' thought were guarantors of either economic prosperity or political democracy, but rather had to be reassessed and reimplemented in light of China's historical experience and circumstances.

It was also in 1997 that Deng Xiaoping died. Jiang Zemin had already given some indication of his neoauthoritarian perspective, and his ability to operate in a highly instrumental manner when it came to the relationship between political and economic reform: economic reform was not just to be permitted but actively fostered in circumstances where it contributed to the political structure that supported him. In Jiang, therefore, could be seen the most overt manifestation of the 'paradoxical' evolution of Chinese political economy – a desire to be a part of the 'modern' world that was matched equally strongly by an insistence that the construction of that modernity within China could only possibly take place under the socio-political auspices of an organization such as the CCP. The death of Deng Xiaoping removed the last check on Jiang's neoauthoritarian instincts (Bramall 2009).

Globalization as 'an objective trend of world economic development' (People's Daily 1998) was therefore a matter for both economic and political reform. The experiences with GITIC, the onset of the AFC, and the change in leadership provoked new consideration within policymaking and intellectual circles as to where new sources of economic growth were to be found and the political mechanisms through which they could be managed. One of the most critical factors in mediating this relationship between the political and the economic in the process of international economic integration was the question of the management of capital. Both the domestic and the transnational dimensions of the financial uncertainty that had emerged in the late 1990s cohered in a hardening of an instrumental attitude towards the relationship between foreign and domestic capital. For Chinese policymakers, the presence of foreign institutional capital in China was linked closely to the process of domestic financial restructuring. Confronted with a need to carve out NPLs and debt restructuring, key officials within both the PBOC and the MOF believed that there were great risks involved in allowing foreign financial institutions to acquire either loan portfolios or take ownership stakes themselves.[12] As was the case for outward-oriented and inward-focused reform alike, maintaining domestic financial stability and preserving centralized macroeconomic control over the flow of capital were to remain the most fundamental policy priorities for China's leadership. Just as perceptions and understandings of the broader global economic order were in flux, China's institutional response reflected significant contingency in how state, market, and Party would evolve in tandem to meet these challenges.

Transforming the state [政企分开]

Following the recognition of the scale of NPLs and the shock of the AFC, calls for a deepening and acceleration of reform resonated throughout the economics profession and policymaking circles (Wu 2000). The policy to 'grasp the large and release the small' [抓大放小] remained the basic guiding line of enterprise reform, and formed in turn the strategic pathway towards the 'going forth' [走出去] objective. The 'large enterprise strategy' [大企业集团战略] and other industrial sector reforms of the 1990s had taken cues from the South Korean *chaebol* model (Heilmann and Shih 2012). The AFC cast doubt upon the soundness of this strategy, although the reaction amongst economic policymakers was not to reject its overall salience, but rather to take steps to ensure that China's 'National Team' would not be vulnerable to the same financial pressures that had so affected South Korea's large enterprises. The link between the real economy and the financial remained the focal point of attention, and in this respect the 'separation of government and business' [政企分开] and reform of the SOE sector were considered central to confronting external threats (Liu 2002).

As Chapter 4 detailed, the origins of this guiding line were clearly to be found earlier in the 1990s, as Zhu Rongji had sought to begin to introduce more modern forms of macroeconomic control [宏观调控] into the financial system. The discourse of regulatory reform and the separation of government and business deepened mark-edly in 1997 with the change in CCP leadership, and terms such as 'corporate governance' began to appear for the first time in CCP documents (Liu 2002). However, just as in the earlier period, it did not produce a linear and unambiguous movement towards a liberal financial system. As Opper (2007, 10) has observed, the 'official policy line was indeed to encourage a separation of government and business to support a rationalization of the economic sphere. In retrospect, however, reforms revealed a high degree of ambivalence and inconsistency'. Rather than being the product of 'partial' or 'failed' reform, though, this inconsistency and ambivalence arises from the fact that even as the state administrative apparatus was rationalized and downsized in order to interfere less with economic processes, the role of the CCP within the broader political economy was preserved, and even bolstered. This took place via a sophisti-cated system of Party committees as 'control mechanisms' (Dotson 2012), buttressed by cadre performance benchmarks and evalua-tion criteria, and the enfolding of career advancement not just into networks or patronage, but further and more fundamentally into broader imperatives of Party-building and progress. In the financial sector, the Central Financial Work Commission (CFWC), estab-lished in 1998, stood at the apex of this system. Government [政] is not synonymous with the Party [党] in either institutional, ideo-logical, or functional terms, and accordingly any efforts to increase the efficiency of the state were not to come at the expense of Party control. As Wu Bangguo, then Vice-Premier of the State Council and Politburo member, stated explicitly in 1997:

> Even if the government administration does not interfere with the enterprises, the Party must absolutely not lose its political leader-ship powers with regard to the enterprises. . . . The Party should take part in the decision-making in the enterprise with regard to major issues. (Xinhua, 14 December 1997)

The result was that the streamlining and rationalization of the state infrastructure simply meant that it became a more effective 'host

147

organism' (Dotson 2012) for the CCP. The desire for China to build up its national economic strength and power was related to the process of ensuring that those big firms that would lead the vanguard of China's economic rationalization and globalization were not only represented within the political system, but were also symbiotically connected to it (Naughton 2003a).

The Central Financial Work Conference of November 1997 was therefore not merely concerned with the threat of the AFC but also the need to address the NPL problem (Yi 2011, 293). In his address to Conference, Zhu Rongji had stressed the opportuneness of deepening reform following the crisis. The failure of GITIC and other TICs provided significant impetus for increasing the stability, transparency, and commercial footing of the banking sector (Lou 2001). Although he argued that great successes had been achieved in the years following the Fourteenth Party Congress in 1992, he also argued that

> We must recognize that deep problems in the financial sector have not yet been touched upon, and that serious historical problems that have built up over many years have not yet been resolved. (Zhu 2000 [1997], 411)

The first of the problems identified by Zhu was that government is neither separate from banking, nor from enterprises (Zhu 2000 [1997]). This was seen as central to a variety of issues afflicting the stability and effectiveness of the financial system, including overheating in real estate and development zones, capital shortage and excessive debt amongst SOEs, redundant investment construction, and inappropriate practices in the process of bank credit appropriation (Zhu 2000 [1997]). As a result, Zhu saw the separation of government and banking as a core component in the streamlining and modernization of the financial system. Nonetheless, he went to great lengths to emphasize that this streamlining was possible only with the reconsolidation of CCP authority within the financial sector, and that the establishment of the CFWC and the Central Financial Disciplinary and Inspection Commission, as well as the concomitant revamping and restructuring of the Party committee system within the PBOC and SOCBs, were all to serve as 'the backbone' [骨干][13] for the rationalization of the state's role in the allocation of financial capital (Zhu 2000 [1997]). Most accounts of financial reform perceive the CCP as a constant source of interference either in the smooth operation of free markets or the technocratic developmentalism of the state bureaucracy. What is clear, however, is that even amongst the most pragmatic and rationalist of the economic policymaking elite, it was precisely the inverse: it was excessive *state* interference that was obstructing 'the centralized and unified leadership of the Party over financial work, . . . the Party's strength in political ideology, and . . . the Party Central Committee's line, programs, and policies' (Zhu 2000 [1997], 325). It was therefore at the nexus of the two trends that the organizational role of the CCP became increasingly apparent, as a functionally crucial structure for maintaining faith in the viability of economic growth in changing circumstances and as a pathway to reconciling the increased role of the market with the continued resilience of a one-party state. This role was to be embodied within the capacity of the CCP to both manage and exploit uncertainty through the course of institutional change in the financial sector.

Institutional transformation: competitiveness over competition

The range of challenges that characterized the policymaking environment in the late 1990s came to influence the priorities of China's leaders as well as conceptions of how those objectives might be achieved. The Beijing economic policymaking community was deeply affected by the experience of the AFC, and the need to confront the challenges of financial globalization through the centralization of political authority over a process of commercialization of the banking sector was reflected across policymaking institutions and networks. The group of 'comprehensive reformers' [整体改革派] led by Wu Jinglian continued to rise within policymaking circles, and the foremost members of this school, including Zhou Xiaochuan, Guo Shuqing, Wang Qishan, and Lou Jiwei would

149

come to occupy some of the highest executive positions within the financial system during the early and mid-2000s. Their ideas and attitudes concerning the goals necessary for the rationalization of the financial sector in the face of increasing globalization were embedded within the broader cognitive frames that placed the CCP at the centre of what otherwise was still seen as an antagonistic relationship between the state and the market – one which all agreed needed to be addressed.[14] Reform embodied movement towards greater international financial integration, a deepening of market-oriented reforms in the ownership, regulation, and organizational behaviour of the state-owned banking sector, and yet also significant bolstering of mechanisms of Communist Party control over how both of these processes would unfold.

The PBOC comes into its own: the growth of mutual dependency

The PBOC underwent significant institutional change in the years following the Asian financial crisis. Its increasingly evident role as lynchpin of macroeconomic coordination was reflected in the bolstering of its independence from both local provincial actors and the SOCBs. This, however, did not produce an increase in the overall independence of monetary policy, exchange rate policy, or the practice of banking supervision. These reforms were part of a process of commercializing state–enterprise relationships, but they did not reduce the nature of interdependence between the core wielders of political authority within the CCP and the key holders of technical financial expertise within the financial bureaucracy. It was thus a transformation that rendered the PBOC more entrenched in a state of mutual dependency with the CCP. Its status within both the bureaucracy and the broader financial community as the deepest repository of technical financial expertise rendered it indispensable in the policymaking process, and lent credibility to the decisions of the State Council.[15] Conversely, the credibility of this status as technocratic macroeconomic manager became closely tied to the positions occupied by the PBOC's leaders within the political hierarchies of the Central Committee and the CCP.

This was a product not just of the rational interplay of bureaucratic interests within either a fragmented post-socialist system (Lampton and Lieberthal 1992), but emerged out of their joint embeddedness as Party elites within a shared understanding of the functional imperatives of the CCP's role as the ultimate authority with responsibility for preserving financial and macroeconomic stability. Even as the deepening reform was viewed as a necessary and inevitable process, China's top financial officials continued to stress the importance of accepting the differences of not only the goals but also the mechanisms of China's monetary policy (Zhou 2006). These dynamics of mutual political dependency remained in place throughout the deepening of reform across the Jiang/Zhu and Hu/Wen regimes, as the institutional framework within which the PBOC operated was seen as highly successful in both managing the expectations of Party elites and stimulating an increasingly active array of financial market actors.

The November 1997 Financial Work Conference produced a wholesale restructuring of the branch network of the PBOC along macro-regional rather than provincial administrative lines (Lou 2001). Until 1998, the PBOC branch network was based on the administrative system, with thirty-one offices located at the provincial level, a situation that provided provincial Party officials with significant leverage to influence local bank branches' decision-making processes. This negatively impacted the allocative efficiency of capital as provinces duplicated investments and pet projects of local administrators were more easily able to attract bank credit (Laurenceson and Chai 2003, 19). The reform merged or closed 148 city-level PBOC branches, and replaced the provincial offices with nine regional branches that were better placed for financial supervision, and which were later to become the architecture of the CBRC (PBOC 1999). This institutional restructuring came into force in 1999, having been preceded in 1997 by the formation of the Monetary Policy Committee. This enhanced the monetary policymaking effectiveness of the PBOC as the monetary policy target began to shift towards overall money supply rather than the scale of credit finance (Wu 2012b).

In 1998 the PBOC abolished the system of directly controlling credit quotas [信贷规模计划] (PBOC 1998; Luo 2003). The transformation of the credit plan from compulsory [控制性] to a consultative target [参考指标] within an overall 'guidance plan' [信贷规划] reflected an intention to move away from direct [直接跳空] to indirect regulation [间接调控].[16] These were all seen as efforts to stymie local provincial officials' efforts to exploit their political superiority over the local branch offices of SOCBs, a dynamic that had produced both NPLs and inflationary pressure (Tong 2007). Yet this notion of 'indirect regulation' was and remains a complex one. It refers to the replacement of the administrative structures of pre-reform central planning with more flexible systems of management more responsive to the exigencies of macroeconomic conditions.[17] This meant also being more attuned to the overall political priorities underpinning monetary policy, and resulted in a much more effective 'crisis management' [危机处理][18] capacity than either the unwieldy strictures of comprehensive credit plans or the unpredictable volatility of market-led corrections.[19] Not merely a matter of controlling lending practices through the promulgation and enforcement of clear legal guidelines, indirect regulation thus manifested in the use of these consultative targets within a broader framework of indirect guidance.

The role of the PBOC in mediating between its political embeddedness and its role in guiding financial markets thus developed into a particular form of 'window guidance',[20] through which the evolving tools of monetary and macroeconomic policy such as open market operations and the frequent adjustment of reserve ratio requirements (RRRs) have been enclosed within a network of officials (including the heads of SOCBs, joint-stock commercial banks (JSCBs), and regulatory officials) who meet regularly in order to develop consistency in the interpretation of policy and manage shared expectations of the macroeconomic and monetary environment.[21] The PBOC began to intervene in the interbank market for government bonds in May 1998,[22] and began to issue its own PBOC bills in 2002. By mid-2008 the PBOC had issued RMB 14.8 trillion of such securities, a forty-fold increase over that at end 2002 (PBOC 2008). As China's current account imbalance deepened after 2003, the capacity of the central bank to credibly sterilize inflows of foreign capital increasingly depended upon a combination of these market operations with the ability of the PBOC to compel SOCBs and other state-owned financial institutions to maintain their holdings of PBOC bills.

Banking reform and 'public' listing

The banking system also underwent radical institutional change between 1998 and 2007. At the end of a long and complex process, the banking system looked a lot more like commercialized, rationalized, and internationally confident financial institutions. Yet even as they were increasingly all of these things, they were nonetheless rationalized tools of the CCP whose key position in supporting the broader macroeconomic demands of reform and development was clear to all stakeholders in this process. The institutional forms that emerged from both the process of disposal of NPLs and the course of 'share reform' [股改] were strongly hierarchical in nature, reflecting the continued paramount position of the political system and also the containment of this hierarchy in modern institutional forms.

The dire state of the balance sheets of the SOCBs was viewed as a significant impediment to China's credibility on the international economic stage just as China was preparing for a significant increase in its interaction with the global economy (Zhan 2000). The AFC further underscored the extent to which a robust financial system was essential for managing this process of globalization, but it further reinforced – to Zhu Rongji especially – the extent to which this 'immunity from the Asian bug' was premised upon a deepening of the 'rectification' [整顿] that had guided financial reform and policymaking since 1993. In this context, a number of research reports emerged that argued for the combination of political retrenchment and greater rationalization of linkages between the state authorities and financial institutions in order to address the problem of debt within the banking sector (SETC and PBOC 1997). The dissemination of these findings and arguments was encouraged by Hua Jianmin, who was Chief of the Office of the Central Financial and Economic Leading Small Group from 1996 until 2003,[23] as well as a variety of Zhu's protégés within the comprehensive reform group.[24]

Through this process of institutional change the SOCBs were recapitalized, large tranches of NPLs were cleaved off from their official balance sheets, and they all began – and in some cases completed – the process of listing publicly on the Shanghai and Hong Kong stock exchanges (HKSE). Mainstream liberal perspectives on this course of banking reform have remained premised on a linear teleological notion of financial reform. Walter and Howie's (2011) effort to trace the strategies adopted through the PBOC and the MOF for disposal of toxic assets, recapitalization, and finally public listing produced an ultimate conclusion that the dependence of China's banking system on opaque transfers of capital through complex channels of ownership, debt, and fiat meant that the artifice was likely to come tumbling down at any moment. Yet a more nuanced analysis of these developments within the institutional sphere of China's banking sector reveals a logic at play that is occluded by Walter and Howie's assumption that the only logical route to an effective role for the financial system is one of unadulterated market liberalization. This underlying presumption of a unidirectional process of transition to a liberal market financial system is problematic. Cai Esheng, then deputy governor of the PBOC, made the point clearly in 1999 when stating that the concept of reform in the financial sector is 'different and more profound' than that used ordinarily by many of those interested in China's 'reform', and that 'the issues . . . today will not be solved simply by principles of market economies' (Cai 1999). At the end of this process, 'like the People's Liberation Army, the banking apparatus would remain a preserve of the Party and subject only to its control'.[25] The principal reason for this was not that conservatives had prevailed in a pitched bureaucratic battle with pro-market reformers, but rather the simple fact that neither a model of free market competition nor one of arm's-length administrative regulation was considered capable of generating the incentives for rapid economic growth whilst also preserving centralized political control. Accordingly, from this perspective it becomes possible to shed deeper light on an otherwise paradoxical trajectory of economic commercialization and political retrenchment. One real motivation *was* to change corporate culture and to modernize the banks themselves in organizational and operational terms. A further real motivation was to draw upon international capital. Both of these were in order to foster economic growth. What made this economic growth possible – and therefore was the most important determinant of partial marketization – was the strengthening of the CCP's capacity to undergird macroeconomic management in the face of greater international market forces and the increasing rationalization of the state. Given the CCP's performance legitimacy, and the growing inevitability of global integration, economic growth was thus only possible through partial marketization.

The restructuring process commenced in 1998. The PBOC reduced the required reserve ratio from 13 to 9 per cent, freeing up RMB 270 billion in spare deposits within the SOCBs. These funds were used to purchase RMB 270 billion of special government bonds issued by the MOF. The MOF then recapitalized the SOCBs directly with these funds.[26] Four asset management companies (AMCs) were established in 1999 between April (Cinda) and October (Huarong, Orient, and Great Wall).[27] They were established as 'solely state-owned non-bank financial institutions' (PRC State Council 2000) whose operations are opaque and financial situations largely undisclosed. These AMCs were capitalized themselves with RMB 40 billion from the MOF, but in order to purchase the troubled assets from the Bank of China (BOC), Industrial and Commercial Bank of China (ICBC), and the China Construction Bank (CCB), issued bonds worth RMB 811 billion to each of the banks (Table 5.1). With a further RMB 604 billion of credit extended from the PBOC, in 2000 they purchased RMB 1.415 trillion of the NPLs held by the SOCBs. This process enabled the SOCBs to replace RMB 1.4 trillion in non-performing debt with an equivalent amount in sound and secure assets ostensibly backed by the MOF.[28] That the MOF stood behind the repayment of these bonds, even as they were evergreened and extended in 2009 for another ten years, has been an open secret within the financial system since the plan was first implemented in the aftermath of the AFC.[29] As one interviewee from a SOCB stated,

> The debt was still there, and of course someone was going to have pay for it, but it made sense to place the debt somewhere between the MOF and the banks themselves whilst it was being worked out. The banks needed it off their books, and the MOF didn't want to write it all down immediately and leave a huge hole on their books, so it was convenient for everyone to put it somewhere else and pretend that it didn't really exist.[30]

Over the course of the ten-year maturation of the bonds issued by the AMCs, the recovery rate was estimated at averaging 20 per cent (CBRC 2010). This was, however, of little consequence; as one interviewee pithily but rather cryptically expressed it, 'the AMCs served their purpose which was to make everything else possible'.[31] One interviewee queried the seemingly insistent focus of some commentators on the desirability of dealing with bad loans through the 'chaos of transparency':

> What would be the preferable option? To abide by abstract principles, or to make sure that there are funds when and where they are needed?[32]

From this perspective, it was the very lack of transparency around the AMCs and the nature of their operations and relationships to other financial institutions that was crucial for generating the conditions necessary for Chinese state officials, domestic depositors, and foreign investors, to each in their own way interpret the process of banking reform as conducive to financial stability. In this way, the use of the AMCs to support the banking sector itself would come to reflect the dependence of financial stability upon the liquidity of financial institutions, rather than their technical solvency per se (Anderson 2006, 85).

Table 5.1. Sources of funds for AMC purchase of NPLs, 1999 (RMB billions)

	PBOC Credit	AMC Bonds	Purchase of NPLs
Cinda	48	347	395
Great Wall	346	0	346
Huarong	95	313	408
Orient	116	151	267
Total	605	811	1,416

Source: Interview, 5 June 2012, Beijing – Chinese Academy of Social Sciences.

This first round of recapitalization and NPL disposal left the SOCBs with a remaining RMB 2.2 trillion of NPLs still on their books. The terms of China's WTO accession in 2001 included a five-year window until 2006 for the granting of full access to China's financial sector to foreign financial institutions. The PBOC was seen as the clear candidate to assume primary responsibility for further reform of the SOCBs, given the technocratic expertise at its disposal and the rising status of its newly appointed governor Zhou Xiaochuan. The MOF-led recapitalization and NPL disposal of 1998–99 had been achieved by drawing upon fiscal resources; these were now overstretched, and it was therefore seen as necessary to either draw upon domestic or foreign private capital. Either option involved change in the ownership structure of the banks, and the PBOC was caught between the expectations of an evolving market environment and an imperative that notwithstanding the status of either foreign or domestic private actors in the process of shareholding reform, the banking system would remain subject to ultimate authority vested in the CCP. In this respect, despite greater receptiveness to the utility of markets in the financial sector on the part of the PBOC (Bell and Feng 2013), the perceptions of MOF and PBOC officials towards the rationale for banking reform were both rooted in Zhu Rongji's plans for rationalization and streamlining of the state, and thus evinced a continuity from the late 1990s to the 2000s following Zhu's retirement. Some sense of this can be seen how, in response to a question about China's 'privatization' process, a 'taken aback' Zhu Rongji remarked to former US President George H. W. Bush in 1998 that,

Mr Bush, China isn't privatizing. We're creating a shareholding system, and a shareholding system is only one of many forms of public ownership. (Zhu 2011, 248)

As Schell and Delury (2013, 342) have argued, 'Zhu was categorical on this point. . . . The ultimate goal of these reforms . . . was not to dismantle the state sector, but to streamline it and thereby make it a stronger element of Deng's new form of marketized socialism.'

The goal of transforming the banking system from a scattered assortment of liabilities into a source of national economic strength was thus closely bound up with the 'public' listing of the SOCBs. Liu Mingkang (2004), chairman of the newly established CBRC, argued in 2004 that the government actions in 1998–99 had been focused on reducing the financial difficulties of banks rather than on overhauling inherent structural problems, and it had become clear that the banks should do more to streamline and rationalize their organizational structures. The policymaking process was underpinned within the Party through the Central Leading Group on Shareholding Reform of the State Banks [中央国有商业银行股份制改革领导小组], which was established by Wen Jiabao in January 2003. This brought together all of the senior financial figures under CCP authority and was chaired by Vice-Premier and PSC member Huang Ju. Zhou Xiaochuan enjoyed Huang's support (Davis 2011), and this further bolstered the ability of the PBOC to enact its vision of banking restructuring reform from 2003 onwards.[33]

Central Huijin Investment Ltd [中央汇金投资有限责任公司] was established as a subsidiary of SAFE, which in turn is an agency subordinate to the PBOC. Guo Shuqing, then also director of SAFE, was therefore its first administrator. It was created in order to bypass the prohibition upon the PBOC from taking a direct ownership stake in any commercial bank (National People's Congress of the People's Republic of China 1995). Huijin was authorized by the State Council to make 'equity investments in major state-owned financial enterprises, and . . . to the extent of its capital contribution, [to] exercise the rights and perform the obligations as an investor on behalf of the State in accordance with applicable laws' (Central Huijin Investment Ltd. 2008). Thus in 2003, when the PBOC determined that BOC and CCB were financially sound enough to write down further capital losses, China's rapidly increasing foreign exchange reserves were utilized through SAFE in order to provide USD 22.5 billion to BOC and CCB for these purposes. In May 2004, RMB 475 billion in NPLs were transferred to the AMCs from these two banks, for consideration from the AMCs of RMB 145 billion. The PBOC then extended direct credit of RMB 700 billion to fund a second tranche of NPL disposal from ICBC, which transferred RMB 705 billion of NPLs to the AMCs. Finally, in 2004 the PBOC extended Special Bills totalling RMB 567 billion to BOC, CCB, and ICBC, which were due to mature in 2009. In 2005, Bank of Communications auctioned off RMB 64 billion in NPLs, for which the bidding AMCs paid RMB 32 billion. On 22 April 2005, following the State Council's approval of the joint stock reform plan, ICBC was again recapitalized, but this time followed the course of BOC and CCB in drawing USD 15 billion from the foreign exchange reserves through SAFE. One month later on 27 May 2005, ICBC then transferred RMB 246 billion of NPLs to Huarong AMC at book value, before signing further agreements on 27 June 2005 with all four AMCs to sell RMB 459 billion in NPLs also at book value.

This second round of recapitalization and NPL disposal was closely oriented towards the goal of attracting foreign capital. Foreign investors were actively encouraged to take direct equity stakes in Chinese banks, which led neither to serious competition from foreign financial institutions within the domestic Chinese market nor to dramatic shifts in the patterns of authority within the banking sector. The dual rationale for reform and internationalization – tapping foreign capital and improving the organizational efficiency of the banking sector – was pursued within the encompassing frames of state rationalization, global integration, and continued supervision and control by the CCP. Following the listing process, the most significant holders of equity in China's banking system are Huijin and the MOF (see Table 5.2).

Table 5.2. Equity structure of China's largest banks, 2010

	Five largest shareholders by stake				
	#1	#2	#3	#4	#5
Agricultural Bank of China	Huijin (40.12%)	Ministry of Finance (39.21%)	HKSCC Nominees Lts (8.99%)	SSF (3.02%)	Ping An Life Insurance Company of China Ltd (0.97)
Bank of China	Huijin (67.60%)	HKSCC Nominees Ltd (29.13%)	Bank of Tokyo-Mitsubishi UFJ Ltd (0.19%)	China Life Insurance Co. Ltd (0.15%)	Asian Development Bank (0.11%)
China Construction Bank	Huijin (57.03%)	HKSCC Nominees Ltd (19.79%)	Bank of America (10.23%)	Fullerton Financial (5.65%)	Baosteel Group (1.41%)
Industrial and Commercial Bank of China	Huijin (35.4%)	Ministry of Finance (35.3%)	HKSCC Nominees Ltd (24.5%)	ICBC Credit Suisse Asset Management Co. Ltd (0.3%)	Ping An Insurances (Group) Company of China (0.3%)
Bank of Communications	Ministry of Finance (26.52%)	HKSCC Nominees Ltd (21.93%)	HSBC (18.63%)	Capital Airports Holding Company (2.01%)	State Grid Asset Management Co. Ltd. (0.92%)
China Minsheng Bank	HKSCC Nominees Ltd (15.44%)	New Hope Investment Co. Ltd (4.99%)	China Life Insurance Company (4.31%)	China Shipowners Mutual Assurance Association (3.39%)	Orient Group Co. Ltd (3.32%)

Industrial Bank	Financial Bureau of Fujian Province (21.03%)	Hang Seng Bank Ltd (12.80%)	Tetrad Ventures Pty Ltd (3.07%)	Fujian Tobacco Haisheng Investment Management Co. Ltd. (2.73%)	COFCO Ltd. (1.78%)
Huaxia Bank	Shougang Corporation (13.98%)	State Grid Corporation of China (11.94%)	Deutsche Bank (11.27%)	Hongta Tobacco Group Co. Ltd (6.00%)	Runhua Group Co. Ltd (4.88%)
China Merchants Bank	HKSCC Nominees Ltd (17.86%)	China Merchants Steam Navigation Co. Ltd (12.40%)	China Ocean Shipping Co. (6.22%)	Shenzhen Yan Qing Investment and Development Co. (2.95%)	Guangzhou Maritime Transport Company (2.93%)

Source: Annual Reports, various years

Note: the year 2010 was selected in order to be able to incorporate ABC, which listed publicly in 2010.

Other state entities that possess major ownership stakes include the National Social Security Fund Council (NSSFC), and a Hong Kong-incorporated entity, Hong Kong Securities Clearing Company Ltd, which is 50 per cent owned by the HKSE and 50 per cent owned by the five largest banks operating in Hong Kong.[34] These changes in the institutional and asset structure of the banking sector following WTO entry were, from one perspective, merely symbolic (Chen 2002). Although now listed publicly on the HKSE and SHSE, these steps reflected an instrumental attitude to the public listing of the institutions, rather than regarding it as an end in itself (Bell and Feng 2013, 281). Whereas the conventional rationale for public listing includes the improvement of corporate governance and transparency in addition to the raising of capital, the non-market tradability of two-thirds of the shares of the state-owned banks and the retention of state control over both traded and non-traded stocks means that market price signals and market-actor oversight still play a highly limited role in determining the market capitalization of the banks.[35]

Following the combination of domestic restructuring and public listing, the core of the banking sector came to resemble an internationally competitive set of institutions dedicated to international best practice. However lines of ownership and the lines of control within the banking sector are not coterminous. The formal ceiling of 25 per cent for foreign ownership in a single domestic bank and that of 20 per cent for any single foreign investor preserved the ongoing paramountcy of formal state ownership. Reflecting the continued paramountcy of the political system to emerge from 'share reform' [股改], the shareholding structure of the SOCBs therefore introduced a new legal entity into the Chinese corporate landscape; that of 'large and small non-[traders]' [大小非].[36] The distinction between these categories is closely related to the nature of the stock market as a 'policy market' [政策市场] in which the hierarchy of political control over the banking sector – and thus its role within the implementation of macroeconomic and monetary policy on a national scale – comes to enter into a symbiotic relationship with the market value of the banks themselves.

Strict ownership is thus not conclusive in determining how control rights are actually exercised over a state-owned entity, even one that has been legally incorporated for the purposes of operating within a competitive market environment.[37] The CCP's powers are not mentioned in the charters of any of the SOCBs, however, neither would it be appropriate to relegate this influence to informal means of control and governance.

The structural embeddedness of the state within the capital markets in this manner, and the concomitant awareness on the part of market participants that these enterprises are in turn embedded within a political hierarchy with the CCP at its apex, is what enables the CCP to act simultaneously as 'the most important controller of risk as well as the largest source of uncertainty'[38] Thus, ownership structures are characterized by retention of predominant state ownership, and it is precisely because those state institutions are embedded in an institutional hierarchy whose coherence depends upon the CCP that they are able to function effectively as mechanisms for corporate governance acceptable to the political elite. The continued role of the CCP anchored the expectations of domestic and foreign investors alike:

> Whilst it is generally acknowledged that privatization goes hand-in-hand with improved efficiency, this might not be the case in China because the very fact that the banks are owned by the state reassures the depositors. (Xie 1999, 329)

Despite the presence of independent directors, foreign strategic investors, and mechanisms for corporate accountability, the most important source of faith and confidence in the banking system remains the simple fact of CCP control over the actions and practices of the biggest banks.[39] What is most important is not whether such a state of affairs is actually always true, but that investors, shareholders, and corporate decision-makers alike construct mutual understandings on the basis of the ultimate repository of power over market risk and uncertainty being retained within political hierarchies that extend from the implementation by banks of regulations on loan classification,[40] to decisions made at the highest levels of the CCP on the impact of interest rate movements.[41]

Upgrading financial discipline: vertical supervision

The problems in the banking sector and the threat the sector posed to the deepening internationalization of the Chinese economy were seen by Zhu Rongji in the aftermath of the AFC as equally a problem of personnel as of institutional structure. The Central Committee and the State Council issued a notice following the November 1997 conference, identifying the following problems as central to the financial situation at the time:

> In the process of transformation from a planned economy towards a socialist market economy, the organization of the financial system has not been appropriate to the needs of reform and development, laws have been incomplete, financial supervision has been weak, management has been disorderly, discipline has been lax, and a small number of employees have demonstrated their inferior quality. (PRC State Council 1997)

According to Liu Mingkang, in 1998 Zhu told the bank presidents:

> Let's say goodbye to all these excuses. No more government-dictated loans. I'll give you money in one shot. Carve off all your existing non-performing loans – I don't care where they came from, but I do care about your future behavior. I'll get proper benchmarks to measure your performance from here on. [For new bad loans] I will hold accountable those who are responsible. (Liu, cited in Kuhn 2010, 266)

There was clear recognition within China's regulatory apparatus of the challenges faced by China's banks by WTO accession, however, the CCP sought the pursuit of increased commercial competitiveness through a deepening of the existing macro-framework of centralized supervision.[42] Zhu's vision of increasing accountability therefore involved the centralization of control and supervision over the banking sector, even as the state bureaucracy was being

164

rationalized and streamlined. This challenge was met through the establishment of the Central Financial Work Commission and the 'correspondingly' established Central Financial Discipline and Inspection Work Committee (CFDIWC) [中央金融纪律检查工作委员会].[43] The CFDIWC was designed to provide far greater capacity for the active monitoring of those engaged in 'financial work' [金融工作], so as to 'strengthen the unified leadership of the Party in financial work' (PRC State Council 1997, n.p.). This also coincided with a restructuring of the Party organization in all the major financial institutions, as emphasis was placed upon the construction of stronger systems of 'vertical leadership', in order that all the necessary duties and functions were carried out according to law.

The overall process of banking and regulatory restructuring was underpinned by the essential guiding principle of 'leadership of the Party' through the Party committees within financial institutions that were each linked vertically to the Central Finance and Economic Leading Small Group (CFELSG) (Dai 2010).[44] As a policymaking and policy coordinating body, the CFELSG was functionally separate from these horizontal and vertical mechanisms of governance, although it exercised ultimate responsibility and control over them as well. The processes of institutional change traced in the previous section were themselves underpinned by an increase in CCP oversight in order to manage uncertainty. As Heilmann (2005, 3–4) observes,

> As soon as China's top leaders had agreed [in 1997] on the need for centralization to counter financial risk, they were able to achieve comprehensive regulatory reform by leaving state institutions intact on the surface for the time being while swiftly changing the internal rules governing Communist Party-appointed 'leadership cadres' and creating a powerful, yet mostly invisible Party body for monitoring financial executives.

Although Zhu Rongji introduced plans to reform the Party structure where organizational overlap existed amongst different parts of the Central Committee, these were not intended to weaken the Party apparatus, but rather to streamline it and increase its efficiency. Where it mattered most to Zhu – the economic realm – the organizational depth and authority of CCP regulatory oversight and capacity for intervention were enhanced. Zhu's response to the problem of reform both in the financial system and SOEs thus emphasized much more strongly the management of people and ideas, rather than institutions and structures. As a senior academic observed in 1998, Zhu did 'not think there [was] anything particularly wrong with the existing structure. He [had] been telling managers that the problem [was] more themselves – sloth, inefficiency, and corruption – than the system' (Yang 1998, 236). This meant that, 'improving the moral quality of cadres was a prerequisite to solving problems ranging from corruption to SOE efficiency' (Lam 1999, 371fn). Just as the evolution of cognitive frames and the path of institutional change reflected the importance of continued CCP control to managing the uncertainty of deepening reform, the most effective mechanism available to Zhu Rongji – and Wen Jiabao after him – for achieving economic growth without permitting the establishment of alternative bases of financial and political power was the control exercised by the CCP over the networks of financial relations.

The primary mechanism for the CCP's tightening of the means of policy diffusion through the financial sector was the CFWC, a body established in 1997 and directly and exclusively answerable to the Central Committee (PRC State Council 1997). In contrast to the agenda setting and decision-making functions of the Leading Small Groups,[45] it was the primary organization devoted to supervision and management of cadres, as the overseer of horizontal networks linking the executive ranks of China's key financial institutions both amongst themselves and to the Central Committee itself. It was mandated explicitly to 'implement the Party line, guidelines, policies, and lead the work of Party-construction throughout the financial system, but not to engage in financial business or provide financial services' (PRC State Council 1997). It complemented the COD, which in 1998 refocused significant attention on the work of cadres within the financial system (Central Organization

Department 1998b). Wen Jiabao, at that stage a Vice Premier and member of the PSC, served as chair of the CFWC. It effectively leapfrogged the PBOC, the MOF, and subsidiaries such as CIC and Huijin in enabling direct CCP appointment of senior management throughout the banking sector (Heilmann 2005). It worked closely in tandem with the COD, which already shouldered responsibility for the 'position-list' system of leading cadre appointment (Central Organization Department 1998a). Thus, between 1998 and 2003 the CFWC controlled the appointment of senior executives across all key institutions in finance, including regulators, administrative agencies, and banks.

In 2003 Wen Jiabao's assumption of leadership over the Central Finance Leading Small Group coincided with a concerted refocusing of attention on the banking sector. Further, his establishment of a new leading small group (the Central Financial Safety Leading Small Group [中央金融安全领导小组]) was not merely a rebranding of the CFWC.[46] Some also saw the CBRC as something of a successor to the CFWC (Naughton 2003a). However, the CFWC, having served its function of reasserting centralized control over personnel and financial leadership following the shock of the GITIC bankruptcy and AFC, saw many of its core functions of cadre appointment transferred to the CCP Organization Department,[47] and thus retrenched within the Party apparatus itself, rather than dispersed through the channels of the governmental bureaucracy ministries (Heilmann 2005). Until the CBRC came into being in 2003, the PBOC retained jurisdiction over supervision of the banking sector. The macro-regional restructuring of 1998 produced the regulatory architecture that would become the institutional foundation for the CBRC, the establishment of which was delayed beyond that of other regulatory bodies,[48] not only because of the reluctance of the PBOC to relinquish jurisdictional turf, but more fundamentally because of broader concerns (both within and beyond the PBOC) that it would usher in instability at a crucial moment in China's financial reform, when the current PBOC-rooted supervisory system was itself being fundamentally restructured.[49]

Upon its establishment, it became increasingly clear that even as the CBRC was intended to assume the regulatory functions of the PBOC and thus present a 'modern' institutional structure for financial regulation, the functional nature of state regulation was to take on a distinctive form that continued to reflect a CCP-dominated political hierarchy. The Chinese notion of regulation embodies the notion that the CCP is both umpire and player, reflected in regulatory authorities asserting a sense of ownership over the banks and their overall regulatory approach.[50] The ambiguity of objective legal standards is intentionally designed to provide space for normative moral standards to be provided by leaders; the CCP therefore commands arbitrary and decisive power. As with other government agencies, the CBRC is subject to an ostensible tension between its roles as both supervisor and CCP agent (Brehm 2008). The regulatory goal of financial stability coexists with the political interpretation of economic needs, providing the legal basis for the CBRC to act within the context of political objectives. This reflects the fact that personal statements by political leaders have institutionalized the norm-setting character in China, and are not just individual personal opinions (Fewsmith 2008). That is to say, they do not reflect simply upon the individual and their position within political structures and discourse, but rather upon the nature of those structures and discourses themselves.

Sterilizing the money markets

Commencing in 1997, a policy of gradual interest rate liberalization was instituted, when a 10 per cent band of flexibility was initially introduced for loans to small and medium enterprises (SMEs). In 1998 this relaxation was extended to all borrowers, before being increased to 20 per cent above the benchmark rate set by the PBOC. This liberalization coincided with the onset of the NPLs crisis in 1997, and represented a concerted effort by the Zhu Rongji administration to instil greater capacity for the pricing of risk within the commercial banks, the previous absence of which had undoubtedly been a significant factor in the buildup of an enormous stock of toxic debt within the banking system.

However, the cap on deposit rates was maintained, and the floor upon lending rates was maintained at 10 per cent below the benchmark rate, thus guaranteeing that a highly profitable interest rate spread remained at the disposal of the banks. The specific management of deposit rates became especially pronounced after 2003. Prior to this, the PBOC would make rapid adjustments to nominal deposit rates to reflect increases and decreases in consumer price inflation. However, beginning in 2004 the PBOC responded to inflation increases with a lag, whilst reducing nominal deposit rates rapidly in line with decreases in inflation (Lardy 2012). With the band of flexibility within which commercial banks were free to deviate from the PBOC-set benchmark rates maintaining a rate floor of 90 per cent of the benchmark, competition amongst the major banks virtually guaranteed the uniformity of lending rates at the lowest level sanctioned by the PBOC.

Deepening economic integration presented clear challenges for the management of China's exchange rate, as reforms were undertaken in a number of domestic manufacturing sectors in order to pave the way for WTO accession (Lardy 2002). As with the institutional change in the banking sector itself, the CCP leadership approached the management of the currency as a further tool with which to pursue economic growth in tandem with the preservation of political control. The confrontation of economic globalization unfolded through the construction of an increasingly rationalized set of relationships between the state and market, yet one that was coordinated and underpinned by the continuing authority of the CCP. From 1998 onwards, monetary policy was subordinated to exchange rate policy. In turn, exchange rate policy was subordinated to preserving internal stability, which demanded the retention of ultimate regulatory authority over capital.

As China acceded to the WTO in the aftermath of the AFC, a 'mercantilist objective' (Yu 2012) became evident in the drive to accumulate foreign reserves as a 'foreign-exchange-creating economy' [创汇经济]. During this period the exchange rate thus was not viewed as 'a price to be determined by the market but rather as a tool in China's broader development strategy' (Kroeber 2011).

The banking sector formed a central component in implementing this policy of exchange rate undervaluation. Beginning in 1998, the PBOC was tasked with two potentially conflicting policy objectives: maintaining export competitiveness through currency devaluation at the same time as ensuring monetary stability. An export-driven current account surplus will have an inflationary effect upon the domestic money supply in the absence of central bank intervention to prevent the capital it expends on accumulation of foreign exchange reserves from entering the domestic money supply. From 2003, the PBOC began to sterilize this surplus capital through two methods. First, it directly imposed bond quotas upon the SOCBs, which require them to hold a certain amount of interest-bearing bills issued by the central bank, thus reducing the money supply.[51] Secondly, it increased the required reserve ratio, forcing banks to deposit greater shares of their capital with the central bank and thus curtailing their lending operations. The effect of these sterilization methods was to reduce the portion of the total money supply in circulation and reduce inflationary pressure (Gang 2010).

The ongoing viability of both of these sterilization methods depended on the maintenance of low interest rates (Zhang 2012). Since the intervention in the foreign exchange markets from 2003 to 2007 was continuous, large scale, and unidirectional, investors in central bank bonds would bet that the sterilization efforts could not remain sustainable and viable in the long run. If interest rates were flexible, this calculation would force up interest rates upon the PBOC bonds, and thus significantly increase the costs of sterilization borne by the central bank, since a difference between the interest earned on foreign currency-denominated debt instruments that comprise official reserves and the interest paid on the bonds issued to the SOCBs would emerge and continuously increase. Thus, by setting interest rates at a low rate, the PBOC avoided these increased sterilization costs, but in doing so implicitly taxed the banks that held these bonds rather than other, more lucrative investments (Zhang 2012). The PBOC then offset this tax by reducing the costs of capital for the banks; it shifted the burden

170

onto household depositors by depressing the benchmark deposit rate. In this manner, the preservation of an exchange rate regime with highly limited flexibility for the purposes of domestic stability within a weak institutional and regulatory environment was symbiotically connected to the broader and deeper repression of the financial system.

Accelerating growth and the deepening of imbalances

These institutional transformations laid foundations for the deepening of a highly unbalanced growth trajectory. As Figure 5.1 indicates, the year 2000 marked a major inflection point in the development of severe imbalances in the composition of GDP growth, when the share of consumption commenced a decrease from 47 per cent to reach 34 per cent, and investment rose from

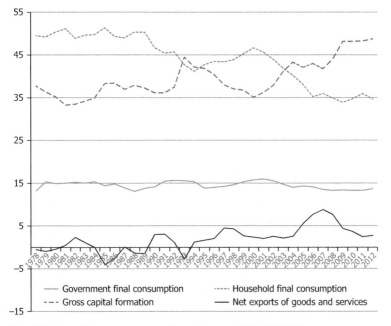

Figure 5.1: Shares of investment, consumption, and exports in GDP, 1978–2012
Source: World Bank, CEIC

171

35 per cent to reach 43 per cent by 2006. Two primary trends therefore emerge from the trajectory of growth between 1998 and 2007: first, the significant increase in investment between 2000 and 2004, and secondly the significant increase in net exports between 2005 and 2008. Following the AFC, therefore, it was first investment and then exports that led to a final headline rate of over 14 per cent in 2007.

Following the AFC, the CCP prioritized the stimulation of domestic demand through expansion in investment projects in order to sustain a rapid pace of economic growth (Chen 1999). Rather than industrial projects, capital was channelled towards infrastructure, which was perceived as still constituting a fundamental bottleneck in the economy. Knight and Ding (2012, 177) have found that from 1998 onwards the return on capital in industry rose substantially across both the state and non-state sectors:

> Enterprise reform and marketization achieved efficiency gains through the reallocation of resources toward more productive uses – from the state sector to the private sector, from agriculture to industry, and from domestic to foreign markets. Entrepreneurial expectations of rapid economic growth were crucial for high investment and the resultant path of economic growth.

The immediate impact of the post-AFC financial restructuring was to produce more effective mechanisms of capital allocation, even if levels of gross capital formation increased relative to other drivers of growth. This is to draw attention to the qualitative nature of that investment in contrast to that of either the investment that produced inflationary pressures in the mid-1990s or the increase in investment that followed the 2008 financial crisis. The newly restructured banking system continued to provide significant loans to enterprises whose loans had been the target of the debt restructuring efforts beginning in 1998. Financial statements indicate that corporate clients still accounted for over three-quarters of total lending by the four SOCBs that had listed publicly by the end of 2007: BOC, Bank of Communications (BOCOM), CCB, and

ICBC (BOC 2007; BOCOM 2007; CCB 2007; ICBC 2007). Of these loans to the corporate sector, loans to SOEs still weighed heavily, with loans to non-SOEs comprising 34 per cent in ICBC's case (ICBC 2007, 167), and 36 per cent in the case of CCB (CCB 2007, 197).

Figure 5.2 demonstrates how, following the rapid reduction in reliance upon government budgetary outlays for the financing of investment, enterprises came increasingly and steadily to rely upon their own savings for their capital outlays. This reflects the fact that China's investment-led growth has been driven by endogenous factors; even as FDI increased, this was directed primarily towards the manufacturing sector, a phenomenon that was increasingly prioritized by the Chinese government as the country's integration proceeded apace following WTO accession (Huang 2003). These investment levels and the entrepreneurial expectations underpinning them were highly dependent on the financial repression engineered through the SOCBs and the interest rate regulation that was a central element in these policies. The direct effect of these negative real interest rates was to repress growth in household disposable income relative to a less repressed financial environment. Two further indirect effects began to emerge. The first was

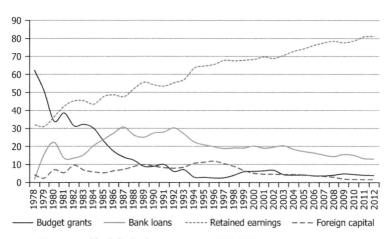

Figure 5.2: Sources of funds for fixed-asset investment, 1978–2012
Source: CEIC

that the savings rate as a portion of household disposable income increased,[52] since the objective of savings in a society without a strong social safety net is to reach a target level of financial assets (Chamon and Prasad 2010). The second was that this financial security-motivated increase in savings, the unattractiveness of depositing these savings with commercial banks, and the limited range of other attractive consumer investment options produced a heightened demand for residential property. As wealthy urban households began to attempt to capitalize upon a speculative real estate bubble, a further transfer of household wealth into the construction and infrastructure sectors began to take hold, accentuating the divergence between consumption and investment.

The roles of investment and exports (as well as the public and private sectors) in China's growth were thus linked closely to the institutional structure and macroeconomic role of the state-dominated financial sector. The overinvestment complex was related to the unbalanced external nature of the growth trajectory, as the relationship between the path of institutional reform in the banking sector and the emergence of overinvestment arose on the basis of policymakers' insistence upon targeting internal balance at the expense of external balance (Yu 2012). This reflects the fact that China's growth story has been one of domestic demand. Figure 5.3 illustrates the minor role that net exports have played in contributing to overall GDP growth, only coming to provide a significant contribution to GDP growth after 2005, the point at which China's current account surplus experienced a significant concomitant increase to reach over 10 per cent in 2007. Yet overall trade as a share of GDP increased since 1978. Although a significant contribution economic growth eventuated from exports directly as well as domestic industries connected through supply-chain and infrastructure needs, this overall investment- and export-dominated growth model remained premised on the ongoing role of the financial system to manage the macroeconomic pressures that resulted from both.

When in 2005 China's GDP growth came to reflect increasingly large shares of exports of goods and services, this did not coincide with a depreciation of the RMB in either real or trade-weighted

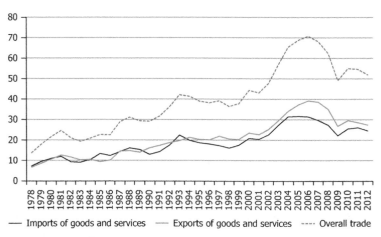

Figure 5.3: Exports and imports in GDP, 1978–2012
Source: World Bank

terms. For this reason, it is not possible to neatly depict the Chinese exchange rate regime as part of a coherent international monetary system in the form of a Bretton Woods II system. Such a system has been characterized by the emergence of a fixed exchange rate periphery in Asia, with China at its core and motivated by an export-led growth strategy (Dooley et al. 2003; 2004a; 2004b). From this perspective, given high savings and policy-driven lending practices, it was purely by virtue of an undervalued exchange rate and the consequent opportunities for export to the US market that China was able to prevent the severe misallocation of capital. This argument focuses on the real effective exchange rate (REER) of the RMB vis-à-vis the USD. The exchange rate regime was fixed rigidly at RMB 8.27 = USD 1 from 1994 until July 2005 when it was reformed into a managed floating rate. However, although the change in exchange rate policy had an effect upon the exchange rate itself in marginal terms (and actually declined in real, trade-weighted value during 2006 and 2007) (Lardy 2012), the current account surplus continued to rise dramatically before peaking in 2008 at 10 per cent of GDP (Figure 5.4) (Gao and Coffman 2013). Were Chinese policymakers genuinely formulating exchange rate policy on the basis of the interests of export-oriented manufacturers, and concerned fundamentally with preserving employment in those export sectors, then it would not have been logical to focus on the REER at the expense of the trade-weighted real exchange rate, for a majority of China's exports flowed and continue to flow to markets whose currencies float against the dollar (Goldstein and Lardy 2009). This trade-weighted exchange rate in fact appreciated by nearly 30 per cent between 1994 and 2002 (Figure 5.4).

Thus the notion that the bilateral USD–RMB was targeted out of consideration for maintaining export-sector employment is ultimately somewhat unconvincing. Rather, it was focused inwards so as to promote faith and confidence in what Calvo and Mishkin (2003, 101) have labelled the 'key to macroeconomic success', the economy's fundamental macroeconomic institutions of fiscal, monetary, and financial stability. In this sense, it is reflective of the need to construct a particular financial regime around the CCP's broader and deeper emphasis on a particular mode of control over the flow of capital within the domestic political economy. Policymakers neglected external macroeconomic balance, focusing instead upon policies beneficial to internal macroeconomic balance. Indeed, as

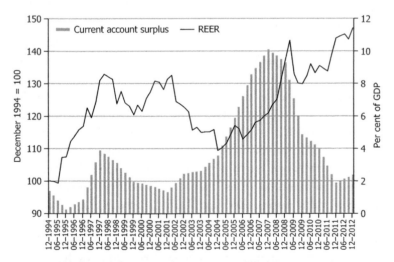

Figure 5.4: Real effective exchange rate and current account, 1994–2012
Source: National Bureau of Statistics, China Statistical Yearbook; CEIC

Yu Yongding has observed, the 'fiscal and monetary blend' of monetary policy to control overheating and fiscal policy to avert downturn had been quite successful in maintaining simultaneously low unemployment and low inflation (Yu 2012, 558). China's economic policymaking can be seen as directed towards maintaining domestic financial stability within a weak regulatory and institutional financial environment (Goldstein and Lardy 2005). In this sense, the peg to the USD was viewed as valuable for reasons of maintaining domestic financial stability and as an anchor for monetary policy.[53]

Conclusion

Zhu Rongji continues to be viewed generally by Western viewers (and to a lesser extent by Chinese financial analysts) as the consummate economic reformer and financial architect concerned with enacting a vision of market-oriented efficiency through economic competition. But what Zhu in fact achieved was the construction of a Chinese capitalism that was at its zenith from 2005 to 2008, as growth surged on the back of an increasingly unbalanced economic growth model. Western bankers, advisors, and commentators who looked to this period of economic opening and integration as commensurate with the diminishment of Party influence within the financial system were mistaken. They saw the growth of market forces and the establishment of modern institutional forms as evidence of the CCP's need to remove itself from the financial system in order to permit continued transformation of the Chinese political economy, and yet it was precisely the opposite; the CCP's continued salience as a crux of reform was exactly what enabled such changes to unfold. Through this system of risk management, the CCP was able to achieve its goals of stability through growth despite the socially regressive effects that this had because it was capable of constructing a system that was both market and state led; it was the CCP that crossed the institutional divide between state and market. In this sense, by strengthening the role of the CCP it strengthened both the market and the state. The course of reform and the resulting growth during this period thereby reflected a fundamental continuity in the economic sociology of China's mode of economic and financial governance. As Schell and Delury (2013, 349) have observed,

> It was an old story, but with a new ending. The Party-state's ultimate ownership rights of the national economy and the total monopoly of political power were no more to be changed, or even tinkered with, than the basic tenets of the Confucian construct were to be altered by the early self-strengtheners a century ago.

In such a vein, this chapter has traced the evolution of the banking sector and its role at the institutional core of this retention of authority over an increasingly capitalist authoritarian political economy as it mediated the relationship between different social groupings both domestic and foreign. The eruption of the financial crisis in 2008 ushered in a new phase in the development of China's financial capitalism, one that continues to unfold around us now and whose dynamics and implications for the longer-run evolution of global capitalism we are only just now beginning to more adequately and rigorously grasp.

Notes

1 Interview, 9 August 2013, Beijing – China Construction Bank.
2 Interview, 21 August 2013, Beijing – PBOC; Interview, 18 April 2014, Beijing – Ministry of Finance.
3 Interview, 6 June 2012, Beijing – Ministry of Finance; Interview, 12 October 2012, Beijing – SAFE.
4 This meeting was notable for the presence of Jiang Zemin, Li Peng, and Zhu Rongji. Participants also included not only central bank officials at the national and provincial level, officials from the headquarters and major provincial branches of the state-owned banks, insurance companies, and many NBFIs, but also provincial governors and provincial level finance officials.
5 Five firms in particular were notable for the scale and rapidity of their demise: China Rural Trust and Investment Corp in January 1997; Hainan Development Bank on 21 May 1998; China New Technology Venture Capital Corp on 22 June 1998; Pudong United Trust and Investment Corporation in October 1998; and Guangdong International Trust and Investment Company in October 1998.

6   USD 3.3 billion and 6.3 billion in the second and third quarters respectively (BIS 1999).

7   Interview, 17 November 2012, Beijing – Shanghai Stock Exchange.

8   These were to place emphasis on 'politics, study, and moral integrity' [讲政治，讲学习，讲正气].

9   This is especially evident in the way that private entrepreneurs navigated around the formal strictures of SOE-centric financing channels in ways that relied upon their ability to gain access to and favour with party officials (Tsai 2007).

10 These included the defeat in 1993 of China's bid to host the 2000 Olympic Games, the action of the US during the 1995–96 Taiwan Straits Crisis, NATO intervention in Kosovo, and particularly the 1999 bombing of the Chinese embassy in Belgrade.

11 As Rana Mitter (2004, 245) has described it, a 'shimmering time of political and cultural promise whose attraction lay in its instability'.

12 Interview, 23 May 2012, Beijing – PBOC; Interview, 23 May 2012, Beijing – Ministry of Finance.

13 Interview, 5 June 2012, Beijing – CASS.

14 As Bell and Feng (2013) have aptly observed (yet underappreciating its significance), these individuals can be characterized neither as Weberian bureaucrats nor Machiavellian politicians.

15 Interview, 23 May 2012, Beijing – PBOC; Interview, 5 June 2012, Beijing – CASS.

16 Interview, 10 October 2012, Beijing – People's Bank of China.

17 Interview, 10 October 2012, Beijing – People's Bank of China; Interview, 16 November 2012, Beijing – China Banking Regulatory Commission.

18 This is reminiscent of Susan Shirk's (1992, 76) notion of leadership and regulatory authority being intertwined together in a system of 'management by exception'.

19 Interview, 21 October 2012, Beijing – People's Bank of China.

20 Although different forms of 'forward guidance' have emerged as a widely recognized and important dimension of central banking internationally (such as Mario Draghi's famous pledge in July 2012 to 'do whatever it takes' to save the Euro), the nature of 'moral suasion' or 'jawboning' in China remains of a qualitatively distinct dynamic between a central bank and financial institutions. Interview 20 June 2012, Beijing – Institute of Finance and Banking, Chinese Academy of Social Sciences.

21 Interview, 10 October 2012, Beijing – People's Bank of China.

22 This interbank bond market itself was only initiated in June 1997.

23 Upon Wen Jiabao's assumption of the Premiership in 2003, Hua was appointed Head of the State Council itself.

24 Interview, 14 April 2014, Beijing – Tsinghua University.

25 Economic cadre (quoted in Lam 1999, 384).

26 RMB 93 billion of this went to BOC and CCB, ICBC received RMB 85 billion, whilst Agricultural Bank of China (ABC) received RMB 92 billion.

27 China Cinda Asset Management Company [中国信达资产管理公司] was closely aligned to CCB; China Huarong Asset Management Company [中国华融资产管理公司] was aligned to ICBC; China Orient Asset Management Company [中国东方资产管理公司] was aligned with BOC; China Great Wall Asset Management Company [中国长城资产管理公司] was aligned with ABC.

28 The CCB listing prospectus stated that 'in the event that Cinda is unable to pay any interest on the bond in full, the MOF will provide financial support, . . . when necessary, the MOF will provide support with respect to Cinda's repayment of the principal of the bond'. Whether this extends to all of the AMCs or just Cinda AMC is unclear (CCB 2005).

29 Interview 12 September 2012, Beijing – Institute of World Economics and Politics, Chinese Academy of Social Sciences.

30 Interview 17 September 2012, Beijing – Agricultural Bank of China.

31 Interview 26 August 2013, Beijing – Minsheng Bank.

32 Interview 21 August 2013, Beijing – People's Bank of China.

33 Interview 27 May 2012, Beijing – Chinese Academy of Social Sciences.

34 Each of the following holds a 10 per cent stake in HKSCC Nominees Ltd: HSBC, Standard Chartered Bank, Hang Seng Bank, Bank of East Asia, and Bank of China. See BIS (2007).

35 Interview 4 June 2012, Beijing – National School of Development, Peking University; Interview 5 June 2012, Beijing – Institute of Finance and Banking, Chinese Academy of Social Sciences.

36 A 'large non-trader' [大非] is a large-scale holder of non-tradeable R-shares, whilst a 'small non-trader' [小非] is a holder of a smaller quantity of such R-shares (typically regarded as less than 5 per cent of the whole stock of the company). See China Securities Depository and Clearing Commission (2008).

37 In functional terms, the similarity between the ownership structures of the publicly listed commercial banks and a non-commercial, non-publicly listed bank such as the China Development Bank is instructive. See (Li Xia 2000). The CDB has three shareholders: MOF (50.18 per cent), Huijin (47.63 per cent), and the NSSFC (2.19 per cent) (China Development Bank 2011).

38 Interview 7 April 2013, Beijing – China Banking Regulatory Commission.

39 Interview 7 September 2012, Beijing – National Development and Reform Commission; Interview 21 November 2012, Beijing – Primavera Capital Group.

40 Interview 9 August 2013, Beijing – China Construction Bank.

41 Interview 26 August 2013, Beijing – Minsheng Bank.

42 Whilst the State Council formally controlled the PBOC, which in turn controlled the SOCBs, the CCP further imposed parallel methods of control through the Central Discipline and Inspection Commission, which was subordinate to the Central Committee of the CCP and which exercised control over staffing the party committees present within all SOEs (Tang 2003).

43 This took place in December 1997, following the November convening of the Central Financial Work Conference (PRC State Council 1997).

44 Interview 4 June 2012, Beijing – National School of Development, Peking University.

45 Wen Jiabao, as the head of the CFWC, clearly saw its role as one of implementation rather than formulation of CCP policy (Heilmann 2005, 8).

46 There was in fact very little continuity in staffing between the two groups (Naughton 2003b).

47 The CFWC's role in horizontal rather than vertical financial supervision will be explored below.

48 The CSRC and the China Insurance Regulatory Commission (CIRC) were both established in 1998.

49 Interview 14 June 2012, Beijing – Baoshang Bank; Interview 28 November 2012, Beijing – Central Leading Group for Finance and Economics.

50 The term for 'regulation' [监督管理] is the conjunction of two different words: *jiandu* [监督]means that of supervision or oversight, whilst *guanli* [管理] refers to management. See He (2014).

51 By the end of 2010, commercial banks had acquired approximately RMB 4 trillion of central bank bills at 1.692 per cent for three-month maturity, and 2.126 per cent for one-year maturity. The discrepancy between these returns and the average lending rate of 6.11 per cent constitutes an implicit tax upon commercial banks (Milana and Wu 2012).

52 Thus China's high savings rate reached an unprecedented level of more than 50 per cent of GDP in the period 2006–10 (Ma and Yi 2010).

53 Interview 16 June 2012, Beijing – China Investment Corporation; Interview 8 June 2012, Beijing – China Construction Bank.

6

Post-crisis challenges: confronting capitalism in the 2010s

The end goal of reform? To increase the wealth of society, to strengthen the nation [国民富强]. Is it possible to really know? But one thing we do know: we cannot ever stop the reform process.

Government official, National Development and Reform Commission[1]

The supposed success of China's developmental model in propelling economic growth was seemingly confirmed in 2008 as China's banking and financial sector was structurally insulated from the financial contagion emanating from the USA. The crisis had two main effects. First, it presented an immediate economic challenge for China's banking system, as the precipitous fall in global demand called for economic stimulus in which the banks, given their extant position within China's political economy, would inevitably play a central role. The second impact was at the ideational level. The crisis had a major impact on how Chinese policymakers and financial elites perceived the financial deregulatory paradigm that had underpinned the Anglo-American financial world prior to the crisis. The rapid and seemingly effective response to China's immediate economic challenges dovetailed with these shifting attitudes to reinforce a sense of vindication for China's financially repressed and gradualist trajectory of financial and economic reform. Yet this was short lived; the discursive challenge in China to the Anglo-American financial paradigm masked the deeper underlying reality of crisis capitalism that is now reconstituting itself in China.

In this chapter I trace how the Chinese leadership has sought to manage the macroeconomic fallout of the previous periods of unbalanced and unsustainable growth without endangering the CCP's political authority. Rather than seeking to insulate the real economy and public finances from the private financial sector, the Chinese crisis response brought financial institutions ever closer to the heart of the Chinese political economy. Financial markets had never been regarded by Chinese policymakers as self-regulating, and thus the central locus of capacity to manage uncertainty and thus not only maintain economic growth as well as financial stability continued to revolve around the CCP itself, and not a nascent regime of technocratic liberal regulation. The response was thus to maintain the duality of the financial system as both economic infrastructure (the governance of uncertainty) and as political tool (the power of uncertainty). China's leaders were clearly not omnipotent in their macroeconomic stewardship following the crisis. But as I argue in this chapter, the economic continuity and stability that has been achieved resulted not only through more-or-less effective macroeconomic policy, but also and just as importantly by virtue of the deeper socio-political centrality of the CCP's role and position at the heart of the financial system.

China's macroeconomic and financial response to the crisis from 2008 to 2012 was thus a product of the use of economic growth to avoid a number of social and political dilemmas whose origins could be traced to 'pre-Modern' China, but which had crystallized most tangibly and viscerally in 1989. After having managed the immediate fallout of that existential political crisis by doubling down on economic growth, and developing the formula of a socialist market economy that would permit the market-oriented economic transformation of society and also institutionalize and entrench the political role of the CCP in socio-economically anchoring that market economy, the CCP had managed to achieve the feat of rapid economic growth without the emergence of any serious threat to its political authority. Chinese capitalism was stable under the authority of the CCP, but it was capitalism nonetheless, containing deeply ingrained logics of accumulation and unbalanced growth that were difficult to disrupt.

This response therefore served to deepen and intensify the country's unsustainable macroeconomic trajectory. The rise of shadow banking and an increasingly inefficient overreliance on debt to support growth through the crisis reflected the unsustainability of the existing developmental trajectory and the inevitable yet unintended consequences of relying upon economic growth as a means of ameliorating deeper social and political fissures. The path dependency embodied in these trends and dynamics was rooted in the continuing salience of the CCP as the manager of financial uncertainty. Within a market economy, volatility and stability are founded upon the mutual expectations of creditors and debtors, and the CCP had never been willing to relinquish the capacity to set those expectations to 'the market' itself. Yet continuity in the relationship between political authority and financial capital does not necessarily equate to stasis either in the institutional structure of the financial system or in the relationship between the financial system and the real economy. The central policymaking challenge long before the crisis had already been of how to shift towards a more consumer-oriented economic growth model without necessarily producing a dramatic movement towards greater private and individual control over financial capital itself. The ultimate objective – of directing capital towards the essential economic bases for shoring up CCP authority – therefore remained the same, but demanded a retooling of the means through which to achieve it.

Contradictions of the crisis [危机（会）]

The onset of the 2008 financial crisis represented both opportunity and challenge to the Chinese leadership. The Chinese word for 'crisis' [weiji 危机] comprises two characters meaning 'peril' [危] and 'opportunity' [机]. The events of 2008 represented both an opportunity for China to increasingly assert itself and its model of political economy more forcefully, yet simultaneously its own developmental trajectory up to that date had become deeply embroiled in a deeply flawed global economic system. It would thus prompt a re-evaluation of China's own path of development and the economic structure that had underlain it, as well as a reconsideration of the desirability of moving along a market-oriented reform trajectory. However, as the crisis was beginning to unfold and spread in the American financial system, the immediate priority was to take necessary steps to ensure that any fallout could be ameliorated through China's own financial system. The CCP viewed the financial system as it always had – as a tool that could be utilized and even manipulated in order to achieve other economic, social, and political goals. In the throes of the crisis, this meant securing support for the real economy. The reasoning was that whereas in the USA the crisis had originated in the financial system and then spread to the real economy, the reverse would be more likely in China: that any major crisis would first emerge in the real economy and then spread to the financial system. The stabilization of output and employment – by any means – was therefore considered the first line of defence against a deeper banking crisis.

China's economic leadership first started to map out a response to the crisis in June 2008, well before most other countries, and despite the distractions of the impending fanfare of the 2008 Summer Olympics in Beijing. The 25 July Politburo meeting established the earliest policy line that would guide the economic leadership through the depths of the crisis: to maintain relatively smooth and fast-paced economic growth whilst guarding against the acceleration of inflation. In preparation for the package itself, a number of steps were taken through the autumn of 2008.[2] The first concerted move was at the Executive Meeting of the State Council on 17 October, where Wen Jianbao resolved to adopt 'flexible and cautionary macroeconomic policies' that would expand domestic demand, improve living conditions, and stimulate overall economic development. Interest rates were steadily lowered throughout the fourth quarter of 2008. This prepared the ground for the announcement and implementation of the fiscal and monetary stimulus package on 9 November, with the formal fiscal policy switching from 'prudent' to 'proactive' and the formal monetary policy stance shifting from 'moderately tight' to 'moderately easy' (Naughton 2009).

The stimulus package could be disaggregated into three primary substantive components. The first was a significant scaling up in scope of the existing investment plan. The second was a funding mechanism for streamlining channels for the flow of investment capital, largely concentrated within the banking sector. The third component was industrial policy, comprising both immediate responses to the specific conditions of the economic crisis, as well as plans for pursuing long-held and longer-term objectives. Although the dimensions of the stimulus package as formulated by a State Council meeting on 5 November 2008 were widely published, they were highly ambiguous and represented little more than satisfying the rhetorical need for a rapid and concerted response that was intended to assure both public and investor confidence, and to forestall any further precipitous drop in domestic demand and overseas sentiment. Yet, as Naughton (2009, 3) has observed and Table 6.1 illustrates, the ensuing 'reservations about the announced Chinese plan were correct, but ultimately irrelevant, because the real action was occurring behind the scenes'. The extent to which the initially announced figures diverged from the reality of capital flows through the fiscal and credit system is apparent.

At the same time as the State Council meeting, a meeting of the CCP Politburo was convened, from which was issued Central Document No. 18 of 2008 [中发 [2008] 18号文件]. Like all secret central Party documents, this was distributed through Party channels and remained unpublished, but in contrast to the vast majority of such documents whose existence remains unknown to all those outside the authorized dissemination channels, this document was abstracted and leaked by individuals in two separate capacities.[2] Of the ten measures listed to 'expand domestic demand and ensure stable rapid growth', the final directive to

Table 6.1. Stimulus package investment plan

Sector	Announced investment	On-balance sheet investment		Off-balance sheet spending
		Centre + local	Local	
Housing security	280	200	120	140
Rural livelihood & affairs	370	200	200	40
Railway, road, airport, water conservation, power grids	1,800	310	310	2,530
Health, education & culture	40	110	110	50
Environmental protection	350	50	50	50
Research & development	160			
Post-disaster reconstruction	1,000	230	210	
Total	4,000	1,100	1,000	2,810

Source: National Development and Reform Commission (NDRC); Interview 14 April 2014, Beijing – Chinese Academy of Social Sciences.

'strengthen the support given by bank credit to economic growth' was universally interpreted as sanctioning the overarching use of the banking system to achieve a range of other objectives, including the foregoing nine (Liu Zebang 2008).[3] The urgency with which the crisis situation and response was received throughout the bureaucracy was palpable. For instance, the National Development and Reform Commission (NDRC) held an 'emergency' [紧急] meeting on 10 November to allocate the RMB 100 billion of increased investment earmarked for the fourth quarter. In the directive issued following the meeting, it was therefore emphasized that 'throughout all regions and departments, the priority amongst all other priorities is to urgently implement the center's increased investment and other measures in order to boost domestic demand'. In so doing, agencies and departments must 'make every second count' (NDRC 2008).

One of the primary mechanisms through which this took place was through local government financing vehicles (LGFVs). Their advent was originally a direct initiative of Chen Yuan upon taking the helm of the CDB in the late 1990s (Sanderson and Forsythe 2012). He informed local officials that 'CDB will provide more loans provided that you provide sound, resilient governance and introduce financial criteria into your system'. The rationale for such action was that

> commercial enterprises can go to commercial banks for loans, but local infrastructure projects, such as highways and urban utilizes, cannot get loans from commercial banks – because these loans are long-term by necessity, and there are no qualified borrowers. … The mechanism worked well. In a few years, we built a nation-wide system. Every province followed the model and could borrow a large amount of money from CDB. (Chen Yuan, quoted in Kuhn 2010, 272)

However, following the crisis LGFVs would take on a different hue – as useful but deeply flawed mechanisms for channelling capital as rapidly as possible to local industry. The explicit freedom with which the central leadership was willing to permit local authorities to 'capture' the banks – which were in no position to resist the CCP's prioritization of infrastructure investment – is testament to the Party's concern with an immediate slump in external demand catalysing a more precipitous and self-fulfilling plunge in domestic sentiment. The CBRC and PBOC (2009) sanctioned the unleashing of local government developmental fervour in January 2009 with Document No. 92:

> Encourage local governments to attract and to incentivize banking and financial institutions to increase their lending to the investment projects set up by the central government. This can be done by a variety of ways including increasing local fiscal subsidies to interest payments, improving rewarding mechanism for loans and establishing government investment and financing platforms compliant with regulations.

Accordingly, the first local government bonds were issued in March 2009 closely on the heels of the stimulus package. The

MOF opened the sales to all investors, issuing RMB 200 billion in three-year bonds. Simultaneously, five government agencies jointly issued a directive on promoting the 'healthy development of credit sales',[4] which advocated credit sales as an important and instrumental mechanisms for boosting post-crisis domestic demand and supporting overall real economic growth, and served as the starting gun for SOCBs to turn on the credit spigots to both SOEs and LGFVs. More important regulatory support came from the MOF, which despite existing regulations on the use of local government revenue and the budget law that prohibits local government borrowing, issued a regulation that allowed local government to finance investment projects using all sources of funds, including budgetary revenue, land revenue, and funds borrowed by local financing vehicles.

The story of the investment spending under the aegis of post-crisis stimulus and its consequences is well known. As Nicholas Lardy (2012) has argued persuasively, it was successful in its fundamental purpose, that of averting a precipitous collapse in employment whilst also ensuring that any risks being generated as a result remained under the purview and control of the central authorities – in other words, by concentrating them in the banking system. It reflected once again the duality of the Chinese financial system – the extent to which the banking system is expected to play a role in dealing with a myriad of policy challenges arising in China's developmental trajectory in addition to the intermediation of credit, all of which must be made compatible with the preservation of ultimate CCP control over financial capital itself. The critical issue was not of how China's leaders averted economic crisis, but of how they then would respond to the reaccumulation of risk and uncertainty within the financial system over the following several years.

Frames: stability with progress

The crisis catalysed a renewed debate about the appropriate direction and way forward for Chinese financial reform and the development of economy and society at large. Intersecting and often conflicting considerations were prominent: the failure of the Anglo-American financial model boosted confidence in China's distinctive approach towards gradual and cautious reform, and retention of political authority over the financial system. But at the same time the flaws in the Chinese trajectory of economic development were clearly apparent, and the role of the financial system in supporting and amplifying the imbalances and tensions in this trajectory were undeniable. The outcome was a muddling through that, whilst at times confused and ineffective, was by no means directionless. Whilst the political objectives of the CCP underlying financial governance would not shift, the role of the financial system in achieving these objectives would slowly start to evolve over the next years, as the national leadership sought to navigate a delicate transition to a new phase of economic growth and development. The trials and tribulations of fragile financial markets and the continuing problems of overcapacity and inefficiency in the state-owned industrial sector demanded progress, but this could only take place without endangering the bottom line of financial governance – macroeconomic stability. The guiding policy line to result was 'making progress while maintaining stability' (Huang et al. 2016, 49).

The events of 2008–09 reinvigorated the New Left debate of the early 1990s when the fundamental characteristics of the socialist market economy were being debated amongst prominent intellectuals. New leftists such as Wang Hui, Wang Shaoguang, and Cui Zhiyuan seized on the chance to forcefully critique the view that China needed to accelerate market-oriented reforms, and that Western 'liberal' financial systems could serve as ideal-types or models for Chinese policymakers (Wang Shaoguang 2011). Yet the New Leftists, Wang Hui particularly amongst them, historically had been deeply critical of how China's embrace of capitalist modernity had reflected many of the worst aspects of neoliberalism and indigenous Chinese bureaucratic authoritarianism. It is accordingly not possible to understand the crisis response through a simple dichotomy of state versus market, since rejecting a greater

190

role for the market did not necessarily entail a corresponding greater role for the state. Wang Shaoguang (2011), writing in the New Leftist journal *Utopia*, argued that just as government should not be seen as the enemy of society, the state was not the enemy of the market. Rather, what was necessary was a socially embedded and ideologically progressive response that could harness both state and market mechanisms for the public interest. Needless to say, for as long as the CCP retained a monopoly on the definition of the public interest, this response would have to be channelled through the ideological and bureaucratic structures of the CCP and embodied within its ongoing political dominance over economy and society.

Relinquishing such a monopoly was precisely what Xi Jinping, recently elevated to the PSC and waiting to take the reins of power, had no intention of doing. Reflecting in 2008 on thirty years of reform and opening, Xi (2008) unsurprisingly placed the Party's leadership at the core of the historic changes to have unfolded in Chinese society over that period. More importantly, he emphasized the importance of the CCP's effectiveness as a ruling Party – as opposed to a revolutionary one – being rooted in both the Party's ability to meet the economic needs of society, but also that confidence and trust in the Party to do so were paramount in this endeavour.[5] In Xi's eyes, the healthy development of the socialist market economy could take place only if the CCP possessed enough authority and power such that no uncertainty existed as to the direction of development. His commitment to such a view would only intensify and deepen over the next several years of the increasingly 'lame duck' post-crisis position of Hu Jintao and Wen Jiabao, as the hangover of the stimulus began to reverberate around the economy. His response upon taking over CCP leadership would be to embrace and deepen the two seemingly contradictory trends that had been the hallmark of financial development since the early 1990s: accelerate the marketization of the financial system and redouble efforts to ensure that the dynamics of such markets were in line with CCP priorities.

In turn, Wen Jiabao's 2010 *Government Work Report* (Wen 2010) provided a clear indication of the conclusions reached by the unified central Party leadership from the experiences of the 2008–09 crisis:

> In the course of the past year … we came to the following conclusions: We must continue to make use of the tools of both market mechanisms and macroeconomic control, that is, at the same time as we keep our reforms oriented towards a market economy, let market forces play their basic role in allocating resources, and stimulate the market's vitality, we must make best use of the socialist system's advantages, which enable us to make decisions efficiently, organize effectively, and concentrate resources to accomplish large undertakings.

The use of both 'market mechanisms' [市场机制] and 'macroeconomic control' [宏观调控] in this context and their juxtaposition is a reflection of the fundamental continuity that had remained in place for almost two decades after the first articulation of the socialist market economy in 1993.

This continuity was present across the highest levels of economic policymaking and leadership. In May 2009 the China's Future Direction Editorial Group (2009) published a book entitled *China's Future Direction: Uniting High-Level Policymaking and National Strategic Arrangements*. The volume makes clear that there were few illusions within the CCP leadership as to the nature and severity of the economic challenges facing China at the outset of the crisis. This mirrored a relatively clear consensus amongst prominent Chinese economists that China's structural economic challenges and constraints were mounting, despite disagreement about the appropriate response. The central leadership was more than aware of these challenges, but they were biding their time and working within these constraints, and one of the key constraints was perceived to be political fragmentation and ineffectiveness. Without a stronger Party, no comprehensive financial or economic reform could possibly be effective.

Institutional inertia: the shadows deepen

The macroeconomic consequences of the stimulus package did not take long to begin to manifest in the financial system. The Central Economic Work conference in December 2009 brought about the first high-level discussion of monetary and fiscal consequences of the stimulus package. This led to a decision to enact monetary tightening as needed, despite the success of the stimulus itself. By early 2010, financial institutions that had rapidly expanded credit under direction from central and local authorities started to receive mixed signals (Hsu et al. 2014; Shen 2016; Tsai 2015). The PBOC was tightening monetary policy in earnest, raising capital adequacy ratios, and imposing credit restrictions on banks, yet there remained significant political pressure – both formal and informal – to continue supporting long-term infrastructure invest-ments (see Figure 6.1). This familiar tension between competing

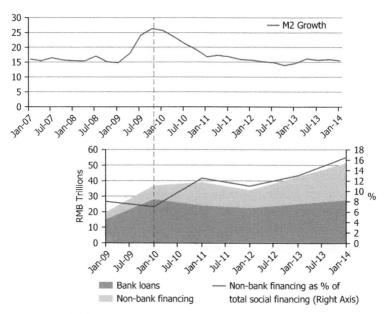

Figure 6.1: 2010 and the emergence of shadow banking
Source: CEIC

policy priorities – financial stability and economic growth – drove financial institutions to seek opportunities for regulatory arbitrage (Huang et al. 2016), resulting in the rapid development of a variety of novel financial products as banks sought to move liabilities off-balance sheet, and non-financial institutions such as trust companies stepped in to extend credit to those borrowers now cut off from access to bank loans. The emergence of China's shadow banking system was thus at its core a story of the financially repressed banking system being pushed to its limits, and struggling to overcome financing and efficiency gaps on both the lending and borrowing sides to SMEs and low-income households (Feyzioğlu 2009; Hsiao et al. 2015). The majority of capital for these securitized and non-securitized products came to be sourced from wealth management products (WMPs), issued directly by banks themselves, trust companies, or through 'bank–trust cooperation', and marketed to ordinary retail investors as alternatives to low-yielding bank deposits.[7]

One motivation for tolerating the growth of shadow banking was to capitalize upon WMPs and shadow banking as both a back door mechanism for introducing market forces into the financial system and as a necessary means of supporting post-crisis economic growth. Historically, the desire for interest rate marketization on the part of the PBOC and CBRC had a strong financial inclusion argument, since doing so would give incentive for greater lending to SMEs, boosting productive employment and increasing financial efficiency (Xie et al. 2001). This gave rise to a policy discourse prioritizing financial inclusion and impact upon the real economy as an important guiding principle for governing WMPs and shadow banking more broadly. The PBOC deputy governor Hu Xiaolian pointed out in 2014 that the shadow banking system had become an alternative channel to finance those restricted from normal bank loans, and that 'regulatory policy should strengthen financial services for the weak areas in the society, such as small firms' (Ruan 2016). This reflected the PBOC's emphasis in its 2013 Financial Stability Report on the benefits of shadow banking, which stated that 'as an integral part of the financial market in a broad sense, shadow banking plays a positive role in facilitating social investment and financing' (PBOC 2013, 199).[8] Similar arguments were made by prominent scholars in central government think tanks, including the State Council Development Research Center (Ba 2010), and leading financial regulators (Yan and Li 2014; Sheng and Soon 2016). Scholars from CASS argued that policy measures should be guided by the overarching principle of ensuring that the financial sector serves the real economy, and that policymakers should accordingly promote the healthy growth and development of the shadow banking sector (CASS 2013; Zhang et al 2014).[9] This influential group of financial policymakers and scholars explicitly linked shadow banking regulation with the prerogatives of economic development, thus laying the basis for a perspective on the risks and rewards of shadow banking that diverged from the negative views prevalent within the global regulatory discourse.

The PBOC and the CBRC cautiously welcomed the growth of WMPs as a diversification of the investment channels available to depositors and retail investors,[10] and the increasing pressure on banks to adopt more market-oriented lending practices played a role in catalysing the acceleration of interest rate marketization in 2012 and 2013 (PBOC 2013). WMPs, however, only provided partial relief to financially repressed economic sectors. Despite the general positive view of shadow banking as a benefit to the real economy, there was limited evidence that WMPs were genuinely either alleviating the credit drought of SMEs or spurring on the growth of consumer finance markets.[11] An estimated 57 per cent of funds from WMPs are channelled to the bond market, with an additional 17 per cent invested in trusts and other non-standardized debt assets, according to research conducted at the Bank of International Settlements (Ehlers et al. 2018). SMEs are of insufficient scale to access capital from bond markets and trusts. And whilst retail investors were a key driver of WMP growth, retail borrowers were not beneficiaries of such funds (Wang et al. 2016; Collier 2017).

The deepest connection between WMPs and the real economy was in their assistance in maintaining growth rates in the aftermath of the credit tightening, by continuing to channel capital to

LGFVs and large firms. In this sense it predominantly fulfilled a credit replacement rather than credit enhancement function, but one which was nonetheless necessary in striking a compromise between countervailing economic and political objectives. The former involves credit that otherwise would have been extended in any case through conventional bank loans, but which has been channelled into off balance sheet financing vehicles. This form of non-bank credit intermediation (NBCI) overlaps significantly but is not coterminous with WMPs and LGFVs, which gives rise to considerable confusion in the discourse on how to conceptualize and regulate Chinese NBCI. The latter credit-enhancing function of NBCI involves credit that would otherwise not be made available, and includes WMPs and other financial products – including the vast majority of fintech (financial technology or digital financial services) – thus serving as useful sources of alternative financing for underserviced enterprises and individuals.[12] That this credit intermediation took place within the shadow banking system rather than through formal banking channels was an inevitable consequence of the PBOC's monetary tightening as the full implications of the 2009 credit expansion became apparent. Between 2011 and 2016, even as the growth in money supply and of bank loans moderated (see Figure 6.1), the WMP market continued to expand relatively rapidly (Figure 6.2).

In this manner, the growth of WMPs served the PBOC's goal of incrementally advancing financial reform without threatening the politically sensitive position of the SOCBs. But shadow banking and WMPs in particular did not benefit the real economy so unambiguously as to justify more concerted efforts to promote it as a force for financial and broader economic reform. Although there was incentive for using the shadow banking system to further promote deeper marketization of the banking sector, doing so at a time of deep uncertainty over headline growth and key employment sectors posed a significant threat to financial stability and therefore broader Party control. The growth of the WMP market as an opaque and increasingly interconnected web of financial relations between banks and NBFIs presented a number of challenges to

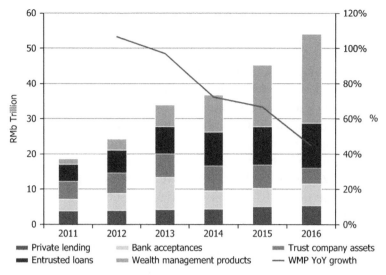

Figure 6.2: Growth of select NBCI product categories, 2011–16
Source: Xi and Xia (2017)

regulatory control over systemic risk in the financial system. At the time these risks were perceived as manageable. In 2012, the PBOC governor Zhou Xiaochuan observed that even though China had its own shadow banking system, it was much smaller in terms of size and risk than those of advanced economies (China Daily 2012). This assessment was backed up by thorough CASS reports in 2013 and 2014 that recognized China's shadow banking sector contains risks derived from maturity and liquidity mismatch and imperfect credit risk transfer, but argued that the risk of triggering a systemic crisis is very small (CASS 2013; Zhang et al. 2014). This is because of the distinction between shadow banking in the wider (NBCI) and in the narrower (those posing systemic risk) sense (Yan and Li 2014). The large majority of China's shadow banking institutions and instruments fall into the first category, and thus were not considered to require tighter regulatory control and oversight.

These policy positions were reflected in the first stage of the regulatory response to shadow banking, which emphasized transparency, disclosure, and monitoring, rather than an attempt to eliminate outright banks' shadow finance operations (Mao 2013). It fell to the CBRC, with responsibility for regulating both banks and trust companies, to address the challenge of tracking the more opaque and convoluted financial products and to attempt to gain a handle on rapidly burgeoning WMP issuance. On 6 July 2009 the CBRC had begun to implement regulation (CBRC 2009) aimed at increasing the visibility and clarity of the risk factors inherent within the rapidly blooming bank–trust cooperative arrangements (Hu and Zheng 2016). More restrictive measures came in January 2011, when the CBRC clarified the risk attribution of bank–trust arrangements, and required them to return such activities to bank balance sheets by the end of 2011 or implement capital-provisioning at 10.5 per cent for such products (CBRC 2011). These regulatory interventions made significant but limited inroads into addressing the transparency problem of the off balance sheet activities of the banks, and also slowed the growth rate of WMPs, contributing to a commensurate decline in overall shadow financing growth (Liang 2016).

The systemic risk challenge posed by WMPs resulted largely from a fragmented regulatory system that was susceptible to regulatory arbitrage, a characteristic that had motivated the initial emergence of WMPs. The PBOC and CBRC accordingly struggled to first monitor and then apportion regulatory responsibility for cross-sectoral NBCI that transcended the traditional boundaries between the securities, insurance, and banking sectors. The CBRC had initially maintained in 2012 that NBCI-related financial activity, such as that of trust companies, finance companies, and the off balance sheet transactions of banks, did not in fact constitute shadow banking (Gao and Wang 2014). This was not a shirking of regulatory responsibility; the agency had already been issuing related regulatory notices for three years. And so in late 2012 at the Eighteenth CCP Congress, CBRC chairman Shang Fulin highlighted that regardless of their status as shadow banking or not, products such as WMPs and trust products were not unregulated but rather within the supervisory perimeter of his agency.[13]

Nevertheless, a fuller regulatory response was required, which came in the form of the late 2013 issuance by the State Council of Document 107 (PRC State Council 2014b), the key foundation text for both clarifying the nature of shadow banking and outlining an effective regulatory framework for monitoring it (Guo and Xia 2014). Document 107 contained the first comprehensive definition of shadow banking. It paved the way for a clearer delineation of regulatory responsibilities over a rapidly changing financial ecosystem, adopting the principle that 'everyone is responsible for their own children', and applying the 1 + 3 (一行三会) regulatory oversight structure (comprising the PBOC and the three commissions) to the development of shadow financial products by financial and non-financial institutions. Rather than offering a reform blueprint for how to harness 'shadow banking' as a positive force for change in the financial system, Document 107 and the regulatory measures surrounding it provided space for WMPs to grow, whilst seeking to articulate a regulatory framework for monitoring the systemic risks accumulating within the system.[14]

Document 107 and the overall policy response to shadow banking was therefore one of cautious tolerance. It recognized both sides of the shadow banking debate, accepting that the emergence of shadow banking was a necessary result of financial development and innovation, and that it functioned as a financing channel that complemented the traditional banking system, but also that its opacity presented regulatory challenges for adequate monitoring and supervision of systemic risk. For as long as the cost benefit calculation of taking more comprehensive steps to either seize the opportunity for broader market-oriented financial reform or to eliminate outright the shadow WMP market and enforce its wholesale return to bank balance sheets remained ambiguous, the policy agenda was stuck in limbo. Neither the scale nor structure of Chinese WMPs presented a risk sufficiently acute to warrant fully fledged intervention and a deeper overhaul of the financial governance structure to minimize opportunities for regulatory arbitrage.

The consequences of this stasis were the seemingly inescapable entrenchment of China's pre-crisis macroeconomic trajectory, as efforts to maintain headline growth and promote the internationalization of the RMB overshadowed incremental progress in increasing domestic consumption. Prior to assuming office in 2003, Wen Jiabao had articulated a vision of economic growth that would be stimulated through domestic rather than foreign demand, and for demand to be sourced from consumers rather than the state. He had argued that

> The long-term strategic direction for China's economic growth has to be rooted in the expansion of domestic demand. Pushing economic development based chiefly on domestic demand requires good handling of 'five combines' – we have to combine the expansion of domestic demand with (1) strategic readjustment of the economic structure (2) deepening of economic system reform (3) increasing employment (4) improvement of the people's standard of living, and (5) sustainable development. (Nathan and Gilley 2002, 174–5)

That this overall goal as outlined by Wen did not eventuate is clear from the macroeconomic picture presented above. The paralysis of the leadership in advancing deeper reform resulted partially from the relatively weak position of Hu Jintao and Wen Jiabao within the upper echelons of the CCP leadership and partially from the overarching consensus that preserving stability in the aftermath of the crisis was the foremost macroeconomic and political priority.

The mounting problems posed by the growth of shadow banking again raised a key issue around which financial reform had revolved since 1993: under what conditions was market-oriented financial reform possible without jeopardizing economic and political stability? Anglo-American finance was considered to represent the apogee of a liberal and deregulated model of financial development, and yet it had just suffered the most devastating financial crisis since the 1920s. In the immediate aftermath of the US subprime meltdown, the scepticism with which financial innovation

[金融创新] and complex financial products generally had always been held in China deepened, as the flawed theoretical linkage between financial sophistication and the productive economy was increasingly exposed. As one financialization pessimist explained,

> The financial system can very easily become far too complicated. Risk management and investment decisions must be based upon common sense and a real understanding of the broader implications of those decisions. This applies to everything. Rather than trying to devise more complicated models that allow for the expansion of the realm of financial products further and further, you need to rely on simpler and more reliable means of understanding risk. It is a major problem for society when all of the best engineers are financial engineers.[15]

Such views were reflected within financial policymaking, with leaders such as CBRC chairman Liu Mingkang (2008b) observing how the seeds of crisis had been sown over a generation of American asset securitization and financial innovation, with disastrous consequences for the banking system and the real economy at large. The 2012 national financial work conference affirmed that in order to avoid the potential for 'financialization' to become a destructive force in the Chinese economy, financial policy would ensure that more capital was dedicated to the country's real economy.[16] Yet such negative views of financial innovation were largely of the Anglo-American vision of deregulated financial markets and the blurring of the lines between equity, credit, and securities markets that occurred. There remained considerable scope for financial innovation in China to develop in a distinct direction, one in which the burgeoning tech and e-commerce sectors, underpinned by big-data analytics and unfolding within the CCP's familiar experimentalist approach to reform and governance, would point a way towards financial liberalization that would endanger neither political authority or macroeconomic stability.

Inclusive innovation: the rise of fintech

At the same time as WMP issuance was expanding in the shadow of the banks, a different form of NBCI was emerging in the guise of digital financial services (DFS). The graduation of Chinese NBCI into the digital realm marked a critical juncture in the policy priorities towards the shadow financial system, which until that point had remained closely tied to an increasingly unsustainable economic growth trajectory. The necessity of a vibrant and growth-facilitating financial system that serves a changing real economy is broadly recognized amongst economic policymakers and has steadily increased since the 2013 CCP third plenum. For this reason, the nascent policy discourse on fintech emphasizes its positive role within China's new economy by furthering financial inclusion and assisting with deeper structural economic rebalancing. This positive role in fostering economic growth is complemented by an increased capacity to control financial risks and enhance political control, the other core priority that has long eluded policymakers interested in deepening financial reform. The contrast with the stasis of policy and reform towards the shadow banking system illustrates how in this latest stage of financial reform and development the underlying developmental priorities of the CCP have not changed, but the role of the financial system in achieving these priorities has.

Fintech and growth in the 'new economy'

The growth of China's DFS sector has been both rapid and sizeable. Although CreditEase, China's first online P2P lending platform, was established in 2006, the industry began to develop exponentially in 2013.[17] Financial innovation linked to e-commerce has utilized new technology infrastructure and big data analytics to grant dramatically improved and faster access to financial services for consumers and SMEs within a system that has traditionally channelled bank credit to large and low-risk SOEs and large private enterprises (Xiang et al. 2017). DFS providers have responded to fundamental changes in the Chinese supply chain

202

production, distribution and consumption, and savings patterns, whilst addressing the genuine needs of the real sector (Sheng and Soon 2016, xxi). In this way they have exploited the gap between logistics and e-commerce businesses and payments systems to enter into various financial services, including funds transfer, wealth management, and lending and investment. The numbers are substantial and belie the fact that as recently as 2013 the market for almost all DFS in China was virtually non-existent. Although online lending is equivalent to less than 5 per cent of domestic bank loans (01Caijing 2017), China rapidly emerged as the largest fintech market worldwide, with a 2015 lending volume of USD 100 billion that dwarfs that of the United States (USD 34 billion) and the United Kingdom (USD 4 billion) (CGFS and FSB 2017). China's largest fintech firm Ant Financial alone has granted loans to more than four million businesses with a total amount of RMB 700 billion in direct lending (Cheng 2017). These trends are highly likely to continue, with China attracting almost 50 per cent of the world's fintech venture capital investment in 2016 (MGI 2017).

The promotion of fintech as a viable avenue for market-oriented financial reform is closely tied to a broader array of efforts to address China's current macroeconomic conditions, which can be described by what is known at the Bank for International Settlements (BIS) as the 'Risky Trinity': rising leverage ratios, declining productivity, and shrinking policy flexibility (BIS 2016). For financial policymakers, fintech is one important element of such progress towards confronting these challenges, by reorienting the credit system towards a more efficient system of risk pricing in financial transactions. It shares many of the same characteristics as other forms of NBCI that undercut the existing banking system by permitting interest rates and capital allocation to be more freely determined by market forces and thus representing an important driving force for financial reform.[18] The crucial difference between fintech and previous NBCI lies in the fact that whilst WMPs alleviated the plight of investors seeking higher returns in a financially repressed environment, fintech offers promise of both generating higher returns for retail investors as well as generating a more efficient and inclusive borrowing environment for the SMEs at the heart of the 'new economy'.

In this context, DFS is seen in China as contributing to three related economic policy goals: deepening China's financial reforms, improvement of the market environment, and the transformation of the overall development model (Xie et al. 2014; Xiang et al. 2017). This is echoed in much of the Western literature, which perceives the rise of fintech as heralding the long-awaited large-scale liberalization of China's financial sector (Huang et al. 2016; Xie et al. 2016a). The close connection of fintech to a broader shift in China's economic growth model has therefore prompted the Chinese state – in contrast to other fintech markets around the world – to take a highly active role in promoting financial inclusion via digital financial innovation (MGI 2017). Premier Li Keqiang encapsulated the sentiment in stating at the opening of Tencent's WeBank that the growth of online banks 'will lower costs for a deliver practical benefits to small clients, while forcing traditional financial institutions to accelerate reforms' (PwC 2015). The growth of DFS represents from this perspective both a source of digital innovation that will spill over into other sectors and a supply-side structural reform in itself. This reflects the changing effects of financial repression from a growth-enhancing 'Stiglitz effect' through the 1990s to a growth-detracting 'McKinnon effect' in the 2000s (Huang and Wang 2011; 2017).[19]

This financial liberalization narrative of the emergence of fintech dovetails with that of financial inclusion [普惠金融]. The Eighteenth Central Committee meeting in November 2013 established an 'inclusive financial system' as a key priority for financial reform. Agencies such as the CBRC had as early as 2006 called for greater financial innovation to promote financial inclusion and household consumption (CBRC 2006).[20] In March 2014, more explicit connections between digital finance and financial inclusion had been drawn by Li Keqiang, one of the most vocal supporters of DFS as well as of financial inclusion, stating that authorities should 'promote the healthy development of digital finance [...] To allow finance to become a liquid pool, better irrigating small and micro-enterprises, the "three rurals", and other trees of the real economy' (Li 2014).[21] A major push in this strategy to develop new growth drivers whilst preserving financial stability came in the 2015 *Internet Plus Plan* that seeks to integrate the mobile Internet, cloud computing, big data, and the Internet of Things with modern manufacturing, to encourage the healthy development of e-commerce, industrial networks, and internet banking (PRC State Council 2015). This policy initiative places financial sector reform front and centre, aiming to enhance China's state capacities and market efficiencies in e-commerce by promoting the contribution of DFS.[22] Following on the heels of the *Internet Plus* plan, on 31 December 2015 the State Council issued its *Plan for Advancing Inclusive Financial Development, 2016–2020 [Inclusive Finance Plan]*, which laid out the basis for developing financial inclusion as a key pillar of national development and financial reform (PRC State Council 2016). The *Inclusive Finance Plan* stressed the central role of big-data analytics, cloud computing, and the integration of offline and online commerce in enabling fintech firms to overcome these historical difficulties through both intra-industry and industry–government cooperation (PRC State Council 2016).

In this broader policy context, the online lending industry was initially subject to a hands-off regulatory approach of 'letting the bullets fly' [让子弹飞] (Sohu 2016), reflecting the goal as stated by the PBOC's deputy governor Pan Gongsheng, who said that the goal of regulation is to 'leave certain space for the development of internet finance while drawing the bottom line clearly' (ECNS 2015). This was followed by a comprehensive regulatory framework coordinated by the PBOC and CBRC in conjunction with eight other central agencies (PBOC 2015b; CBRC 2016) that attempted to ensure that online financing channels are structured so as to allocate capital to genuine SMEs and individual entrepreneurs, rather than opening up another shadow banking avenue through which large-scale borrowers can skirt regulatory controls (Caixin 2016). Early empirical research indicated that despite the risks of fraud and embryonic governance in the sector, online lending was generating meaningful opportunities for individuals to access consumer credit, as well as for SMEs to finance short-term financing gaps in their business operations (Shen 2016). There was accordingly growing recognition that large and increasingly influential 'upstart' lenders entering into financial territory that Chinese banks traditionally ignored constituted a potential future driver of economic growth through empowering consumers and small businesses and breaking away from the long-standing dependence on big infrastructure projects funded by state-owned banks (Shen 2016; Yan and Li 2014).[23]

Both the initial laissez-faire attitude towards and later regulation of the online lending industry indicate significant political will for harnessing digital financial inclusion as a force for economic growth (Gruin and Knaack 2019), framed squarely within this policy discourse of 'inclusive financial liberalization'. The belief that DFS and P2P lending genuinely addresses a financing gap for SMEs and fosters greater financial inclusion as a whole is reinforced by the rise of the Chinese consumer as both a key driver of China's economic growth model over the next decades, as well as the 'financial empowerment' of the individual in an increasingly materialistic society (Xie et al. 2014; Huang et al. 2016).[24] From this perspective, the economic policy incentives for promoting online financial inclusion and innovation as a means of capitalizing upon the Chinese consumer class as an economic force were relatively clear (Li and Yi Tin 2016). Such economic rationales for fintech development are supplemented with visions of a deeper transformation of Chinese socio-economic life deeply and irresistibly for the better – as Ant Financial's Chief Strategy Officer and respected academic economist Chen Long (2016, 231) describes it, 'from Fintech to Finlife'. In this process, 'real life demand is the mother of innovation … the reason why China's fintech developed so fast is that its development is tightly knitted to and supports consumption growth. As a result, technology, finance, and real-life need form a virtuous circle'. The policy support given to DFS as a means for furthering this objective by expanding access to financial services to SMEs and consumers has been matched by widespread societal support for fintech, thereby generating enthusiasm for a future imaginary of liberalized financial markets and access to financial services for individuals and entrepreneurs unadulterated by the strictures of state authority over financial institutions and their lending activities (Wang 2017).[25] This underscores the receptivity of this rapidly burgeoning consumer class to the reshaping of lifestyles and consumption patterns around the growth of e-commerce, fintech, and the big data-driven business practices that underpin them. It further embeds the rise of fintech within a socially legitimated policy discourse of economic development and modernization.

As the sector began to gradually mature, the broader infrastructural foundation of Chinese DFS began to take clearer shape. The core source of financial value in Chinese online lending is the collection of information on consumer and business economic behaviour, predominantly oriented thus far around e-commerce (Tang et al. 2014). Yet an early challenge lay in developing usable credit scores, given the underdeveloped state of Chinese consumer finance and the historical exclusion of SMEs from formal credit channels (CFI 2016). In early 2015 eight private technology firms were granted permission through a PBOC pilot programme to commence preparatory work on establishing formal credit databases and scoring methodologies. Sesame Credit, developed by Ant Financial's subsidiary Zhima Credit, is the largest and most well known of these, and its superficial resemblance to *Black Mirror*-type visions of social dataveillance have led it to be mistaken in popular media accounts as the basis for the broader social credit system (SCS) (Botsman 2017). This is not entirely accurate, although as detailed below there are substantive links between the PBOC's pilot programme and the broader work of constructing a social credit system. Nevertheless, through Alibaba's extensive reach into all aspects of consumer's online behaviours, Sesame Credit has access to data on online purchases, utility bill payments, social network behaviour, mobile phone history, and previous micro-finance history (Caixin 2017), whilst other tech giants, Baidu, Tencent, and Jingdong, are seeking to develop equally comprehensive credit scoring databases (Millward 2016; Caixin 2017).

Online lending and the emergence of digital credit scoring is facilitating shifts in China's model of growth and development, enabling the expansion of new digital economies and markets, whilst also accelerating a rupture with the financial repression that has long-characterized the role of finance and particularly the banking system in China's economic reform and development. MYbank, Ant Financial's online-only private bank, provides a '310' loan service (three-minute application, one-second approval and grant, and zero manual intervention) that is specifically geared towards micro- and small entrepreneurs that have grown up within the Alibaba e-commerce ecosystem (Cheng 2017). The use of big-data analytics in credit risk assessment has led to JD Finance serving over 100,000 SMEs with supply chain finance solutions that amount to a total of RMB 250 billion, concentrating not on a traditional loan model but on using big-data analytics to offer loan packages with characteristics tailored to individual enterprises, such as flexible amortization rates (Dong 2017). The real economic impact of DFS has been felt in a variety of sectors and regions, with early empirical studies evidencing a correlation between the penetration of DFS and economic activity in the new economy sectors prioritized by the central government (Shen et al. 2016).[26] As a means of capitalizing upon the Chinese consumer class as an economic force central to China's broader structural economic rebalancing (Barton, Chen, and Jin 2013), the economic incentives for promoting online financial inclusion and innovation are clear to Chinese policymakers, and are increasingly forming the basis for economic development plans (Li and Yi Tin 2016, 175).

Governing fintech: consolidation and control

The rise of DFS as a foundation for inclusive financial liberalization thus marks a subtle but significant shift in the financial underpinnings of Chinese reform and economic development. Who controls this process of financialization,[27] and how do they use technology to do so? Accelerating China's financial inclusion in this way begins to shift the locus of financial authority from the traditional network of commercial banks to those overseeing and exploiting the infrastructure of digital finance: the databases and data-processing techniques at the heart of algorithmic credit scoring. As Mader (2015) observed with reference to the implications of the broader financial inclusion movement, 'digital financial inclusion, if fulfilled, would immensely empower whoever controls the new monetary infrastructures'. Digital financial inclusion involves a potentially rapid diffusion of previously centralized control over personal data, data that is useful not just for making financial decisions, but which can also be used to influence wider social attitudes and interests. The newest stage of financial reform thus continues to present numerous risks, not just to financial stability, but to the deeper resilience of Communist Party authority over an increasingly diversified economy and market-oriented social structure. Put simply, the financial system has long functioned as the bedrock of the CCP's gradualist and experimentalist mode of economic reform, a function that is threatened by 'liberalization' and the attendant increasing power of new actors wielding influence over market dynamics and the capital allocation process. The answer to this conundrum for the CCP has been to develop mechanisms for control and oversight over all actors involved in the emerging fintech ecosystem. Financial governance in the digital realm has begun to evolve into a structure that is increasingly rationalized and effective in its operations, but one that also deepens the capacity for the CCP to exercise authority and control over the financial system. This marks a distinct shift from the immediate post-crisis period, when the supposedly technocratic regulatory agencies established in the 2000s were largely sidelined in favour of the 'comprehensive agencies' such as the NDRC that responded first and foremost to policy signals emanating directly from the central CCP authorities (Pearson 2010, 2).

One of the key policy objectives of the 2015 *Guiding Proposal* was to achieve industry consolidation within the rapidly burgeoning online lending industry, and both broaden and deepen the financial services offered by large companies.[28] Whilst regulatory arbitrage beyond the banks in a financially repressed and conservative regulatory environment had been one of the initial catalysts for the emergence of digital finance, industry consolidation was now seen as both reducing financial risk and increasing monitoring capacity.[29] This consolidation also took on greater political significance, as the large tech firms could be regulated in a more balanced manner, and are both amenable to and dependent on close coordination with the government in order to preserve their political support and market position (Feng 2017).[30] In addition to such organizational ties, the CCP is assuming a role as a direct investor in tech firms through the development of special management shares, in which the Party takes a minor financial stake in exchange for board representation and input into firm strategy and operations (Li 2017). At a time of steady consolidation of CCP power under Xi Jinping, it is clear to firms that in order to pursue business strategies that involve market-oriented financial and the opening up of new modes of capital allocation, deepening Party–firm cooperation is not only a necessary survival strategy, but also constitutes a key source of competitive advantage.

Industry–government coordination in digital credit scoring took more tangible form in March 2016, when the National Internet Finance Association (NIFA) was established in Shanghai, with CreditEase as executive director, and Li Dongrong, former PBOC deputy governor, serving as president. Firmly under the administrative purview of the PBOC, the NIFA represents one element of the government's efforts to exercise control over the evolution of the country's digital credit scoring infrastructure. One of its early projects was to establish the new digital Credit Information Sharing Platform [全国信用信息共享平台] (CISP), launched in September 2016 in conjunction with the PBOC. With seventeen NIFA members including Ant Financial, JD Finance, and Lufax present from its inception, this platform brought Chinese credit scoring genuinely into the algorithmic era (Yang 2016). The platform offered the promise of solving one of the biggest problems of online lending platforms operating in the absence of traditional in-depth credit assessment procedures. Information asymmetry

and completeness, as well as data sharing across multiple platforms, have proven significant hurdles in the way of an accurate
and reliable credit scoring mechanism. It operates by way of a gen-
eralized information dissemination system, so that customer and
competitive information remains protected. The synergy between
the interests of the sector and the government are apparent in Li
Dongrong's statement at the CISP's launch:

> the credit information recorded through the platform can not
> only improve the internet finance industry credit system, but also
> complement with the existing data in the national financial credit
> information database and other industry credit databases, further
> consolidating the social credit system's information foundation.
> (NIFA 2016)

The NIFA's pursuit of this objective through the CISP has been
bolstered by wider national policy support. The PBOC and
NDRC (2017) have sought to propagate successful local social
credit systems by identifying twelve 'demonstration cities', of
which Yiwu, China's leading trade hub for manufactured goods,
was earmarked for special recognition on account of its integration of social credit with finance, foreign trade, and market supervision (Xinhua 2018a).[31] The NIFA has paid special attention to
the Yiwu plans, seeking ways to integrate the CISP with both
national and local government efforts to compile usable credit
databases, including by developing integrated cloud storage for
financial information managed by an SOE under the control of the
CBRC (STCN 2018).

These patterns of industry–government control, coordination,
and cooperation are part of what Creemers (2018, 1) refers aptly to
as an 'evolving practice of control'. The largest lending platforms
have been central to this push for regulation and the direction of
its development. Key members of the NIFA have spoken of the
close working relationship between regulators and industry players (CNTV 2016). The essence of the compact reached between
the new heavyweight DFS providers and the government is clear:

from the industry's perspective, their efforts to break existing banking monopolies grant them access to the front lines of the Chinese consumer revolution, as long as they fully meet central government expectations for the sharing, analysis, and utilization of underlying data.[32] Just as with the establishment of its wider e-commerce empire, Ant Financial has been closely aligned with the priorities of regulators in the development of its financial business (Elliott and Qiao 2015). Ant Financial is now prepared to open its systems and data to the central bank and other authorities for real-time monitoring and supervision (ECNS 2015).[33] There remains little doubt that regulatory authorities are in control of the overall agenda.[34]

The government in turn has a clear interest in exercising control over such firms as Ant Financial, as one source with knowledge of Ant's mounting pressure and scrutiny from regulatory authorities states: 'as a non-bank, non-state-owned institution in China, it's not allowed to independently grow too big to manage' (Zhang and Ruwitch 2018). Party committees do not merely exist at the country's largest tech firms, but have been effective in monitoring their alignment with government priorities and policies.[35] This renders less surprising the 2017 decision by the PBOC not to renew the eight pilot licences to develop consumer credit scores owing to the potential conflict between the commercial interests of the institutions and those of the PBOC in establishing reliable and comprehensive individual scores across platforms (Hornby 2017). Rather, the eight firms involved have in conjunction with NIFA formed a further third-party credit scoring organization, Baihang Credit Scoring, which is China's first unified private platform that provides personal credit information services and is intended to supplement the existing state-run personal credit database (Xinhua 2018b). Recast in this light, the decision underscores how financial inclusion is not only about developing new domains from which to extract economic value, but also – and potentially more importantly – about ensuring that the potentials offered through digital credit scoring techniques remain under CCP control and management.

Conclusion

The post-crisis period laid bare the contradictions and tensions of the role played by the financial system in China's economic development. The CCP's swift action to ameliorate the effects of the crisis on unemployment and output deepened what were already unsustainable trends within the financial system, yet maintaining macroeconomic stability remained the leadership's paramount goal. As in previous instances of confronting political-economic uncertainty, the banking system provided an array of mechanisms through which the government could maintain macroeconomic growth and stability, and manage the financial risk entailed by rapid credit expansion, whilst also ensuring that economic growth trends remained under the Party's control. Pursuing such a balancing act resulted in the emergence of a large network of shadow loans and wealth management products, as banks sought to transfer financial assets off balance sheets whilst pursuing regulatory arbitrage in an increasingly competitive environment. This same regulatory arbitrage in the context of the explosive growth of digital technology and e-commerce firms in turn catalysed the rise of digital financial services and big data-driven lending practices as an alternative to the traditional state-owned banking system. The growth of the DFS sector has been both promoted as a means of accelerating China's broader economic restructuring towards a domestic consumption-led economy, whilst at the same time potentially transferring political power to private financial actors, thus giving rise to new governance challenges for the Party leadership.

The political economy of the growth of Chinese fintech highlights enduring features of the CCP's relationship to financial capital. The traditional banking system remains the beating heart of the financial system, responsible in large portion for realizing the CCP's goals of growth and stability under the aegis of Party dominance. There are signs nevertheless that the duality of purpose defining this system since 1989 is being replicated gradually in the relationship between the CCP and key actors at the heart of the new digital economy. Fintech represents potential for increasing efficiency of capital allocation, but the attendant financial 'liberalization' continues to be underpinned by CCP authority and control, both at sectoral and macroeconomic levels. The CCP is seeking to transform the threat of losing control over the online financial landscape into an opportunity to establish the new infrastructural foundations of governance over an authoritarian capitalist society.

Notes

1 Interview, 7 September 2012, Beijing – National Development and Reform Commission.
2 The PBOC started to loosen credit restrictions on commercial banks in early August, directing them to focus their lending as much as possible on the SME sector. Credit quotas were raised by 5 per cent for the SOCBs and the national JSCBs, whilst regional and local JSCBs were permitted to increase lending amounts by 10 per cent. On 18 September, the State-owned Assets Supervision and Administrative Commission announced that it would support central SOEs to increase their holdings of listed firms or to embark on share buybacks. Central Huijin Investment Company immediately bought approximately RMB 1.2 billion of shares in ICBC, BOC, and CCB. On 25 September the PBOC reduced the RRR for all deposit-taking banks and financial institutions by one percentage point, except for the big five SOCBs. This was followed by a further 0.5 per cent reduction in the RRR for all banks on 15 October.
3 Interview, 27 April 2012, Beijing – Chinese Academy of Social Sciences.
4 Interview, 27 April 2012, Beijing – Chinese Academic of Social Sciences.
5 These were the MOF, the Ministry of Commerce, the PBOC, the CBRC, and the China Insurance Regulatory Commission.
6 This transition from a 'revolutionary' to a 'ruling' or 'governing' party is one that is astutely perceived by Timothy Heath (2014) in his analysis of the evolution of the CCP's national strategic direction.
7 For an up-to-date description of commercial bank cooperation with different NBFIs, see the 2017 PBOC Financial Stability Report (2017).
8 In slightly more colourful language, the PBOC (2013, 204) also observed that 'the whole financial market gets a shot in the arm from shadow banking'.
9 For a recent comprehensive analysis of transferability and contagion risks within the shadow banking system that supports these conclusions, see Wang and Hu (2016).
10 This had the further advantage of alleviating pressure from overheating property markets.

11 The empirical evidence on the benefits that shadow banking brings to economic growth is mixed, with numerous Chinese academic studies support both positive and negative views of shadow banking as a driver of real economic growth (Chao and Ee 2017).

12 For a related discussion of how this distinction relates to the triple-tiered framework for assessing systemic risk, see a Fung Global Institute report by Sheng et al. (2015).

13 Stating that 'WMPs generally do not involve the generation of additional leverage or the securitisation of loan assets, and because banks manage the activity, they are subject to CBRC regulation' (Green 2014).

14 Document 107 was never released publicly or as a formal legal document, but as a normative administrative document [行政规范性文件] of the general office of the State Council, addressed directly towards local governments, regulatory agencies, and financial institutions themselves.

15 Interview, 28 November 2012, Beijing – China Investment Corporation.

16 Interview, 29 November 2012, Beijing – Development Research Center of the State Council.

17 Having even been described as 'Year One of China's Internet Finance Era' (China IRN 2013). In July 2013, Jack Ma summarized succinctly yet controversially his challenge to the banks: 'if the banks don't change, we will change the banks' (Ma 2013).

18 Whilst at the end of 2016 the Shanghai interbank rate was 3 per cent and the Wenzhou informal curb rate was 15 per cent, the average P2P investment rate hovered around 10 per cent (Huang and Wang 2017).

19 Stiglitz (1993) reasons that at early stages of economic development, underdeveloped financial markets are often not capable of efficient financial capital allocation, and financial repression in the form of state intervention can promote confidence and enhance conversion of savings into effective investment. At a more advanced level of financial development, in line with McKinnon (1973) the effect of financial repression on economic growth becomes negative by virtue of less effective capital allocation and the emergence of moral hazard.

20 The CBRC department responsible for internet finance is now called the financial inclusion department [普惠金融部].

21 Referring to the three issues of peasantry, rural areas, and agriculture.

22 Lin Nianxiu, vice-chairman of the NDRC, provided the most definitive statement of connection between inclusive finance and the *Internet Plus* plan (Lin 2016).

23 Interview 11 September 2016, Beijing – CreditEase.

24 McKinsey estimates that by 2022 more than 75 per cent of China's urban consumers will earn RMB 60,000 to 229,000 (US 9000 to 34,000) a year (annual household disposable income, in real (2010) terms) (Barton et al. 2013).

25 The close connection between internet finance and financial inclusion strategies was made clear by Bai (2016), stating that 'Inclusive finance and internet finance have a lot in common, being open, inclusive, and equal. Internet finance reaches the bottom of the financial sector, and heightens financial inclusion, while financial inclusion serves as policy guidance for internet-based finance'. Bai Chengyu is division director of the Poverty Alleviation of China International Center for Economic and Technical Exchanges (CICETE), and also the director of CICETE/UNDP Poverty Alleviation Program Management Office.

26 Interview 13 September 2017, Beijing – Institute for Digital Finance.

27 Some of the broader implications of this process will be taken up in the concluding chapter. On financialization, see Zwan (2014) generally, and examining the intersection of social media and financialization in the Chinese case, Wang (2017).

28 Interview 23 September 2016, Beijing – Chinese Academy of Social Sciences.

29 Interview 27 September 2016, Beijing – Pandai; Interview 3 October 2016, Beijing – Chinese Academy of Social Sciences.

30 Interview 4 October 2016, Beijing – Ant Financial. As JD.com vice president (and Party Secretary) Long Baozheng (Liang 2017) put it:

> Under the guidance of the Party, JD.com is a major beneficiary of the deepened reform and constant improvement of business environment … We will assist the structural supply-side reform and rejuvenate the real economy by opening up our platforms and capabilities, and shoulder more corporate social responsibilities.

31 Yiwu municipality formed a 'multidimensional credit database' comprising over 180 million records covering over 370,000 enterprises and organizations and 2.2 million natural persons (NIFA 2018).

32 Interview 4 October 2016, Beijing – Ant Financial; Interview 15 September 2017, Beijing – Yirendai.

33 Likewise WeChat, the source of significant credit data for Tencent and already the world's most heavily monitored messaging app, shares users' private data with the government in compliance with 'applicable laws or regulations' (Huang 2017).

34 Interview 29 September 2016, Beijing – Chinese Academy of Social Sciences; Interview 4 October 2016, Beijing – Ant Financial.

35 Interview 14 September 2018, Beijing – Ant Financial.

7

Chinese finance and the future of authoritarian capitalism

The jury is very much out on how epiphenomenal the West's post-1800 advantage will be.

Kenneth Pomeranz (2009)

Reevaluating China's financial development in historical comparative context challenges existing ways of thinking about the dynamics of global order and China's place within it. This global order is in a deep state of flux and uncertainty, yet our posing of questions surrounding the fate of the liberal world order occlude the possibility that China is constructing its own version of capitalist modernity. As Wolfgang Streeck (2012, 3–4) observes,

> Capitalism must be studied, not as a static and timeless ideal type of an economic system that exists outside of or apart from society, but as an historical social order that is precisely about the relationship between the social and the economic – a social order that came into its own in Western Europe in the early nineteenth century and has been continuously evolving since.

The evolution of Chinese capitalism challenges us to reflect on the contingency – both material and ideational – of liberal democratic capitalism as a sustainable political form. This demands an understanding of Chinese development as a distinctive, unique, yet nonetheless thoroughly modern process of confronting the contradictions and tensions of capitalist governance.

This book has argued that one path towards this is to focus upon the mechanisms through which trust is achieved, thereby managing the inherent uncertainty of socio-economic action. China's capitalism has achieved this through a gradual deepening of the market's role in financial intermediation and the bureaucratization of the state, accompanied by the rationalized consolidation of the CCP's role as political authority over both. China's otherwise paradoxical path of development has flowed principally from conceptions of reform that saw the harnessing of capital as both a means of fostering economic growth, as well as of shaping the foundational political parameters of Chinese society. These conceptions revolved around the idea of capital and the markets through which it could be allocated as tools, rather than the subject of normative ends and policy objectives in themselves. Thus, even as the financial system has become increasingly commercialized and devoted to supporting economic growth, it has simultaneously lain at the heart of the ability of the CCP to ensure that this economic growth continuously supported the political needs of the Party.

Re-evaluating the course of Chinese financial development

What are the implications of this experience of reform and opening for China's development of a specific socio-economic formation that we can identify as constituting contemporary capitalism? The uniqueness of China's new capitalist society resides in the determination of the CCP to maintain its explicit role as custodian of the power of capital. This interpenetration of the market and the state in the pursuit of capital accumulation is thus unfolding in a direction distinct from that of Western conceptions of free-market, individualistic, and bottom-up capitalist development. This brings to the fore the illusion of a distinction between a liberal and illiberal politics in the structuring of capitalist society. What Redding sought to identify in his pioneering *Spirit of Chinese Capitalism* was less the spirit of capitalism, and more the sociological foundations of market exchange with Chinese characteristics. Capitalism as a mode of social organization is rooted firmly in discrete socio-historical circumstances, and it is

218

only possible to identify something akin to its spirit by examining the macro-social processes through which it emerges, develops, and becomes entrenched within the cognitive, institutional, and structural matrices of social relations.

The way in which ideas, interests, and institutions have emerged and evolved in China's political economy is the product of the emergence and evolution of Chinese capitalist modernity. Just as the experience of modernity in the West is a process of historical change that has roots extending far beyond the contemporary era of global capital, contemporary China can only be understood as the latest iteration of the deeply historical interplay of political, economic, and social forces, steadily accumulating through lineages and junctures that serve to both reinforce and disrupt ideational paradigms, institutional configurations, and networked topographies. To argue that the features of premodern China remain analytically salient in the study of modern China is not to mount a culturalist argument, but rather to decentre the Western experience of modernity as the only available theoretical and conceptual lens through which to study modern Chinese development. As we saw in Chapter 2, the Chinese experience of economic development in imperial China constituted a rational and sophisticated economic sociology of market behaviour and economic development that was distinct from that which led to European-style capitalism, but was not necessarily incompatible with it. Accordingly, the construction of a capitalist system in contemporary China – one that is now deeply embedded in the competitive dynamics of an integrated global economy – represents potentially the coalescence of logics of politico-economic organization that are as equally rational as they are qualitatively distinct.

Decentring the universality of the Western historical experience therefore places us then in a difficult position. Compelled to undertake a reflexive reappraisal of those concepts that have underlain the study of Western political economy but which may prove inadequate for the study of Chinese political economy, we must search for alternative conceptual foundations for the analysis of rational social action that provide useful insight into the construction of modernity, without assuming that actors embedded in such modernities abide by the same conception of rationality. This means also being ecumenically pluralistic about the study of capitalism, and to this end the analytic framework developed in this book has revolved around the role of uncertainty as one core conceptual feature of social action that enables one to marshal together theories of economic development and theories of political power. It does so, however, without ascribing a priori to a sociological or politico-economic ontology that focuses deterministically on concepts such as the Weberian bureaucratic state or Marxian creative destruction that may have been prominent in the experience of Western capitalism, but which cannot be assumed to be central to the story of Chinese capitalism. Rather, the concept of uncertainty, and the cognitive frames and the social institutions that enable us to manage it, can be deployed in order not only to develop better explanations of empirical phenomena such as the patterns of authority and power exercised by the CCP in the construction of a capitalist political economy, but also to place those explanations in the broader comparative context of global capitalist development and evolution.

What has been central to the story of Chinese capitalism is the economic role and political implications of capital itself. Harnessing the flow of capital throughout the economy can be conceived as a process of managing the uncertainty inherent in financial decision-making, one that has been underpinned in China through the role of the CCP at the nexus of the state and the market. Control over the flow of financial capital is a source of both the power to incentivize economic growth, as well as the power to distribute the benefits of this growth in uneven ways. Yet as this study has sought to demonstrate, the ways in which these flows of capital are managed and controlled are not deterministically reducible to either 'the market' or 'the state'; rather, they must be assessed on the basis of a broader array of mechanisms that allow actors to generate stable reciprocal expectations, and thereby to manage the fundamental uncertainty that afflicts all social action. In China the CCP itself has grown and evolved to comprise a fundamental and crucial element in this array, and the reason that China's path of development is too often mischaracterized and misinterpreted is because of an assumption that the institutions of capitalist modernity must all somehow be pressed out of the same mould. As we have seen, China presents many reasons to recognize that this is not in fact the case. Accordingly, this book has highlighted the complex, obscure, but critically important role of the CCP in underpinning China's path of financial reform and economic development more broadly. It has argued that the CCP's role is both the reflection as well as the source of particular ideas about how to manage the flow of capital that are reducible neither to the endogenous self-interested rationality of bureaucratic institutions nor to relapses into a premodern – and thus exogenous – set of interests that manifest in parochial personal networks or local biases. By placing specific ideas at the centre of the analysis and the role that they played in underpinning expectations of financial growth and stability, it becomes possible to cast China's development in a new light by refracting it through the socio-economic foundations of capitalist development, rather than as a process of transition from a centrally planned economy to a market-oriented one.

Jettisoning such assumptions opens up space for deeper analytic appreciation of the role of different factors and variables in the study of China's economic reform. The interests of financial elites within the Chinese political economy could not be determined *ex ante* in an environment characterized by extreme uncertainty, and there is no a priori reason to presume that the immediate institutional or networked positions or identities of particular actors would be determinative in shaping material interests over and above the ideas and frames to emerge out of a significantly broader social context comprising multiple and overlapping institutional contexts, the historical lineages of Chinese political and economic development, and the deeply rooted hierarchies and structures that continue to reside at the heart of Chinese society. The story of how these interests come into existence, and the effect that they had on the path of institutional change and the production of real socio-economic outcomes therefore cannot be recounted in ignorance of

221

particular ideas about the relationship between financial capital and political authority. Yet this is not just to say that ideas mattered; this book has been concerned with developing a broader and more holistic understanding of *how* these ideas mattered, and in order to do this it has been necessary to displace analytic perspectives that locate China's experience of modernity squarely within the parameters of the Western experience of modernity – assuming that as China embraces modernity it relinquishes and severs its ties to an equally modern historical experience of social, political, and economic development. The ideas that have guided intellectual debate, the politics of policymaking, and economic behaviour are firmly rooted in this historical experience, and this experience and its impact upon China's contemporary development must be assessed on its own terms and in its own light.

Such a perspective compels us to rethink our analyses of a number of issues and areas within China's financial system and its role in the country's developmental trajectory. Increasing liberalization in the financial sector will not necessarily produce a more ecumenical and broad-based path of growth: as this book has argued, the process of marketization is itself contingent upon the continued role of the CCP as the guardian of financial stability. The nature of this role is changing along with the constitutive foundations of the CCP itself, as the institutions and networks of power that in aggregate comprise the CCP increasingly straddle the expanding private sector. As a result, the deepening contradictions and tensions of capitalist development will be reflected less in the evolving balance between state intervention and market autonomy and more in the variegated distribution of power and agency amongst actors according to their connections to existing structures of authority and control. The development of China's financial system and its capacity to support broad-based and sustainable real economic growth is therefore tied closely to the ways in which the CCP manages and adapts to this process of constitutive change in the foundations of its ruling mandate and authority. As the market plays an increasingly significant role in allocating the flow of financial capital through the real economy, stability within the financial sector will be generated through its continued embeddedness in the political system, rather than as a product of unfettered market forces or an independent and technocratic regulatory regime.

The algorithmic foundations of authoritarian capitalism

This returns us to the banker mentioned in the opening passage of this book, who despite holding a position at the very centre of an increasingly modern, commercial, and international Chinese banking sector, remains firmly entrenched in the broader political system of control and authority over the flow of capital. As China's new leadership under Xi Jinping has taken the reins of power, it has become ever clearer that the dynamics of continuous capitalist transformation and authoritarian governance are two sides of the same Chinese coin. That the CCP continues to pursue the 'rejuvenation of the great Chinese nation' without seemingly any indication of loosening its grip on the levers of political power yet is now firmly committed to deepening and enhancing the role of the market is testament to the need for more nuanced and reflective appraisals of the relationship between the market, the state, and society. China's experience of financial development has brought it once again to the question of how to utilize the market, as Deng Xiaoping envisaged all along, as an 'economic tool' [经济手段] that has little bearing on the fact of a society's 'socialism' or 'capitalism'.

Both the CCP's vision for the Chinese nation, and the tools with which this vision can be pursued, have evolved continuously throughout the opening and reform era. In an era of deepening ideological and political consolidation, coupled with the advance of new modes of increasingly indirect data-driven governance and the embeddedness of Chinese corporate power in a CCP-dominated power structure, the implications for how we assess the future of authoritarian capitalism are profound. This is most apparent in the latest stage of the CCP's nascent plans to interweave big-data driven financial services and broader regimes of social credit scoring. The former constitutes an essential infrastructural foundation for what Creemers (2017a) describes as the CCP's placing of technology at the centre of an ambitious agenda for comprehensive reform of social and economic governance. The SCS provides an insight into the novel mechanisms of 'algorithmic governance' (Campbell-Verduyn et al. 2017) that will play an increasingly significant role in underpinning the political-economic stability of China's authoritarian capitalism.

The preliminary plan for a comprehensive SCS was announced in 2014 (PRC State Council 2014) and forms the overarching blueprint of the broader plan of upgrading both social and economic supervision through technological innovation. The holistic systems-oriented focus of Chinese governance that blurs the boundaries between public and private also complicates liberal notions of public and private data. As Chen Gang (2016) opened a prominent *Seeking Truth* article, 'in the present era, data has become a fundamental national strategic resource'.[1] Accordingly, the process of constructing usable digital credit databases is taking place along two tracks within the private and state sectors. The construction by large e-commerce and tech platforms of large repositories of financially valuable consumer data is being complemented by coordinated efforts between financial regulatory bodies such as the PBOC and other central government agencies including the NDRC and the State Internet Information Office, charged with control over China's internet censorship and propaganda regimes (see Table 7.1).

The core public repository of credit information is the PBOC Credit Reference Center (CRC), providing a high quality of existing historical credit data. The CRC system was initially established in 2004 and will constitute an important foundation for the broader SCS (PBOC 2015a). Amongst other existing certified financial institutions, the Postal Savings Bank of China, with the largest branch network in the country, is supplying financial data on otherwise difficult to evaluate rural customers (CFI 2016). Additionally, uncertified credit institutions provide lending information, alongside data from public sector entities handling

Table 7.1. Illustrative data sources for private and public financial credit scoring mechanisms

System		Ant Financial credit system	PBOC credit system
Number of businesses	Corporate credit	>6 million (TaoBao alone)	>10 million
	Individual credit	>145 million (TaoBao alone)	>600 million
Nature of credit information	Corporate credit	All information relating to business operation, including identification, volume, activity level, inventory, rating, cash flow, and utility bills, etc.	Identification, credit information, social security payments and housing acquisition fund, quality control information, salary arrears, utility payments
	Individual credit	Buyer's information and corporate credit system, buyers' identification, online expenditures histories, social activity	Personal credit information, identification, social security, payments, property dealings, legal records
Data source		Automatic recording	Commercial banks and government agencies

Source: Ant Financial, October 2016; PBOC

credit transactions such as phone bills and property tax payments, information from law enforcement agencies, and from the court system. All of this is being further being integrated into the CISP, which has been operational since October 2015, and which currently includes almost 400 datasets from more than thirty central ministries and governmental agencies (NDRC 2016). These two data collection and processing infrastructures – one borne directly out of consumers' online activities and the other founded upon public records and existing databases – are expected to merge over the next years, even if the intention is not to produce one single credit score as a result, but to enable data to be utilized for a variety of different purposes.[2] This mutability between private sector initiatives to support commercial business and the government's objective to implement broader systems of social governance is a natural reflection of China's distinctive political tradition.

The initial plan for the SCS did not refer explicitly to the use of algorithmic big data analytics. Yet to assume that this means data collected purely for the purposes of financial risk management will never play a role in the broader matrix of social governance mechanisms would appear wilfully naïve. As one industry professional observed, the 2014 SCS plan extended through to 2020, but 'that is not the end of the process. There will obviously be a new plan after that.'[3] In this light it is less surprising that the more recent 2017 State Council notice on the Thirteenth Five-Year Plan for Market Supervision (PRC State Council 2017) refers specifically to establishing and 'perfecting' [完善] new regulatory mechanisms involving 'credit supervision, big data supervision, multidimensional collective governance etc'. [信用管理，大数据管理，以多元公职等]. The same document also places the role of technology front and centre in undergirding this system of market supervision that expands the concept of credit ratings far beyond financial metrics, to include social, political, and environmental factors both in terms of data inputs and rating outputs (PRC State Council 2017). Likewise, in the implementation of the *Internet Plus Plan* the State Council has underscored the importance of big-data analytic techniques to enhance 'social governance ability' at all levels of government, and the expectation of collaboration and cooperation between government and tech firms in establishing the necessary credit information sharing platforms (PRC State Council 2015). Unsurprisingly, the substantive details of the algorithms themselves that produce these evaluations are as yet and will likely remain unknown. But the intent is clear: a constant monitoring presence of automatically generated and updated credit rating scores, which will – in the terms of official discourse – constitute 'self-disciplining enforcement' mechanisms at the level of both the individual citizen [个体自我约束] and the corporate entity [企业自我约束] (PRC State Council 2017).

Both the empirical data sources as well as the algorithmic scoring techniques being developed across the range of DFS

226

players are thus integral elements in transferring the practice and methodologies of financial credit rating to a broader range of quantifiable social and political benchmarks (Yan and Li 2014; Xie et al. 2016b). Although unsurprisingly there is little public acknowledgement of this process, the extent to which the laws and regulations defining the limits of data-sharing between tech firms and the government reflect Beijing's policy priorities is widely known amongst officials and industry alike.[4] Xie et al. (2016a) describe this process of melding together the private and public functions of digital credit scoring thus:

> Financial services will be available to all, and everyone will enjoy the benefits. In this way, internet finance is more democratic than a finance controlled by professional elites. ...
>
> Individuals (or institutions) have many stakeholders, who all have some information about their wealth, employment status, personality, and so on. If all stakeholders' information is released and pooled on social networks, and inaccurate information is disputed or filtered through social networks and search engines, we will get a reliable picture of their creditworthiness. Social networks also enable the accumulation of 'social capital' among people, with which costs of financial activities will drop considerably and opportunistic behaviors will be constrained.[5]

Such visions underscore just how fine a line there is between the use of credit scoring algorithms for evaluating financial creditworthiness on the one hand and socio-political trustworthiness on the other. As part of China's evolving regime of social management, those technologies underpinning financial data collection and processing are capable of taking on different functions and serving different functions, both political and economic.

Coda: a global capitalist order in flux

These nascent transformations raise questions that extend beyond the study of Chinese political economy. What do they inform us about how China is confronting the dilemma of authoritarian governance in a capitalist society increasing in its economic prosperity, technological sophistication, and cultural pluralism? And what are the implications of this for how we understand the further evolution of capitalism as a socio-political system on a global scale?

Heeding the above plea to decentre the Western experience when evaluating Chinese capitalism reframes questions surrounding the relationship between technology, political authority, and financial capital. Rather than merely asking how fintech is affecting Chinese politics and society, the question is one of how the significance of fintech – and underlying relationships between technology and society – are affected by its entry into a highly complex and historically formed political culture.[6] As this book has argued, one key component of the Chinese political tradition in which fintech is developing is an emphasis upon systemic stability underpinned by a holistic integration or harmony of its constituent parts. As Hoffman (2017) has argued, in China's ICT governance this tradition found form in a form of complex systems-thinking traceable to the 1970s that views technology as a mechanism for achieving Leninist social management. This conceptualization of governance evaluates elements with reference to their utility or function in achieving system-objectives: social harmony and economic development (Creemers 2018). The process blurs divisions between public and private, and lays responsibility for overall social development upon the citizenry, party members, commercial enterprises, social organization, and government officials alike (Thornton 2007). This has evolved into a 'cyber-Leninism' (Creemers 2017b) that has in turn undergone substantial upgrading since the start of the Xi administration, a turning point in the CCP's approach to utilizing and exploiting technology to restructure the Party's governing framework. New financial technologies are linked to this broader project of social engineering, seeking to form a 'more civilized' society via improvements in the natural, psychological, and social 'quality' (*suzhi* 素质) of the citizenry (Barmé and Goldkorn 2013). This objective has taken on particular significance by virtue of the rise of the Chinese consumer, a socio-economic process now subject to careful 'ideology management' by the CCP (Goodman 2014). This represents a transmutation of the duality of the financial system as both political and economic tool, reflecting the twin imperatives of shifting the growth model towards domestic consumption, and harnessing rather than combating the political power of digital connectivity.

A key issue at the heart of this process of digitizing authoritarianism is one of how normative ideas and social institutions generate sufficient trust and mutual understanding between individuals to enable solidarity and cooperative activity. The CCP's twenty-first-century challenge is to construct institutions that enable trust in an increasingly digitized market economy. At the same time, it must retain sufficient trust in the political system that contains and supports this market economy. For much of the twentieth century, Chinese society experienced numerous waves of eroding social solidarity, reaching a nadir during the Cultural Revolution when trust between individuals and within communities was replaced by blind and exclusive faith in Mao Zedong. Since 1978, the CCP has endeavoured to preserve residual trust and credibility in its guarantee of social and economic progress, which for much of the reform period has taken the form of rising living standards and greater personal freedom in choices of work and lifestyle. The intersection of these changes with technological progress therefore has deep and broad politico-economic implications. The reach of social media into all regions and strata of Chinese society is transforming existing social relationships and enabling experimentation with new relationship forms (McDonald 2016). The CCP seeks – however imperfectly – to guide, shape, and manipulate the social trust norms underlying these relations, a process involving now the use of technological infrastructures, without destroying trust in the CCP's authority to largely control the process of norm generation itself.

This book began with the premise that a proper understanding of the evolution of global capitalism requires an understanding of the political economy of China's financial development on its own historical, cultural, and conceptual terms. The duality of the financial system within China's emergent algorithmic governance is emblematic of the blurring of boundaries between public and private that is possible in this current era of economic growth and development. Crucially, it is neither marketization nor state intervention that is responsible for China's future course of technology-saturated development, but rather the CCP's shaping of trust and confidence in both as necessary elements of this developmental path. The Chinese example illustrates how enfolding this socio-economic power of big data more closely within complex yet ideologically cohesive political structures may be establishing the foundations for a mode of capitalist governance that mitigates the political risks of authoritarian rule. This refracts in a different light the power struggles at the heart of Western liberal democracies, as the political agency wielded by those controlling the algorithms behind our multitudinous screens – tracking consumption preferences, spending patterns, financial proclivities – potentially comes to encompass not just how we spend our capital, but how we define the purpose and meaning of capital itself. Liberal democratic capitalism's normative prioritization of a market exchange rationality occludes a fuller perspective on the social foundations of this agency, and how to sustainably control and harness it. In this respect, China's nascent authoritarian capitalism at once represents a learning opportunity, a societal forewarning, and a politico-economic challenge.

Notes

1 *Seeking Truth* [求是] is the pre-eminent journal of political theory published by the CCP.
2 Interview 2 October 2016, Beijing – China Construction Bank; Interview 30 September 2016, Beijing – 01Caijing; Interview 29 September 2016, Beijing – Chinese Academy of Social Sciences; Interview 15 September 2017, Beijing – Yirendai.
3 Interview 15 September 2017, Beijing – Yirendai.

4 Interview 13 September 2017, Beijing – Peking University.
5 This passage is worth quoting at length. The book's lead author Xie Ping is one of the most respected senior financial policymakers in the Chinese financial system and one of the leading proponents of the Chinese fintech revolution.
6 See further Creemers (2017b).

References

01Caijing. 2017. '2017中国互联网接待服务行业发展报告' ['2017 Report on the Development of China's Online Lending Service Industry']. Beijing: 01 Caijing.

Abolafia, Mitchel. 2010. 'Narrative Construction as Sensemaking: How a Central Bank Thinks'. *Organization Studies* 31(3): 349–67.

Abrams, Philip. 1988. 'Notes on the Difficulty of Studying the State'. *Journal of Historical Sociology* 1(1): 58–89.

Akerlof, George, and Robert Shiller. 2009. *Animal Spirits: How Human Psychology Drives the Economy, and Why it Matters for Global Capitalism*. Princeton, NJ: Princeton University Press.

Allen, Franklin, Jun Qian, and Meijun Qian. 2005. 'Law, Finance, and Economic Growth in China'. *Journal of Financial Economics* 77(1): 57–116.

Anderson, Jonathan. 2006. 'Which Way Out for the Banking System'. *Asian Economic Perspectives Research Report*. Hong Kong: UBS Global Economic & Strategy Research Institute.

Anderson, Perry. 1974. *Lineages of the Absolutist State*. London: New Left Books.

Ang, Yuen Yuen. 2016. *How China Escaped the Poverty Trap*. Ithaca: Cornell University Press.

Arrighi, Giovanni. 2008. *Adam Smith in Beijing: Lineages of the Twenty-First Century*. London; New York: Verso.

Arrighi, Giovanni. 2009 [1994]. *The Long Twentieth Century: Money, Power, and the Origins of Our Times*. London: Verso.

Arrighi, Giovanni, Po-keung Hui, Ho-fung Hung, and Mark Selden. 2003. 'Historical Capitalism, East and West'. In *The Resurgence of East Asia: 500, 150, and 50 Year Perspectives*, edited by Giovanni Arrighi, Takeshi Hamashita, and Mark Selden. Oxford: Routledge.

Ba, Shusong. 2010. 中国金融大未来 *[China's Great Financial Future]*. Beijing: Huawen Publishers.

Bai, Chengyu. 2016. 'The Origin and Role of Inclusive Finance in China'. *China Development Gateway*. http://en.chinagate.cn/2016–06/06/content_38610696. htm. Accessed 19 October 2017.

Barmé, Geremie, and Jeremy Goldkorn, eds. 2013. *Civilizing China: China Story Yearbook 2013*. Canberra: ANU Press.

Barton, Dominic, Yougang Chen, and Amy Jin. 2013. 'Mapping China's Middle Class'. *McKinsey Quarterly* 3: 54–60.

Beckert, Jens. 1996. 'What is Sociological about Economic Sociology? Uncertainty and the Embeddedness of Economic Action'. *Theory and Society* 25: 803–40.

Beckert, Jens. 2002. *Beyond the Market: The Social Foundations of Economic Efficiency*. Princeton, NJ: Princeton University Press.

Beckert, Jens. 2009. 'The Social Order of Markets'. *Theory and Society* 38: 245–69.

Beckert, Jens. 2010. 'How Do Fields Change? The Interrelations of Institutions, Networks, and Cognition in the Dynamics of Markets'. *Organization Studies* 31(5): 605–27.

Beckert, Jens. 2013. 'Capitalism as a System of Expectations: Toward a Sociological Microfoundation of Political Economy'. *Politics and Society* 41(3): 323–50.

Beckert, Jens, and Wolfgang Streeck. 2008. Economic Sociology and Political Economy: A Programmatic Perspective. *MPIfG Working Paper 08/04*. Köln: Max-Planck-Institut für Gesellschaftsforschung.

Bell, Daniel. 2015. *The China Model: Political Meritocracy and the Limits of Democracy*. Princeton, NJ: Princeton University Press.

Bell, Stephen, and Hui Feng. 2013. *The Rise of the People's Bank of China: The Politics of Institutional Change*. Cambridge, MA: Harvard University Press.

Bernstein, Thomas, and Lü Xiaobo. 2003. *Taxation without Representation in Contemporary Rural China*. Cambridge: Cambridge University Press.

BIS. 1999. *Consolidated International Banking Statistics*. Basel: Bank for International Settlements.

BIS. 2007. *Securities Settlement System Disclosure Statement: HKSSC Ltd*. Basel: Bank for International Settlements.

BIS. 2016. *BIS 86th Annual Report, 2015–16*. Basel: Bank for International Settlements.

Blecher, Marc. 2003. *China Against the Tides: Restructuring Through Revolution, Radicalism, and Reform*. London: Continuum.

Blue, Gregory. 1999. 'China and Western Social Thought in the Modern Period'. In *China and Historical Capitalism: Genealogies of Sinological Knowledge*, edited by Timothy Brook and Gregory Blue. Cambridge: Cambridge University Press.

Blue, Gregory, and Timothy Brook. 1999. 'Introduction'. In *China and Historical Capitalism: Genealogies of Sinological Knowledge*, edited by Gregory Blue and Timothy Brook. Cambridge: Cambridge University Press.

Blyth, Mark. 2002. *Great Transformations: Economic Ideas and Institutional Change in the Twentieth Century*. Cambridge: Cambridge University Press.

BOC. 2007. Annual Report. Beijing: Bank of China.

BOCOM. 2007. Annual Report. Shanghai: Bank of Communications.

Boltanski, Luc, and Laurent Thévenot. 2006. *On Justification: Economic Ideas and Political Change in the Twentieth Century*. Princeton, NJ: Princeton University Press.

Bonney, Richard, ed. 1999. *The Rise of the Fiscal State in Europe*. Oxford: Oxford University Press.

Botsman, Rachel. 2017. 'Big Data Meets Big Brother as China Moves to Rate Its Citizens'. WIRED UK. https://www.wired.co.uk/article/chinese-government-social-credit-score-privacy-invasion. Accessed 26 October 2017.

Bourdieu, Pierre, and Loïc Wacquant. 1992. *An Invitation to Reflexive Sociology*. Cambridge: Cambridge University Press.

Bramall, Chris. 2009. *Chinese Economic Development*. Abingdon: Routledge.

Bramall, Chris, and Peter Nolan. 2000. 'Introduction: Embryonic Capitalism in East Asia'. In *Chinese Capitalism, 1522–1840*, edited by Xu Dixin and Wu Chengming. Basingstoke: Macmillan.

Brandt, Loren, Debin Ma, and Thomas Rawski. 2012. From Divergence to Convergence: Re-evaluating the History Behind China's Economic Boom. In *Department of Economic History Working Papers No. 158/12*. London: London School of Economics and Political Science.

Braudel, Fernand. 1977. *Afterthoughts on Material Civilization and Capitalism*. Baltimore, MD: Johns Hopkins University Press.

Braudel, Fernand. 1981. *Civilization and Capitalism, 15th – 18th Century*, Vol. 1: *The Structure of Everyday Life*. New York: Harper & Row.

Braudel, Fernand. 1982. *Civilization and Capitalism, 15th – 18th Century*, Vol. 2: *The Wheels of Commerce*. Berkeley: University of California Press.

Braun, Benjamin. 2015. 'Governing the Future: The European Central Bank's Expectation Management During the Great Moderation'. *Economy & Society* 44(3): 367–91.

Braun, Benjamin. 2016. 'From Performativity to Political Economy: Index Investing, ETFs and Asset Manager Capitalism'. *New Political Economy* 21(3): 257–73.

Brehm, Stefan. 2008. 'Risk Management in China's State Banks: International Best Practice and the Political Economy of Regulation'. *Business and Politics* 10(1): 1–29.

Brown, Kerry. 2016. 'A Response to Francis Fukuyama's "Reflections on Chinese Governance"'. *Journal of Chinese Governance* 1(3): 392–404.

Béland, Daniel, and Robert Henry Cox, eds. 2011. *Ideas and Politics in Social Science Research*. Oxford: Oxford University Press.

Cai, E'sheng. 1999. 'Financial Supervision in China: Framework, Methods, and Current Issues'. In *Strengthening the Banking System in China: Issues and Experience*, edited by Bank for International Settlements. Basel: Bank for International Settlements.

Caixin. 2016. 'P2P 监管'双负责' '银监会负责第三方存管' ['Within P2P Regulation "Dual Responsibility" System the CBRC Assumes Responsibility for Third Party Deposits']. 24 August 2016. http://finance.caixin.com/2016–08–24/100981355.html. Accessed 18 August 2016.

Caixin. 2017. 'Ant Financial's Credit Scoring Ambitions Crawl Ahead with Two New Deals'. 10 May 2017. http://www.caixinglobal.com/2017–05–10/101088774.html. Accessed 15 September 2017.

Callon, Michel. 1998. 'Introduction. The Embeddedness of Economic Markets in Economics'. In *The Laws of the Market*, edited by Michel Callon. London: Routledge.

Calvo, Guillermo, and Frederic Mishkin. 2003. 'The Mirage of Exchange Rate Regimes for Emerging Market Countries'. *Journal of Economic Perspectives* 17(4): 99–118.

Campbell-Verduyn, Malcolm, Marcel Goguen, and Tony Porter. 2017. 'Big Data and Algorithmic Governance: The Case of Financial Practices'. *New Political Economy* 22(2): 219–36.

Carstensen, Martin, and Vivien Schmidt. 2016. 'Power Through, Over and In Ideas: Conceptualizing Ideational Power in Discursive Institutionalism'. *Journal of European Public Policy* 23(3): 318–37.

CASS. 2013. 中国影子银行体系研究报告 [*Intermediate Research Report on the Shadow Banking System*]. Beijing: Chinese Academy of Social Sciences Press.

CBRC. 2006. 商业银行金融创新之音 [*Guidelines on Commercial Banks' Financial Innovation*]. Beijing: China Banking Regulatory Commission.

CBRC. 2009. 中国银监会关于进一步规范商业银行个人理财业务投资管理有关问题的通知 [*Notice of the China Banking Regulatory Commission on the Relevant Issues concerning Further Regulating the Investment Management of the Personal Financial Management Business of Commercial Banks*]. Beijing: China Banking Regulatory Commission.

CBRC. 2010. 2009 年鉴 [*2009 Annual Report*]. Beijing: China Banking Regulatory Commission.

CBRC. 2011. 中国银行业监督管理委员会关于进一步规范银信理财合作业务的通知 [*Notice of the China Banking Regulatory Commission on Further*

Regulating Wealth Management Cooperation between Banks and Trust Companies]. Beijing: China Banking Regulatory Commission.

CBRC. 2016. 网络借贷信息中介机构业务活动管理暂行办法 *[Interim Law on the Management of Internet Lending Information Intermediaries]*. Beijing: China Banking Regulatory Commission.

CBRC, and PBOC. 2009. 中国人民银行、中国银行业监督管理委员会关于进一步加强信贷结构调整促进国民经济平稳较快发展的指导意见 [Guiding Opinions of the People's Bank of China and China Banking Regulatory Commission on Further Adjusting the Credit Structure to Promote the Rapid yet Steady Development of the National Economy]. Beijing: People's Bank of China.

CCB. 2005. *Global Offering Prospectus*. Hong Kong: Hong Kong Exchanges and Clearing Limited.

CCB. 2007. *Annual Report*. Beijing: China Construction Bank.

Central Committee of the CCP. 1998. 中共中央关于成立财经, 政法, 外事, 科学文教各小组的通知 [CPC Central Committee Notice on the Establishment of the Finance and Economy, Politics and Law, Foreign Affairs, Science, and Culture and Education Small Groups]. In 中国共产党组织史资料 *[Materials on the Organizational History of the Communist Party of China]*, Vol 9., edited by CPC Party History Research Office, CPC Organization Department and Central Archives. Beijing: CPC Party History Publishers.

Central Committee of the CCP. 1990. 中共中央关于进一步治理整顿和深化改革的决定 [Decision of the Central Committee on Steps to Re-establish Order and to Deepen Reform]. Beijing: Central Committee of the Communist Party of China.

Central Committee of the CCP. 1993a. 中共中央关于建立社会主义市场经济体制若干问题的决定 [Decision of the Central Committee of the CCP on Issues Concerning the Establishment of a Socialist Market Economic System]. Beijing: Central Committee of the Communist Party of China.

Central Committee of the CCP. 1993b. 中共中央和国务院关于当前经济情况和加强宏观经济调控的意见 [Proposal of the CPC Central Committee and State Council on the Current Economic Situation and the Strengthening of Macroeconomic Control]. Beijing: Central Committee of the Communist Party of China.

Central Huijin Investment Ltd. 2008. 'About Us'. http://www.huijin-inv.cn/hjen/aboutus/aboutus_2008.html?var1=About. Accessed 17 April 2013.

Central Organization Department. 1998a. 中共中央金融工作委员会关于中央各金融机构党组改为党委有关问题的通知 [Notice of the Central Financial Work Conference on Issues Related to the Transformation of Central Financial Institutions' Party Organizations into Party Committees]. Edited by

Central Organization Department of the Chinese Communist Party. Beijing: Central Organization Department of the Chinese Communist Party.

Central Organization Department. 1998b. 中央金融工委组织部关于金融系统党的领导体制调整后金融系统转移党员组织关系等有股烟问题的通知 [Notice of the Organization Department of the Central Financial Work Commission on Issues Related to the Transformation of Relations Between Party Personnel Organizations in the Financial System Following the Restructuring of the Party Leadership System of the Financial System]. Edited by Central Organization Department of the Chinese Communist Party. Beijing: Central Organization Department of the Chinese Communist Party.

Cetina, Karin Knorr, and Urs Bruegger. 2002. 'Global Microstructures: The Virtual Societies of Financial Markets'. *American Journal of Sociology* 107(4): 905–50.

CFI. 2016. 'How New Credit Scores Might Help Bridge China's Credit Gap'. *Center for Financial Inclusion Blog*. https://cfi-blog.org/2016/06/06/how-new-credit-scores-might-help-bridge-chinas-credit-gap/. Accessed 29 October 2017.

CGFS, and FSB. 2017. 'FinTech Credit: Market Structure, Business Models and Financial Stability Implications'. *Working Group Report of the Committee on the Global Financial System and the Financial Stability Board*. Basel: Bank for International Settlements.

Chamon, Marcos, and Eswar Prasad. 2010. 'Why are Savings Rates of Urban Households in China Rising? '. *American Economic Journal: Macroeconomics* 2(1): 93–130.

Chan, Wellington. 1982. 'The Organizational Structure of the Traditional Chinese Firm and Its Modern Reform'. *Business History Review* 56(2): 218–35.

Chang, Ta-kuang. 1998. 'SAFE and Sound'. *China Business Review* 25(4): 31–5.

Chang, Ta-kuang. 1999. 'The East is in the Red'. *International Financial Law Review* 18(3): 43–6.

Chang, Xiangqun. 2010. *Guanxi or Li Shang-Wanglai? Social Support, Reciprocity, and Social Creativity in a Chinese Village*. Taipei: Airiti Press.

Chao, Chi-Chur, and Mong Shan Ee. 2017. 'Shadow Banking and Economic Development in Developing Countries: Evidence from China'. In *EFMA 2017 Symposium Papers*. Frankfurt: European Financial Management Association.

Chaudhuri, K. N. 1985. *Trade and Civilisation in the Indian Ocean: An Economic History from the Rise of Islam to 1750*. Cambridge: Cambridge University Press.

Chaudhuri, K. N. 1990. *Asia Before Europe*. Cambridge: Cambridge University Press.

Chen, Aiming. 2002. 'China One Year After WTO Entry'. In *The Chinese Economy after WTO Accession*, edited by Bao Shuming, Lin Shuanglin, and Zhao Changwen. Abingdon: Ashgate.

Chen, Gang. 2016. '运用大数据思维和手段提升政府治理能力 ['Use Big Data Thinking and Methods to Enhance the Government's Governing Capacity']. 求是 [Seeking Truth] 12.

Chen, Jiagui, ed. 2008. 中国金融改革开放 30 年研究 [Research on 30 Years of China's Financial Reform and Opening-Up]. Beijing: Economy & Management Publishing House.

Chen, Jinhua. 2005. 国事忆述 [Remembering State Affairs]. Beijing: CCP Party History Publisher.

Chen, Long. 2016. 'From Fintech to Finlife: the case of Fintech Development in China'. China Economic Journal 9(3): 225–39.

Chen, Yuan. 1991. '我国经济的深层问题和选择 [Deep-Seated Issues and Choices of China's Economy]'. 经济研究 [Economic Research] 3:18–26.

Chen, Yuan. 1992. '我国经济运行研究的几个方法和理论问题 [Several Methodological and Theoretical Questions on Research into China's Economic Operations']. 经济研究 [Economic Research] 1: 29–37.

Chen, Yuan. 1999. 'Warding off Policy-Oriented Financial Risks and Promoting Effective Growth of the National Economy'. In Strengthening the Banking System in China: Issues and Experience, edited by Bank for International Settlements. Basel: Bank for International Settlements.

Chen, Yuming, ed. 2000. 中国加入 WTO 各行业前景分析 [An Analysis of Each Industry's Prospects as China Enters the WTO]. Beijing: Economics Press.

Cheng, Ming 1994. '东亚模式的美丽' ['The Glamour of the East Asian Model']. 战略与管理 [Strategy and Management] 2: 18–27.

Cheng, Ouyang. 2017. Inclusive Growth and E-Commerce: China's Experience. Hangzhou: AliResearch.

China Daily. 2012. 十八大新闻中心举行 '中国银行改革与科学发展' 集体采访. [18th Party Congress News: "Chinese Banking Reform and Scientific Development" Collective Interview', 12 November.

China Development Bank. 2011. Annual Report. Beijing: China Development Bank.

China Finance and Banking Society. 1991. 中国金融年鉴 1990 [Almanac of China's Finance and Banking 1990]. Beijing: China Financial Publishing House.

China Finance and Banking Society. 1994. 中国金融年鉴 1993 [Almanac of China's Finance and Banking 1993]. Beijing: China Financial Publishing House.

China IRN. 2013. '2013 年被称为互联网金融元年' ['2013: Year One of China's Internet Finance Era']. 2013. http://www.chinairn.com/news/20131231/120642562.html. Accessed 10 September 2017.

China Securities Bulletin. 1998. 'China Central Banker Tries to Assure Hong Kong Bankers on ITICs'. China Securities Bulletin, 5 November.

China Securities Depository and Clearing Commission. 2008. 中国证券登记结算统计年鉴 [*China Securities and Settlement Statistical Yearbook*]. Shanghai: China Securities Depository and Clearing Commission.

China's Future Direction Editorial Group. 2009. 中国未来走向：聚集高层决策与国家战略布局 [*China's Future Direction: Uniting High-Level Policymaking and National Strategic Arrangements*]. Beijing: People's Publisher [人民出版社].

CNTV. 2016. 'PBOC Sets up Advisory Body'. 26 March 2016. http://english.cntv.cn/2016/03/26/VIDEKOJJSIzIFLaMsCd9gkQE160326.shtml. Accessed 18 September 2016.

Cohen, Myron. 1991. 'Being Chinese: The Peripheralization of Traditional Identity'. *Daedalus* 120(2): 113–34.

Collier, Andrew. 2017. *Shadow Banking and the Rise of Capitalism in China*. Singapore: Palgrave Macmillan.

CCP Research Department. 2002. 江泽民论有中国特色社会主义 [*Jiang Zemin: On Socialism with Chinese Characteristics*]. Beijing: Communist Party of China Research Department.

Creemers, Rogier. 2017a. 'Cyber China: Upgrading Propaganda, Public Opinion Work and Social Management for the Twenty-First Century'. *Journal of Contemporary China* 26 (103): 85–100.

Creemers, Rogier. 2017b. 'Cyber-Leninism: The Political Culture of the Chinese Internet'. In *Speech and Society in Turbulent Times*, edited by Monroe Price and Nicole Stremlau. Cambridge University Press.

Creemers, Rogier. 2018. 'China's Social Credit System: An Evolving Practice of Control'. *SSRN Paper 3175792*. Rochester, NY: Social Science Research Network.

CSRC. 2008. *China Capital Markets Development Report*. Beijing: China Securities Regulatory Commission.

Cui, Zhiyuan. 1997. 第二次思想解放与制度创新 [*The Second Thought Liberalization and Institutional Innovation*]. Hong Kong: Oxford University Press.

Cull, Robert, and Colin Xu. 2000. 'Bureaucrats, State Banks, and the Efficiency of Credit Allocation: The Experience of Chinese State-owned Enterprises'. *Journal of Comparative Economics* 28: 1–31.

Cull, Robert, and Colin Xu. 2003. 'Who Gets Credit? The Behaviour of Bureaucrats and State Banks in Allocating Credit to Chinese State-owned Enterprises'. *Journal of Development Economics* 71(2): 533–59.

Dai, Xianglong. 1993. '把交通银行办成社会主义商业银行' ['Transform the Bank of Communications into a Socialist Commercial Bank']. In 戴相龙金融文选 [*Dai Xianglong: Collections on Banking and Monetary Policy*], edited by Xianglong Dai. Beijing: China Financial Publishing House.

239

Dai, Xianglong. 2001. 领导干部金融知识读本 *[Instructional Reader in Finance for Leadership Cadres]*. Beijing: China Financial Publishing House.

Dai, Xianglong. 2010. '回顾1997全国金融工作会议' ['Looking Back on 1997's Financial Work Conference']. 中国金融 *[China Finance]* 55: 19–20.

Davis, Bob. 2011. 'Political Overlords Shackle China's Monetary Mandarins'. *The Wall Street Journal*, 15 April.

de Tocqueville, Alexis. 1978. *The Old Regime and the French Revolution*. Translated by Stuart Gilbert. Gloucester: Peter Smith.

Deng, Gang. 1999. *Maritime Sector, Institutions, and Sea Power of Premodern China*. Westport: Greenwood Press.

Deng, Xiaoping. 1984. *Selected Works of Deng Xiaoping (1975–1982)*. Edited by Chung-kuo Kung. 1st ed. Beijing: Foreign Languages Press.

Deng, Xiaoping. 1993. 邓小平文选第三卷 *[Selected Works of Deng Xiaoping, Volume 3]*. Beijing: Renmin Press.

Deng, Xiaoping. June 9, 1989. 在接见首都戒严部队军以上干部时的讲话 [Speech Made While Receiving Cadres of the Martial Law Units in the Capital at and Above the Army Level].

Dickson, Bruce. 2003. *Red Capitalists in China: The Party, Private Entrepreneurs, and Prospects for Political Change*. Cambridge: Cambridge University Press.

Ding, Jianming, and Jianxin Li. 1998. '东南亚金融危机的启示' ['Revelations of the Southeast Asian Financial Crisis']. 人民日报 *[People's Daily]*, 5 January.

Dipchand, Cecil, Yichun Zhang, and Mingjia Ma. 1994. *The Chinese Financial System*. Westport, CT: Greenwood Press.

Dirlik, Arif. 1989. *The Origins of Chinese Communism*. New York: Oxford University Press.

Dong, Tongjian. 2017. 'Quick Take: JD.Com Finance Unit Launches Microlending in Chongqing'. *Caixin Global* 19 October 2017. https://www.caixinglobal.com/2017–10–19/101158477.html. Accessed 23 October 2017.

Dooley, Michael, David Folkerts-Landau, and Peter Garber. 2003. An Essay on the Revived Bretton Woods System. In *NBER Working Paper 9971*. Cambridge, MA: National Bureau of Economic Research.

Dooley, Michael, David Folkerts-Landau, and Peter Garber. 2004a. Direct Investment, Rising Real Wages and the Absorption of Excess Labor in the Periphery. In *NBER Working Paper 10626*. Cambridge, MA: National Bureau of Economic Research.

Dooley, Michael, David Folkerts-Landau, and Peter Garber. 2004b. The Revived Bretton Woods System: The Effects of Periphery Intervention and Reserve Management on Interest Rates and Exchange Rates in Center Countries. In *NBER Working Paper 10332*. Cambridge, MA: National Bureau of Economic Research.

Dotson, John. 2012. The China Rising Leaders Project, Part 1: The Chinese Communist Party and its Emerging Next-Generation Leaders. In *Staff Research Report*. Washington, DC: US-China Economic and Security Review Commission.

Duke Law School. 2005. 'Gao Xiqing '86: Reformer and Optimist'. *Duke Law Magazine* 23(2): 22–3.

Eaton, Sarah. 2016. *The Advance of the State in Contemporary China: State-Market Relations in the Reform Era*. Cambridge: Cambridge University Press.

ECNS. 2015. 'China to Issue Guidelines for Web Finance Companies'. 5 March 2015. http://www.ecns.cn/business/2015/03–05/156739.shtml. Accessed 26 September 2016.

Ehlers, Torsten, Steven Kong, and Feng Zhu. 2018. 'Mapping Shadow Banking in China: Structure and Dynamics'. *BIS Working Papers 701*. Basel: Bank for International Settlements.

Elliott, Douglas, and Yu Qiao. 2015. 'Reforming Shadow Banking in China'. *Research Report*. Washington, DC: Brookings Institution.

Fairbank, John K., and Merle Goldman. 2006. *China: A New History*. Cambridge, MA: Belknap Press of Harvard University Press.

Fang, Xing. 2000 [1985]. 'The Retarded Development of Capitalism'. In *Chinese Capitalism, 1522–1840*, edited by Xu Dixin and Wu Chengming. Basingstoke: Macmillan.

Fang, Xing, Qi Shi, Rui Jian, and Shixin Wang. 2000. 'The Growth of Commodity Circulation and the Rise of Merchant Organisations'. In *Chinese Capitalism, 1522–1840*, edited by Xu Dixin and Wu Chengming. Basingstoke: Macmillan.

Fei, Xiaotong. 2006 [1948]. 乡土中国 *[From the Soil: The Foundations of Chinese Society]*. Shanghai: Shanghai People's Press.

Feng, Emily. 2017. 'Chinese Tech Groups Display Closer Ties with Communist Party'. *Financial Times*, 10 October.

Feuchtwang, Stephan. 2009. 'Social Egoism and Individualism: Surprises and Questions that Arise from Reading Fei Xiaotong's Idea of "The Opposition" between East and West'. In *Fei Xiaotong and Sociology-Anthropology in China*, edited by Ro Ma. Beijing: Beijing Social Science Academic Press.

Feuerwerker, Albert. 1984. 'The State and the Economy in Late Imperial China'. *Theory and Society* 13(3): 297–326.

Fewsmith, Joseph. 2008. *China Since Tiananmen: From Deng Xiaoping to Hu Jintao*. Cambridge: Cambridge University Press.

Fewsmith, Joseph, and Andrew Nathan. 2018. 'Authoritarian Resilience Revisited'. *Journal of Contemporary China*. Published online 23 September.

Feyzioğlu, Tarhan. 2009. Does Good Financial Performance Mean Good Financial Intermediation in China? In *IMF Working Paper 09/170*. Washington, DC: International Monetary Fund.

Florini, Ann, Hairong Lai, and Yeling Tan. 2012. *China Experiments: From Local Innovations to National Reform*. Washington, DC: Brookings Institution Press.

Fourcade, Marion, and Kieran Healy. 2007. 'Moral Views of Market Society'. *Annual Review of Sociology* 33: 285–311.

Gang, Fan. 2010. 'China's Monetary Sterilization'. accessed 15 July. http://www.project-syndicate.org/commentary/china-s-monetary-sterilization.

Gao, Debu. 1997. '全球化还是民族化?' ['Globalization or Nationalization?']. 中国党政干部论坛 *[Chinese Cadres' Forum]* 5: 44.

Gao, Shangqun, and Sen Ye. 1990. *China Economic Systems Reform Yearbook*. Beijing: China Reform Publishing House.

Gao, Simin, and Qianyu Wang. 2014. 'Chasing the Shadow in Different Worlds: Shadow Banking and Its Regulation in the US and China'. *Manchester Journal of International Economic Law* 11: 421–58.

Gao, Yuning, and D'Maris Coffman. 2013. 'Renminbi Internationalization as a Response to the Global Imbalance'. *Journal of Chinese Economic and Business Studies* 11(2): 139–51.

Gardella, Robert. 1992. 'Squaring Accounts: Commercial Bookkeeping and Capitalist Rationalism in Late Qing and Republican China'. *The Journal of Asian Studies* 51(2): 317–39.

Goffman, Erving. 1986. *Frame Analysis: An Essay on the Organization of Experience*. London: Northeastern University Press.

Goldstein, Morris, and Nicholas Lardy. 2005. China's Role in the Revived Bretton Woods System: A Case of Mistaken Identity. In *Working Paper No. WP05–02*. Washington, DC: Institute for International Economics.

Goldstein, Morris, and Nicholas Lardy. 2009. *The Future of China's Exchange Rate Policy*. Washington, DC: Peterson Institute for International Economics.

Goodman, David. 2014. 'Middle Class China: Dreams and Aspirations'. *Journal of Chinese Political Science* 19(1): 49–67.

Goody, Jack. 2006. *The Theft of History*. Cambridge: Cambridge University Press.

Gore, Lance. 2001. 'Dream On: Communists of the Dengist Brand in Capitalistic China'. In *The Nanxun Legacy and China's Development in the Post-Deng Era*, edited by John Wong and Yongnian Zheng. Singapore: Singapore University Press.

Gore, Lance. 2014. 'The Social Transformation of the Chinese Communist Party: Prospects for Authoritarian Accommodation'. *Problems of Post-Communism* 62(4): 204–16.

Green, Stephen. 2014. 'China: A Primer on Banks' Wealth Management'. *Research Note* Hong Kong: Standard Chartered.

Gruin, Julian. 2013. 'Asset or Liability: The Role of the Financial System in the Political Economy of China's Rebalancing'. *Journal of Current Chinese Affairs* 42(4): 73–104.

Gruin, Julian. 2016. 'The Social Order of Chinese Capitalism: Socio-economic Uncertainty, Communist Party Rule, and Economic Development, 1990–2000'. *Economy & Society* 45(1): 24–50.

Gruin, Julian, and Peter Knaack. 2019. 'Not Just Another Shadow Bank: Chinese Authoritarian Capitalism and the "Developmental" Promise of Digital Financial Innovation'. *New Political Economy* (forthcoming).

Guo, Li, and Daile Xia. 2014. 'In Search of a Place in the Sun: The Shadow Banking System with Chinese Characteristics'. *European Business Organization Law Review* 15(3): 387–418.

Hall, Peter, ed. 1989. *The Political Power of Economic Ideas: Keynesianism across Nations*. Princeton, NJ: Princeton University Press.

Hamilton, Gary. 1996. 'The Organizational Foundations of Western and Chinese Commerce: A Historical and Comparative Analysis'. In *Asian Business Networks*, edited by Gary Hamilton. Berlin: Walter de Gruyter.

Hamilton, Gary. 2010. 'World Images, Authority, and Institutions A Comparison of China and the West'. *European Journal of Social Theory* 13(1): 31–48.

Hamilton, Gary, and Wei-An Chang. 2003. 'The Importance of Commerce in the Organization of China's Late Imperial Economy'. In *The Resurgence of East Asia: 500, 150 and 50 Year Perspectives*, edited by Giovanni Arrighi, Takeshi Hamashita, and Mark Selden. Abingdon: Routledge.

Hamilton, Gary, Robert Feenstra, Wongi Choe, Chung Ku Kim, and Eun Mie Lim. 2000. 'Neither States nor Markets: The Role of Economic Organization in Asian Development'. *International Sociology* 15: 288.

Hamilton, Gary, and Wang Zheng. 1992. 'Introduction'. In 乡土中国 / *From the Soil: The Foundations of Chinese Society]*, edited by Fei Xiaotong. Los Angeles: University of California Press.

Hamrin, Carol Lee, and Suisheng Zhao. 1995. 'Introduction: Core Issues in Understanding the Decision Process'. In *Decision-Making in Deng's China: Perspectives from Insiders*, edited by Carol Lee Hamrin and Suisheng Zhao. Armonk: M.E. Sharpe.

Han, Yuting. 1995. '把银行变成真正的银行' ['We Should Transform the Banks into Real Banks']. 人民日报 *[People's Daily]*, 21 April.

Harding, James. 1999. 'Downgrade for Five Financial Institutions'. *Financial Times*, 2 March.

243

Hausmann, Ricardo, and Dani Rodrik. 2003. 'Economic Development as Self-Discovery'. *Journal of Development Economics* 72(2): 603–33.

Hay, Colin. 2014. 'Neither Real nor Fictitious but 'As If Real'? A Political Ontology of the State'. *British Journal of Sociology* 65(3): 459–80.

He, Guoqian. 1998. 中国经济市场化进程中的货币政策 [China's Monetary Policy in the Midst of Economic Liberalization]. Doctoral Dissertation, School of Economics, Peking University.

He, Weiping. 2014. *Banking Regulation in China: The Role of Public and Private Sectors*. New York: Palgrave Macmillan.

Heath, Timothy. 2014. *China's New Governing Party Paradigm: Political Renewal and the Pursuit of National Rejuvenation*. Surrey: Ashgate.

Heilmann, Sebastian. 2005. 'Regulatory Innovation by Leninist Means: Community Party Supervision in China's Financial Industry'. *The China Quarterly* 181: 1–21.

Heilmann, Sebastian, and Elizabeth Perry. 2011. 'Embracing Uncertainty: Guerrilla Policy Style and Adaptive Governance in China'. In *Mao's Invisible Hand: The Political Foundations of Adaptive Governance in China*, edited by Sebastian Heilmann and Elizabeth Perry. Cambridge, MA: Harvard University Press.

Heilmann, Sebastian, and Lea Shih. 2012. 'The Rise of Industrial Policy in China, 1978–2012'. *Harvard-Yenching Institute Working Paper Series*. Cambridge, MA: Harvard-Yenching Institute.

Hellman, Joel. 1998. 'Winners Take All: The Politics of Partial Reform in Postcommunist Transitions'. *World Politics* 50(2): 203–34.

Hellmann, T., K. Murdock, and J. Stiglitz. 1997. 'Financial Restraint: Towards a New Paradigm'. In *The Role of Government in East Asian Economic Development: Comparative Institutional Analysis*, edited by M. Aoki, H.-K. Kim and M. Okuno-Fujuwara. Oxford: Clarendon Press.

Heytens, Paul, and Harm Zebregs. 2003. 'How Fast Can China Grow?' In *China: Competing in the Global Economy*, edited by Wanda Tseng and Markus Rodlauer. Washington, DC: International Monetary Fund.

Historical Research Unit of the Central Committee of the CCP. 1999. 中共十一届三中全会以来大事记－下 [*Major Events after the Third Session of the Eleventh Central Committee of the Communist Party of China (III)*]. Beijing: Central Document Press.

Hobson, John. 2004. *The Eastern Origins of Western Civilisation*. Cambridge: Cambridge University Press.

Hodgson, Geoffrey. 2006. 'What are Institutions?', *Journal of Economic Issues* 40(1): 1–25.

Hoffman, Philip. 2015. *Why Did Europe Conquer the World?* Princeton, NJ: Princeton University Press.

Hoffman, Samantha. 2017. 'Programming China: The Communist Party's Autonomic Approach to Managing State Security'. *China Monitor*. Berlin: Mercator Institute for Chinese Studies.

Hornby, Lucy. 2017. 'China Changes Tack on "Social Credit" Scheme Plan'. *Financial Times*. 4 July 2017.

Hsiao, Cheng, Yan Shen, and Wenlong Bian. 2015. 'Evaluating the Effectiveness of China's Financial Reform: The Efficiency of China's Domestic Banks'. *China Economic Review* 35: 70–82.

Hsu, Sarah, Jianjun Li, and Ying Xue. 2014. 'Shadow Banking and Systemic Risk in China". *Political Economy Research Institute Working Paper No. 349*. Amherst: University of Massachusetts Amherst.

Hu, Angang. 1998. 'Background to Writing the Report on State Capacity'. *Chinese Economy* 31(4): 5–29.

Hu, Bin, and Liansheng Zheng. 2016. 'China's Shadow Banking System – Scale, Risks and Regulation: Research from the Perspective of Non-Traditional Credit Financing'. In *Development of China's Financial Supervision and Regulation*, edited by Bin Hu and Liansheng Zheng. Abingdon: Palgrave Macmillan.

Hu, Shuli, Kan Huo, and Zheyu Yang. 2012. '改革是怎样重启的 — 社会主义市场经济体制的由来' ['How is Reform to be Restarted? The Origins of the Socialist Market Economy']. *中国改革 [China Reform]* 12. http://magazine.caixin.com/2012-11-29/100466603.html. Accessed 7 January 2013.

Hu, Wei. 1995. '中国发展的比较优势何在？ 超越纯经济观点的分析 [Where does China's Comparative Advantage Lie for its Development? An Analysis Beyond a Pure Economic Point of View]'. *战略与管理 [Strategy and Management]* 5: 69–78.

Huang, Paul. 2017. 'WeChat Confirms: It Shares Just About All Private Data with the Chinese Regime'. *The Epoch Times*, 13 September 2017.

Huang, Philip. 1985. *The Peasant Economy and Social Change in North China*. Stanford, CA: Stanford University Press.

Huang, Yasheng. 2003. *Selling China: Foreign Direct Investment During the Reform Era*. Cambridge: Cambridge University Press.

Huang, Yasheng. 2008. *Capitalism with Chinese Characteristics: Entrepreneurship and the State*. Cambridge; New York: Cambridge University Press.

Huang, Yiping, Yan Shen, and Qiuzi Fu. 2016. 'China's Macroeconomic Balancing Act: Shifting to New Drivers of Growth and Sustaining Financial Stability'. In *China's New Sources of Economic Growth: Reform, Resources, and Climate Change*, edited by Ligang Song, Ross Garnaut, Cai Fang, and Lauren Johnston. Canberra: ANU Press.

Huang, Yiping, Yan Shen, and Jingyi Wang. 2016. 'Can the Internet Revolutionise Finance in China?' In *China's New Sources of Economic Growth: Reform, Resources, and Climate Change*, edited by Ligang Song, Ross Garnaut, Cai Fang, and Lauren Johnston. Canberra: ANU Press.

Huang, Yiping, and Xu Wang. 2017. 'Building an Efficient Financial System in China: A Need for Stronger Market Discipline'. *Asian Economic Policy Review* 12(2): 188–205.

Huang, Yiping, and Xu Wang. 2011. 'Does Financial Repression Inhibit or Facilitate Economic Growth? A Case Study of Chinese Reform Experience'. *Oxford Bulletin of Economics and Statistics* 73(6): 833–55.

Huang, Zi. 1992. '是否需要设立政策性银行' ['Whether There is a Need to Establish Policy Banks']. 经济体制改革内参 *[Internal Reference of Economic System Reform]* 3:35–7.

ICBC. 2007. *Annual Report*. Beijing: Industrial and Commercial Bank of China.

Institute for Industrial Economics. 1998. 中国工业发展报告 1997 [Chinese Industrial Development Report 1997]. Beijing: Beijing Economic Management Press.

Jia, Heping. 2004. 'The Three Represents Campaign: Reform the Party or Indoctrinate the Capitalists?' *The Cato Journal* 24(3): 261–75.

Jiang, Zemin. 1996. 领导干部一定要讲政治 *[Leading Cadres Must Emphasize Politics]*. Beijing: People's Press.

Jiang, Zemin. 2001. 'Speech at the Gathering to Celebrate the 80th Anniversary of the Founding of the Chinese Communist Party' ['在庆祝中国共产党成立八十周年大会上的讲话']. *Renmin Ribao [人民日报]*, 2 July 2001.

Jiang, Zemin. 2006 [1997]. '深化金融改革; 防范金融风险 [Deepen Financial Reform; Guard Against Financial Risks]'. In 江泽民文选 *[Collected Works of Jiang Zemin]*, edited by Editorial Committee of the Central Document Bureau. Beijing: Central Document Publisher.

Johansson, Anders. 2012. 'Financial Repression and China's Economic Imbalances'. In *Rebalancing and Sustaining Growth in China*, edited by Huw McKay and Ligang Song, 45–64. Canberra: ANU E-Press.

Johansson, Anders, and Xun Wang. 2011. 'Financial Repression and Structural Imbalances'. *Working Paper No. 2011–19*. Beijing: China Economic Research Center.

Johansson, Anders, and Xun Wang. 2012a. 'Financial Repression and External Imbalances'. *Working Paper No. 2012–20*. Beijing: China Economic Research Center.

Johansson, Anders, and Xun Wang. 2012b. 'Financial Sector Policies, Poverty and Inequality'. *Working Paper No. 2012–24*. Beijing: China Economic Research Center.

Kalecki, Michael. 1943. 'Political Aspects of Full Employment'. *Political Quarterly* 14(4): 322–30.

King, Robert, and Ross Levine. 1993. 'Finance and Growth: Schumpeter Might be Right'. *Quarterly Journal of Economics* 53: 715–37.

Kirby, William. 1990. 'Continuity and Change in Modern China: Economic Planning on the Mainland and on Taiwan, 1943–1958'. *Australian Journal of Chinese Affairs* 24: 121–41.

Knight, Frank. 1985 [1921]. *Risk, Uncertainty, and Profit*. Chicago: Chicago University Press.

Knight, John. 2014. 'China as a Developmental State'. *The World Economy* 37(10): 1335–1447.

Knight, John, and Sai Ding. 2012. *China's Remarkable Economic Growth*. Oxford: Oxford University Press.

Krippner, Greta. 2011. *Capitalizing on Crisis: The Political Origins of the Rise of Finance*. Cambridge, MA: Harvard University Press.

Kroeber, Arthur. 2011. 'The Renminbi: The Political Economy of a Currency'. *Foreign Policy*, 7 September.

Kuhn, Robert. 2010. *What China's Leaders Think: The Inside Story of China's Reform and What This Means for the Future*. Singapore: John Wiley.

Kwan, Man-bun. 1990. 'The Merchant World of Tianjin: Society and Economy of a Chinese City'. Doctoral Dissertation, Stanford University.

Kwong, Charles. 2011. 'China's Banking Reform: The Remaining Agenda'. *Global Economic Review* 40(2): 161–78.

Lam, Willy Wo-Lap. 1995a. *China After Deng Xiaoping: The Power Struggle in Beijing since Tiananmen*. Armonk, NY: M.E. Sharpe.

Lam, Willy Wo-Lap. 1995b. 'Jiang's Men Clash with Top Officials'. *South China Morning Post*, 9 February.

Lam, Willy Wo-Lap. 1999. *The Era of Jiang Zemin*. Singapore: Prentice Hall.

Lampton, David, and Kenneth Lieberthal, eds. 1992. *Bureaucracy, Politics, and Decision-Making in Post-Mao China*. Berkeley: University of California Press.

Landler, Mark. 1999. 'Bankruptcy the Chinese Way: Foreign Bankers are Shown to the End of the Line'. *New York Times*, 22 January.

Lardy, Nicholas. 1995. 'The Role of Foreign Trade and Investment in China's Economic Transformation'. *The China Quarterly* 144: 1065–82.

Lardy, Nicholas. 1998. *China's Unfinished Economic Revolution*. Washington, DC: Brookings Institution.

Lardy, Nicholas. 2002. *Integrating China into the Global Economy*. Washington, DC: Brookings Institution Press.

Lardy, Nicholas. 2012. *Sustaining China's Economic Growth After the 2008 Financial Crisis*. Washington, DC: Peterson Institute for International Economics.

Laurenceson, James, and Joseph Chai. 2003. *Financial Reform and Economic Development in China*. Cheltenham: Edward Elgar.

Leigh, Lamin, and Richard Podpiera. 2006. 'The Rise of Foreign Investment in China's Banks: Taking Stock'. *IMF Working Papers*. Washington, DC: International Monetary Fund.

Leng, Jing. 2009. *Corporate Governance and Financial Reform in China's Transition Economy*. Hong Kong: Hong Kong University Press.

Levine, Ross. 2005. 'Finance and Growth: Theory, Mechanisms, and Evidence'. In *Handbook of Economic Growth*, edited by Philippe Aghion and Steven Durlauf. London: Elsevier.

Li, Cheng. 2012. 'The End of the CCP's Resilient Authoritarianism? A Tripartite Assessment of Shifting Power in China'. *The China Quarterly* 211: 595–623.

Li, Cheng. 2016. *Chinese Politics in the Xi Jinping Era: Reassessing Collective Leadership*. Washington, DC: Brookings Institution Press.

Li, David. 2001. 'Beating the Trap of Financial Repression in China'. *Cato Journal* 21 (1): 77–90.

Li, Kui-Wai. 1994. *Financial Repression and Economic Reform in China*. Westport, CT: Praeger.

Li, Kehua. 2000. '十年股市他们这样富起来' ['Stock Markets: Rising to Riches This Way in Ten Years']. *中国证券报 [China Securities Report]* 12: 7–8.

Li, Keqiang. 2014. *2014 政府工作报告 [2014 Government Work Report]*. Beijing: PRC State Council.

Li, Lanqing. 2009. *Breaking Through: The Birth of China's Opening-Up Policy*. Oxford: Oxford University Press.

Li, Liming, and Renxiong Zeng. 2007. *1979–2006: China's Financial Transformation [1979–2006: 中国金融大变革]*. Shanghai: Shanghai People's Publishing House.

Li, Sai Yau, and Cathleen Yi Tin. 2016. 'Impact of Technology on China's Financial System'. In *Shadow Banking in China: An Opportunity for Financial Reform*, edited by Andrew Sheng and Ng Chow Soon. Hoboken, NJ: Wiley & Sons.

Li, Tao. 1994. '分析专业银行的点贷做法 [Analysis of the Specialized Banks' Practice of Designated Loans]'. *经济日报 [Economic Daily]*, 16 September.

Li, Xia. 2000. '实施债转股企业的防卫与条件' ['The Parameters and Circumstances for Enterprises in the Debt-Equity Swap']. *金融时报 [Financial News]*, 15 September.

Li, Xinning. 1998. '从东亚金融危机看我国的金融隐患:对啊国有肚子商业银行资产运营现状的分析'. *改革 [Reform]* 3: 31–40.

Li, Yiuan. 2017. 'Beijing Pushes for a Direct Hand in China's Big Tech Firms'. *The Wall Street Journal*, 11 October.

Li, Zhenzhi. 1998. '也要推动政治改革' ['It is Necessary Also to Push Forward Political Reform']. *改革 [Reform]* 1: 17–21.

Liang, Meichen. 2017. 'Xi's Vision to Drive Internet Firms'. *China Daily*, 24 October.

Liang, Yan. 2016. 'Shadow Banking in China: Implications for Financial Stability and Macroeconomic Rebalancing'. *The Chinese Economy* 49(3): 148–60.

Lin, Kun-Chin. 2008. 'Macroeconomic Disequilibria and Enterprise Reform: Restructuring the Chinese Oil and Petrochemical Industries in the 1990s'. *The China Journal* 60: 49–79.

Lin, Nanxiu. 2016. *State Council Policy Briefing*. Beijing. CN: PRC State Council.

Lin, Yifu, Fang Cai, and Zhou Li. 1994. 中国的奇迹: 发展战略葛经济改革 *[China's Miracle: Development Strategy and Economic Reform]*. Shanghai: Sanlian Publishers.

Lin, Yutang. 1941. *My Country, My People*. London: Heinemann.

Liu, Guangdi, Genyou Dai, and Jian Li, eds. 1997. 中国经济体制转轨时期的货币政策研究 *[Research on Monetary Policy during China's Period of Economic Transition]*. Beijing: China Finance Publishing House.

Liu, Mingkang. 2004. The State-Owned Banks in China: Reform, Corporate Governance, and Prospects. Speech at the Beijing International Financial Forum: China Banking Regulatory Commission.

Liu, Mingkang. 2008a. '全球金融稳定与全球文明' ['Global Financial Stability and Global Civilization']. *Speech at the Annual Conference on 'World Civilization', 2 May*. British Museum, London.

Liu, Mingkang. 2008b. '在多变市场环境下维护银行业稳定' ['Maintenance of Banking Stability in a Changing Market Environment']. *Speech at China Banking Regulatory Commission 25 September*. Beijing.

Liu, Xirui. 2002. '服务型政府: 经济全球化背景下中国政府改革的目标选择' ['Service-Style Government: China's Choice of Reform Goal Under Conditions of Globalization']. 中国行政管理 *[Chinese Administration and Management]* (7): 5–8.

Liu, Zebang. 2008. '关于中共中央 18 号文件 [On the Central Committee's Document No. 18]'. http://liuzebang.2000.blog.163.com/blog/static/4224889 2008102644556842/. Accessed 8 July 2014.

Lothian, Tamara. 2012. 'Beyond Macroprudential Regulation: Three Ways of Thinking about Financial Crisis, Regulation and Reform'. *Global Policy* 3(4): 410–20.

Lou, Jianbo. 2001. *China's Troubled Bank Loans: Workout and Prevention*. London: Kluwer Law International.

Lou, Jiwei. 2018. 'Speech at 16th Enterprise Development High-Level Forum'. 28 January. Beijing.

Luo, Dezhi. 2003. '1949–2002: 中国银行制度变迁研究' ['1949–2002: Research on Changes in China's Banking System']. Doctoral Dissertation, Fudan University.

Lü, Xiaobo. 2000. *Cadres and Corruption*. Stanford, CA: Stanford University Press.

Ma, Jack. 2013. '马云：金融行业需要搅局者 [Jack Ma: The Finance Industry Needs Disruptors]'. 2013. http://cpc.people.com.cn/pinglun/n/2013/0621/c78779–21920452.html. Accessed 10 September 2017.

Ma, Guonan, and Wang Yi. 2010. 'China's High Savings Rate: Myth and Reality'. *BIS Working Paper No. 312*. Basel: Bank for International Settlements.

McDonald, Tom. 2016. *Social Media in Rural China*. London: UCL Press.

Mackenzie, Donald, and Yuval Millo. 2003. 'Negotiating a Market, Performing Theory: The Historical Sociology of a Financial Derivatives Exchange'. *American Journal of Sociology* 109(1): 107–45.

McKinnon, Ronald. 1973. *Money and Capital in Economic Development*. Washington, DC: The Brookings Institution.

Mader, Philip. 2015. *The Political Economy of Microfinance: Financializing Poverty*. New York: Palgrave Macmillan.

Mann, Susan. 1987. *Local Merchants and the Chinese Bureaucracy, 1750–1950*. Stanford, CA: Stanford University Press.

Mann, Susan. 1992. 'Household Handicrafts and State Policy in Qing Times'. In *To Achieve Security and Wealth: The Qing State and the Economy*, edited by Jane Leonard and John Watt. Ithaca, NY: Cornell University Press.

Mao, Qizheng. 2013. 'Measuring the Off-balance-sheet Wealth Management Business of Commercial Banks'. *International Financial Corporation Bulletin* 36:68–76.

Mao, Zedong. 1967. 毛泽东选集 *[Selected Works of Mao Zedong]*. Beijing: People's Press.

Marshall, Gordon. 1982. *In Search of the Spirit of Capitalism: An Essay on Max Weber's Protestant Ethic Thesis*. New York: Columbia University Press.

Maswana, Jean-Claude. 2011. 'China's Financial Development and Economic Growth: Exploring the Contradictions'. *Journal of Chinese Economics and Finance* 3: 15–27.

MGI. 2017. *China's Digital Economy: A Leading Global Force*. Hong Kong: McKinsey Global Institute.

Milana, Carlo, and Harry Wu. 2012. 'Growth, Institutions, and Entrepreneurial Finance in China: A Survey'. *Strategic Change* 21: 83–106.

Millward, Steven. 2016. 'China Lacks a US-Style Credit Scoring System. But Big Data and AI Are Filling the Gap.' *Tech in Asia*. https://www.techinasia.com/baidu-china-credit-score-system-ai-big-data. Accessed 9 February 2017.

Misra, Kalpana. 1998. *From Post-Maosim to Post-Marxism: The Erosion of Official Ideology in Deng's China*. London: Routledge.

Mitter, Rana. 2004. *A Bitter Revolution: China's Struggle with the Modern World*. Oxford: Oxford University Press.

Moody's Investor Service. 1999. *Banking System Outlook: China*. Singapore: Moody's.

Nathan, Andrew, and Bruce Gilley, eds. 2002. *China's New Leaders: The Secret Files*. London: Granta Books.

National People's Congress of the People's Republic of China. 1995. 中华人民共和国中国人民银行法 *[Law of the People's Republic of China on the People's Bank of China]*. Beijing: China Democracy and Legal System Publishers.

Naughton, Barry. 1995. *Growing Out of the Plan: Chinese Economic Reform, 1978–1993*. Cambridge: Cambridge University Press.

Naughton, Barry. 1996. 'China's Macroeconomy in Transition'. In *China's Transitional Economy*, edited by Andrew Walder. Oxford: Oxford University Press.

Naughton, Barry. 2002. 'China's Economic Think Tanks: Their Changing Role in the 1990s'. *The China Quarterly* 171: 625–35.

Naughton, Barry. 2003a. 'Government Reorganization: Liu Mingkang and Financial Restructuring'. *Chinese Leadership Monitor* 7: 1–10.

Naughton, Barry. 2003b. 'The Emergence of Wen Jiabao'. *Chinese Leadership Monitor* 6: 36–47.

Naughton, Barry. 2009. 'Understanding the Chinese Stimulus Package'. *China Leadership Monitor* 28: 1–12.

Naughton, Barry. 2014. 'After the Third Plenum: Economic Reform Revival Moves Toward Implementation'. *China Leadership Monitor* 43: 1–14.

Naughton, Barry, and Dali Yang. 2004. 'Holding China Together: Introduction'. In *Holding China Together: Diversity and National Integration in the Post-Deng Era*, edited by Barry Naughton and Dali Yang. Cambridge: Cambridge University Press.

NDRC. 2008. 明确任务抓落实扩大内需促增长 *[Clarify Responsibility and Grasp Implementation; Expand Domestic Demand and Promote Growth]*. Edited by National Development and Reform Commission. Beijing: National Development and Reform Commission.

NDRC. 2016. 全国信用信息共享平台信用信息目录 (部际联席会议成员单位 2016 年版) *[Credit Information Catalogue of the National Credit Information Sharing Platform (Interdepartmental Joint Membership Conference Unit 2016 Edition)]*.

Nee, Victor. 1989. 'A Theory of Market Transition: From Redistribution to Markets in State Socialism'. *American Sociological Review* 54(5): 663–81.

Nee, Victor, and Sonja Opper. 2012. *Capitalism from Below: Markets and Institutional Change in China*. Cambridge, MA: Harvard University Press.

Needham, Joseph. 1956. *Science and Civilisation in China, Vol 2: History of Scientific Thought*. Cambridge: Cambridge University Press.

Nettl, J. P. 1968. 'The State as a Conceptual Variable'. *World Politics* 20(4): 559–92.

NIFA. 2016. 'Internet Finance Industry Credit Information Sharing Platform Launched'. http://www.nifa.org.cn/nifaen/2955875/2955895/2964303/index.html. Accessed 21 October 2017.

NIFA. 2018. '信用有价值守信有力量' ['Credit Has Worth, Promises Have Power']. http://www.nifa.org.cn/nifa/2961652/2961654/2972545/index.html. Accessed 17 June 2018.

North, Douglass. 1990. *Institutions, Institutional Change and Economic Performance.* Cambridge: Cambridge University Press.

North, Douglass. 2005. 'The Chinese Menu (For Development)'. *The Wall Street Journal*, 7 April.

North, Douglass, and Robert Thomas. 1973. *The Rise of the Western World: A New Economic History.* Cambridge: Cambridge University Press.

Oi, Jean. 1995. 'The Role of the Local State in China's Transitional Economy'. *The China Quarterly* 144: 1132–49.

Oksenberg, Michel. 2001. 'China's Political System: Challenges of the Twenty-First Century'. *The China Journal* 45: 21–35.

Opper, Sonja. 2007. 'Going Public Without the Public: Between Political Governance and Corporate Governance'. In *The Chinese Economy in the 21st Century: Enterprise and Business Behaviour*, edited by Barbara Krug and Hans Hendrischke. Cheltenham: Edward Elgar.

Padgett, John, and Christopher Ansell. 1993. 'Robust Action and the Rise of the Medici, 1400–1434'. *American Journal of Sociology* 98(6): 1259–1319.

Pagano, Marco. 1993. 'Financial Markets and Growth: An Overview'. *European Economic Review* 37: 613–22.

Pang, Zhongying 1998. '国际金融体系酝酿改革' ['International Financial System Deliberates Reform']. 人民日报 *[People's Daily]*, 9 April.

PBOC. 1988. 关于加强利率管理工作的暂行规定 *[Provisional Regulation on Strengthening Interest Rate Management].* Beijing: People's Bank of China.

PBOC. 1996. '转制中的国有企业银行债券问题的调查报告' ['Research Report on the Issues of Bank Loans to State-Owned Enterprises during Transition']. 经济研究参考 *[Economic Research Reference]* 63: 33–8.

PBOC. 1998. 中国人民银行关于该经过有商业银行贷款规模规例的通知 *[Notice on improving the Management of Loan Size for State-Owned Commercial Banks].* Beijing: People's Bank of China.

PBOC. 1999. *China Financial Outlook 1998.* Beijing: China Financial Publishing House.

PBOC. 2008. *China Monetary Policy Report Quarter Two, 2008.* Beijing: People's Bank of China.

PBOC. 2013. *China Financial Stability Report 2013.* Beijing: People's Bank of China.

PBOC. 2015a. '征信系统建设运行报告' (2004–2014) ['Report on the Construction and Operation of the Credit System (2004–2014)']. People's Bank of China.

PBOC. 2015b. 关于促进互联网金融健康发展的指导意见 [*Guiding Proposal on Promoting the Healthy Development of Internet Finance*]. Beijing: People's Bank of China.

PBOC. 2017. 中国金融稳定报告 2017 [*China Financial Stability Report 2017*]. Beijing: People's Bank of China.

Pearson, Margaret. 2010. 'The Impact of the PRC's Economic Crisis Response on Regulatory Institutions: Preliminary Thoughts'. *China Analysis Working Paper*. Trier: Trier University.

Pei, Minxin. 1998. 'The Political Economy of Banking Reforms in China, 1993–1997'. *Journal of Contemporary China* 7(18): 321–50.

Pei, Minxin. 2006. *China's Trapped Transition: The Limits of Developmental Autocracy*. Cambridge, MA: Harvard University Press.

Peng, Xinwei. 1994. *A Monetary History of China*, Vol. 2 [中国货币史, 第二卷]. Bellingham, WA: Center for East Asian Studies.

People's Daily. 1993. '什么是社会主义市场经济? 主要内容与编写特点 [What is the Socialist Market Economy? Primary Content and Characteristics]'. 人民日报 [*People's Daily*], 19 November.

People's Daily. 1998. '江泽民主席参加香港代表团审议时强调坚定不移贯彻 "一国两制" 方针继续保持香港繁荣稳定' ['Whilst Participating in a Delegation to Hong Kong, General Secretary Jiang Zemin Emphasizes the Unswerving Implementation of the "One Country, Two Systems" Policy to Continue Protecting Hong Kong's Prosperity and Stability']. 人民日报 [*People's Daily*], 10 March.

Pistor, Katharina. 2013. 'The Governance of China's Finance'. In *Capitalizing China*, edited by Joseph Fan and Randall Morck. Chicago: Chicago University Press.

Pomeranz, Kenneth. 1997. ''Traditional' Chinese Business Forms Revisited: Family, Firm, and Financing in the History of the Yutang Company of Jining, 1779–1956'. *Late Imperial China* 18(1): 1–38.

Pomeranz, Kenneth. 2000. *The Great Divergence: China, Europe, and the Making of the Modern World Economy*. Princeton, NJ: Princeton University Press.

Pomeranz, Kenneth. 2009. 'Putting Modernity in its Place(s): Reflections on Jack Goody's *The Theft of History*'. *Theory, Culture & Society* 26(7–8): 32–51.

Potter, Pitman. 2001. 'Liberation and Control: Deng Xiaoping's Nanxun Legacy and the Chinese Legal System'. In *The Nanxun Legacy and China's Development in the Post-Deng Era*, edited by John Wong and Yongnian Zheng. Singapore: Singapore University Press.

Prasad, Eswar, Kenneth Rogoff, S. Wei, and A. Köse. 2003. 'Effects of Financial Globalization on Developing Countries: Some Empirical Evidence'. *Occasional Paper*. Washington, DC: International Monetary Fund.

PRC State Council. 1992a. 国务院关于加强对固定资产投资和信用配额宏观调控的通知 *[Notice on Strengthening Macroeconomic Control over Fixed-Asset Investments and Credit Quotas]*. Beijing: State Council of the People's Republic of China.

PRC State Council. 1992b. 国务院关于进一步加强证券市场宏观管理的通知 *[Notice of the State Council Concerning Further Strengthening Macroeconomic Management of the Financial Markets]*. Beijing: State Council of the People's Republic of China.

PRC State Council. 1993. 国务院关于金融体制改革的决定 *[Decision of the State Council Concerning Reform of the Financial System]*. Beijing: State Council of the People's Republic of China.

PRC State Council. 1994. 国务院关于组建国家开发银行的通知 *[Notice of the State Council on the Establishment of the State Development Bank]*. Beijing: State Council of the People's Republic of China.

PRC State Council. 1997. 中共中央国务院关于深化金融改革，整顿金融秩序，防范金融风险的通知 *[Notice of the State Council Concerning Deepening Financial Reform, Rectifying Financial Order, and Guarding Against Financial Risk]*. Beijing: State Council of the People's Republic of China.

PRC State Council. 2000. 金融资产管理公司条例 *[Regulation on Financial Asset Management Companies]*. Beijing: State Council of the People's Republic of China.

PRC State Council. 2014a. 国务院关于印发社会信用体系建设 规划纲要 （2014 – 2020年）的通知 *[Notice of the State Council on the planning outline for the construction of a social credit system]*. Beijing: State Council of the People's Republic of China.

PRC State Council. 2014b. 国务院办公厅关于加强影子银行监管有关问题的通知 *[Document No. 107: Notice of the State Council on Strengthening Regulation of Shadow Banking]*. Beijing: State Council of the People's Republic of China.

PRC State Council. 2015. 国务院关于积极推进'互联网＋'行动的指导意见 [State Council Guiding Opinions concerning Vigorously Moving Forward the 'Internet Plus' Plan]. Beijing: State Council of the People's Republic of China.

PRC State Council. 2016. 推进普惠金融发展规划 *(2016 – 2020 年) [Plan for Advancing Financial Inclusion Development (2016–2020)]*. Beijing: State Council of the People's Republic of China.

PRC State Council. 2017. 国务院关于印发'十三五'市场监管规划的通知 *[Notice of the State Council on the 13th Five-Year Plan for Market Regulation]*. Beijing: State Council of the People's Republic of China.

PwC. 2015. *Banking and Finance in China: The Outlook for 2015*. Hong Kong: PricewaterhouseCoopers.

Qin, Hui. 2008. '共识破裂：改革争论的激化' ['Rupturing Consensus: The Intensification of the Reform Debate']. *Notice of the State Council on the planning outline for the construction of a social credit system 南方周末 [Southern Weekend]*, 21 February. Accessed 22 November 2013. http://news.sina.com.cn/pl/2008–02–21/121114987351.shtml.

Rawski, Thomas. 1989. *Economic Growth in Prewar China*. Berkeley: University of California Press.

Redding, S. Gordon. 1990. *The Spirit of Chinese Capitalism*. Berlin: Walter de Gruyter.

Rein, Martin, and Donald Schon. 1996. 'Frame Critical Policy Analysis and Frame Reflective Policy Practice'. *Knowledge and Policy: The International Journal of Knowledge Transfer and Utilization* 9: 85–104.

Riedel, James, Jing Jin, and Jian Gao. 2007. *How China Grows: Investment, Finance, and Reform*. Princeton, NJ: Princeton University Press.

Roubini, Noriel, and Xavier Sala-i-Martin. 1992. 'Financial Repression and Economic Growth'. *Journal of Development Economics* 39: 5–30.

Rowe, William. 1990. 'Modern Chinese Social History in Comparative Perspective'. In *Heritage of China: Contemporary Perspectives on Chinese Civilization*, edited by P. S. Ropp. Berkeley: University of California Press.

Ruan, Victoria. 2016. 'China Central Bank sees Role for Shadow Banking'. *South China Morning Post*, 1 November.

Sanderson, Henry, and Michael Forsythe. 2012. *China's Superbank: How China Development Bank is Rewriting the Rules of Finance*. Somerset, NJ: Wiley.

Sartori, Giovanni. 1970. 'Concept Misformation in Comparative Politics'. *American Political Science Review* 64(4): 1033–53.

Schell, Orville, and John Delury. 2013. *Wealth and Power: China's Long March to the Twenty-First Century*. London: Little, Brown.

Searle, John. 1995. *The Construction of Social Reality*. Cambridge: Cambridge University Press.

Searle, John. 2005. 'What is an Institution?' *Journal of Institutional Economics* 1(1): 1–22.

SETC, and PBOC. 1997. 关于下达核销贷坏账准备金分配规模和编制企业兼并破产和职工再就业工作计划的通知 *[Notice Concerning the Scale of Distribution of Bad-Loan Reserves and the Drafting of Plans for Enterprise Bankruptcy and Reemployment of Workers]*. Beijing: People's Bank of China.

Shaw, Edward. 1973. *Financial Deepening in Economic Development*. New York: Oxford University Press.

Shen, Wei. 2016. *Shadow Banking in China: Risk, Regulation and Policy*. Cheltenham: Edward Elgar Publishing.

Shen, Yan, Minggao Shen, and Qin Chen. 2016. 'Measurement of the New Economy in China: Big Data Approach'. *IIF Working Paper*. Beijing: Institute of Digital Finance.

Sheng, Andrew, Christian Edelmann, Cliff Sheng, and Jodie Hu. 2015. 'Bringing Light Upon the Shadow: A Review of the Chinese Shadow Banking Sector'. *FGI Working Paper*. Hong Kong: Fung Global Institute.

Sheng, Andrew, and Ng Chow Soon. 2016. *Shadow Banking in China: An Opportunity for Financial Reform*. Hoboken, NJ: John Wiley & Sons.

Shih, Victor. 2008. *Factions and Finance in China: Elite Conflict and Inflation*. Cambridge: Cambridge University Press.

Shirk, Susan. 1992. 'The Chinese Political System and the Political Strategy of Economic Reform'. In *Bureaucracy, Politics, and Decision Making in Post-Mao China*, edited by Kenneth Lieberthal and David Lampton. Berkeley: University of California Press.

Shirk, Susan. 1993. *The Political Logic of Economic Reform in China*. Berkeley: University of California Press.

Skinner, William. 1977. 'Cities and the Hierarchy of Local Systems'. In *The City in Late Imperial China*, edited by William Skinner. Stanford, CA: Stanford University Press.

Snooks, Graeme. 1996. *The Dynamic Society: Exploring the Sources of Global Change*. London: Routledge.

Sohu. 2016. 'P2P 网贷平台怎么管? [How to control P2P lending platforms?]' http://mt.sohu.com/20160803/n462375447.shtml. Accessed 21 September 2016.

Sombart, Werner. 1913. *Krieg und Kapitalismus*. Munich: Duncker & Humblot.

Song Ping. 1991. '加强党的建设，提高党的战斗力' ['Strengthen the Party's Construction, Elevate the Party's Fighting Ability']. 党建研究 *[Party Construction Studies]* 4.

Staal, Frits. 1979. 'Oriental Ideas on the Origin of Language'. *Journal of the American Oriental Society* 99(1): 1.

STCN. 2018. 云上战争" 打响! 监管牵头 16 家金融机构自建 "融联易云 [The war on the cloud has started! Regulators lead 16 financial institutions in the construction of a unified financial cloud]. *Securities Times, 8 March 2018. http://www.stcn.com/2018/0308/14011763.shtml*. Accessed 18 June 2018.

Steinfeld, Edward. 1998. *Forging Reform in China: The Fate of State-Owned Industry*. Cambridge: Cambridge University Press.

Stent, James. 2017. *China's Banking Transformation: The Untold Story*. New York: Oxford University Press.

Stiglitz, Joseph. 1994. 'The Role of the State in Financial Markets'. In *Proceeding of the World Bank Annual Conference on Development Economics, 1993:*

Supplement to the World Bank Economic Review and the World Bank Research Observer, edited by Michael Bruno and Boris Pleskovic. Washington, DC: World Bank.

Stiglitz, Joseph. 2000. 'Capital Market Liberalization, Economic Growth, and Instability'. *World Development* 28: 1075–86).

Strauss, Julia. 2006. 'Morality, Coercion and State Building by Campaign in the Early PRC: Regime Consolidation and After, 1949–1956'. *The China Quarterly* 188(1): 891–912.

Streeck, Wolfgang. 2009. *Reforming Capitalism: Institutional Change in the German Political Economy*. Oxford: Oxford University Press.

Streeck, Wolfgang. 2010. 'Taking Capitalism Seriously: Toward an Institutionalist Approach to Contemporary Political Economy'. *MPIfG Discussion Paper 10/15*. Cologne: Max Planck Institute for the Study of Societies.

Streeck, Wolfgang. 2012. 'How to Study Contemporary Capitalism?' *European Journal of Sociology* 53(1): 1–28.

Sugihara, Kaoru. 2003. 'The East Asian Path of Economic Development: A Long-Term Perspective'. In *The Resurgence of East Asia: 500, 150, and 50 Year Perspectives*, edited by Giovanni Arrighi, Takeshi Hamashita, and Mark Selden. Abingdon: Routledge.

Sun, Liping. 2012. 'On the Practice of Market Transition'. In *Sociology and Anthropology in Twentieth-Century China: Between Universalism and Indigenism*, edited by Arif Dirlik. Hong Kong: The Chinese University Press.

Tam, On Kit. 1988. 'Rural Finance in China'. *China Quarterly* 113: 60–76.

Tam, On Kit, ed. 1995. *Financial Reform in China*. London: Routledge.

Tamagna, Frank. 1942. *Banking and Finance in China*. New York: Institute of Pacific Relations.

Tang, Shuangning. 2003. '应对 WTO 挑战 加快中国银行业改革开放步伐 Coping with WTO Challenges by Accelerating the Pace of China's Banking Sector Reform and Opening Up'. *Speech at China Banking Regulatory Commission*. Beijing: China Banking Regulatory Commission.

Tang, Tjun, Yue Zhang, and David He. 2014. 'The Rise of Digital Finance in China: New Drivers, New Game, New Strategy'. *Strategy Report*. Hong Kong: Boston Consulting Group.

Tang, Tsou. 1998. 'Further Thoughts on Chinese Politics at the Top: the Past, the Present, and the Future'. *Journal of Contemporary China* 7(17): 167–99.

Thornton, Patricia. 2007. *Disciplining the State: Virtue, Violence, and State-Making in Modern China*. Cambridge, MA: Harvard University Press.

Tilly, Charles. 1992. *Coercion, Capital, and European States, AD 990–1992*. Oxford: Blackwell Publishing.

Tong, Shiqing. 2007. 'The Vicissitudes and Logic of Change in China's Credit System'. *Shanghai University of Finance Working Paper*. Shanghai: Shanghai University of Finance.

Tsai, Kellee. 2007. *Capitalism Without Democracy: The Private Sector in Contemporary China*. Ithaca, NY: Cornell University Press.

Tsai, Kellee. 2013. 'China's Political Economy and Political Science'. *Perspectives on Politics* 11(3): 860–71.

Tsai, Kellee. 2015. 'The Political Economy of State Capitalism and Shadow Banking in China'. *Issues & Studies* 51(1): 55–97.

Tu, Weiming. 1993. *Way, Learning and Politics: Essays on the Confucian Intellectual*. Albany: State University of New York Press.

Underhill, Geoffrey. 2000. 'State, Market, and Global Political Economy: Genealogy of an (Inter-?) Discipline'. *International Affairs* 76(4): 805–24.

Underhill, Geoffrey, and Xiaoke Zhang. 2005. 'The Changing State-Market Condominium in East Asia: Rethinking the Political Underpinnings of Development'. *New Political Economy* 10(1): 1–24.

Usher, Abbott. 1943. *The Early History of Deposit Banking in Mediterranean Europe*. Cambridge, MA: Harvard University Press.

Vries, Peer. 2002. 'Governing Growth: A Comparative Analysis of the Role of the State in the Rise of the West'. *Journal of World History* 13(1): 67–138.

Walder, Andrew. 1995. 'Local Governments as Industrial Firms: An Organizational Analysis of China's Transitional Economy'. *American Journal of Sociology* 101(2): 263–301.

Walter, Carl, and Fraser Howie. 2003. *Privatizing China: Inside China's Stock Markets*. Singapore: Wiley.

Walter, Carl, and Fraser Howie. 2011. *Red Capitalism: The Fragile Financial Foundation of China's Extraordinary Rise*. Singapore: Wiley & Sons.

Wang An. 2000. 股爷您上座 *[Mister Share, You to the Head of the Table]*. Beijing: Huayi Publishing House.

Wang, Bingcai. 1998. 与狼共舞：中国加入 *[Dancing with Wolves: China Enters the World]*. Beijing: China Literary Publishing House.

Wang, Hao, Honglin Wang, Lisheng Wang, and Hao Zhou. 2016. 'Shadow Banking: China's Dual-Track Interest Rate Liberalization'. *SSRN Paper no. 2606081*. Rochester, NY: Social Science Research Network.

Wang, Hui. 2009. 现代中国思想的兴起 (全四册) *[The Rise of Modern Chinese Thought (Four Volumes)]*. Beijing: New Knowledge Joint Publishing.

Wang, Hui. 2011. 'Weber and the Question of Chinese Modernity'. In *The Politics of Imagining Asia*, edited by Wang Hui and Theodore Hunter. Cambridge, MA: Harvard University Press.

Wang, Hui. 2003 [1998]. 'Contemporary Chinese Thought and the Question of the Modern'. In *China's New Order: Society, Politics, and Economy in Transition*, edited by Wang Hui. Cambridge, MA: Harvard University Press.

Wang, Huning. 1988. '中国变化中的中央和地方政府的关系: 政治的含义' ['Central and Local Government Relations in the Midst of China's Transformation: The Implicit Meaning of Governance']. 负担学报 (社会科学版) [*Fudan Journal: Social Sciences Edition*] 5: 1–8.

Wang, Jing. 2017. "Stir-Frying' Internet Finance: Financialization and the Institutional Role of Financial News in China'. *International Journal of Communication* 11: 22.

Wang, Qinghua. 2011. 'The 'State of the State' in Reform-Era China'. *Asian Perspective* 35: 89–110.

Wang, Qishan. 2015. '王岐山会见参加中美政党高层对话美国代表团' ['Wang Qishan Engages in High-level China-US Political Party Talks with an American Delegation']. *Xinhua*. 8 May 2015.

Wang, Shaoguang. 2011. '小政府大社会从根本上是错的' ['The Notion of Small Government and Big Society is Fundamentally Wrong']. 乌有之乡 [*Utopia*], http://www.wyzxsx.com/Article/Class17/201103/219956.html. Accessed 21 September 2014.

Wang, Shaoguang, and Angang Hu. 1993. 加强中央政府在市场经济转型中的主导作用: 关于中国国家能力的研究报告 [*Strengthening the Guiding Role of the Central Government During the Transition to a Market Economy: A Research Report on China's State Capacity*]. New Haven & Beijing: Yale University & Chinese Academy of Sciences.

Wang, Yao, and Jodie Hu. 2016. 'Inherent Risks in Chinese Shadow Banking'. In *Shadow Banking in China: An Opportunity for Financial Reform*, edited by Andrew Sheng and Ng Chow Soon. Hoboken, NJ: Wiley & Sons.

Wang, Yeh-chien. 1992. 'Secular Trends of Rice Prices in the Yangzi Delta, 1638–1935'. In *Chinese History in Economic Perspective*, edited by Thomas Rawski and Lillian Li. Berkeley: University of California Press.

Wang, Yong. 2013. 'Courting Financial Innovation'. *Caixin*, 9 December.

Wei, Shang-Jin, and Tao Wang. 1997. 'The Siamese Twins: Do State-owned Banks Favor State-owned Enterprises in China?' *China Economic Review* 8(1): 19–29.

Weimer, David, ed. 1997. *The Political Economy of Property Rights: Institutional Change and Credibility in the Reform of Centrally Planned Economies*. Cambridge: Cambridge University Press.

Weingast, Barry, and Donald Wittman. 2008. 'Introduction: The Reach of Political Economy'. In *The Oxford Handbook of Political Economy*, edited by Donald Wittman and Barry Weingast. Oxford: Oxford University Press.

Wen, Jiabao. 2010. 在第十一届全国人民代表大会第三次会议上的政府工作报告 [Report on the Work of the Government, Delivered at the Third Session of the Eleventh National People's Congress]. Beijing, CN.

Wong, R Bin. 1997. *China Transformed: Historical Change and the Limits of European Experience*. Ithaca, NY: Cornell University Press.

Wong, R Bin. 1999. 'The Political Economy of Agrarian Empire and its Modern Legacy'. In *China and Historical Capitalism: Genealogies of Sinological Knowledge*, edited by Timothy Brook and Gregory Blue. Cambridge: Cambridge University Press.

World Bank. 1993. The East Asian Miracle: Economic Growth and Public Policy. In *World Bank Policy Research Report*. Washington, DC: World Bank.

World Bank. 1995. China: Macroeconomic Stability in a Decentralized Economy. Washington, DC: World Bank.

World Bank. 1996. The Chinese Economy: Fighting Inflation, Deepening Reform. In *World Bank Country Study*. Washington, DC: World Bank.

Wright, Arthur. 1962. 'Values, Roles, and Personalities'. In *Confucian Personalities*, edited by Arthur Wright and Denis Twitchett. Stanford, CA: Stanford University Press.

Wu, Chengming. 2000 [1985]. 'Introduction: On Embryonic Capitalism'. In *Chinese Capitalism, 1522–1840*, edited by Xu Dixin and Wu Chengming. Basingstoke: Macmillan.

Wu, Guoguang. 2001. 'The Return of Ideology? Struggling to Organize Politics during Socio-Economic Transitions'. In *The Nanxun Legacy and China's Development in the Post-Deng Era*, edited by John Wong and Yongnian Zheng. Singapore: Singapore University Press.

Wu Guoguang. 1995. 'Documentary Politics: Hypotheses, Process, and Case Studies'. In *Decision-Making in Deng's China: Perspectives from Insiders*, edited by Carol Lee Hamrin and Suisheng Zhao. Armonk, NY: M.E. Sharpe.

Wu, Jinglian. 2000. 'China's Transition to a Market Economy: How Far Across the River?' *Working Paper No. 69*. Stanford, CA: Center for Research on Economic Development and Policy Reform.

Wu, Jinglian. 2012a. '1993年：经济改革进入"整体推进"的新阶段 [1993: Economic Reform Enters a New Period of "Comprehensive Reform"'. In 中国经济改革：二十讲 *[Chinese Economic Reform: Twenty Essays]*. Beijing: Sanlian Publishers.

Wu, Jinglian. 2012b. '重建金融系统 [Reconstruct the Financial System]'. In 中国经济改革：二十讲 *[Chinese Economic Reform: Twenty Essays]*. Beijing: Sanlian Publishers.

Wu, Jinglian, Xiaochuan Zhou, and Jingben Rong. 1995. 建设市场经济的总体构想与方案设计 *[The Road to a Market Economy: A Comprehensive Framework and Working Proposals]*. Beijing: Central Compilation & Translation Press.

Wu, Xiaoqiu. 2005. 市场主导型金融体系: 中国的战略选择 *[Market-Oriented Financial System: China's Strategic Choice]*. Beijing: China Renmin University Press.

Xi, Jinping. 2008. '改革开放30年党的建设回顾与思考' ['Thoughts and Reflections on 30 Years of Party-Building, Reform and Opening']. 学习时报 *[Study Times]* 1.

Xiang, Xiao, Lina Zhang, Yun Wang, and Huang Chengxuan. 2017. 'China's Path to Fintech Development'. *European Economy* 2: 143–59.

Xiao, Zhengqin 1999. '朱镕基运用智囊团知会的技巧' ['Zhu Employs the Wisdom of his Think Tanks']. 新报 *[HK Daily News]*, 25 January.

Xie, Ping. 1994. '关于国有企业的改革 [On the Reform of State-owned Enterprises]'. 经济研究 *[Economic Research]* 2: 25–33.

Xie, Ping. 1999. 'Options for China's Financial System'. In *Strengthening the Banking System in China: Issues and Experience*, edited by Bank for International Settlements. Basel: Bank for International Settlements.

Xie, Ping, Yiliang Liu, Jiansheng Cheng, and Yin Zheng. 2001. 从通货膨胀到通货紧缩 *[From Inflation to Deflation]*. Chengdu: Southwest University of Finance and Economics Press.

Xie, Ping, Chuanwei Zou, and Haier Liu. 2014. 互联网金融手册 [Internet Finance Handbook]. Beijing: Renmin University of China Press.

Xie, Ping, Chuanwei Zou, and Haier Liu. 2016a. *Internet Finance in China*. Abingdon: Routledge.

Xie, Ping, Chuanwei Zou, and Haier Liu. 2016b. 'The Fundamentals of Internet Finance and its Policy Implications in China'. *China Economic Journal* 9 (3):1–17.

Xinhua. 1997. '副总理吴邦国强调党在改革过程中的领导地位 [Vice-Premier Wu Bangguo Stresses the Party's Leadership Position in Reform]'. 14 December.

Xinhua. 2018a. '社会信用体系建设示范城市典型经验介绍之十一: 义乌市' ['Social Credit System Construction Demonstration Cities, Introduction of Typical Experience No. 11: Yiwu Municipality']. 6 February 2018. http://credit.xinhua08.com/a/20180214/1748625.shtml. Accessed 15 June 2018.

Xinhua. 2018b. 'China Approves Personal Credit Platform for Online Lending'. 22 February 2018. http://www.xinhuanet.com/english/2018–02/22/c_136991905.htm. Accessed 15 June 2018.

Xu, Xiaoping. 1998. *China's Financial System under Transition*. Basingstoke: Macmillan.

Xue, Muqiao. 1996. 薛暮桥回忆录 *[Memoir of Xue Muqiao]*. Tianjin: Tianjin People's Publisher.

Yan, Qingmin, and Jianhua Li. 2014. 国影子银行监管研究 *[Research on China's Shadow Banking Regulation]*. Beijing: Renmin University of China Publishing House.

Yang, C. K. 1959. 'Some Characteristics of Chinese Bureaucratic Behaviour'. In *Confucianism in Action*, edited by David Nivison and Arthur Wright. Stanford, CA: Stanford University Press.

Yang, Dali. 2004. 'Economic Transformation and State Rebuilding in China'. In *Holding China Together: Diversity and National Integration in the Post-Deng Era*, edited by Barry Naughton and Dali Yang. Cambridge: Cambridge University Press.

Yang, Felix. 2016. 'China's National Internet Finance (Fintech) Association Finally Launches Credit Scoring System'. September 14, 2016. https://www.kapronasia.com/china-banking-research/china-s-national-internet-finance-fintech-association-finally-launches-credit-scoring-system.html. Accessed 29 September 2016.

Yang, Shengchun. 2000. 中国最高领导班子的左右手: 中共中央直属机构档案1949–1998 *[The Assistants of the Top Leadership Groups of the CCP: A Record of Directly Subordinate Institutions, 1949–1998]*. Taipei: Yongye Publishers.

Yang, Yabin. 2001. 近代中国社会学 *[Modern Chinese Sociology]*. Beijing: Chinese Social Sciences Press.

Yang, Zhongmei. 1998. 朱镕基传 *[A Biography of Zhu Rongji]*. Taipei: China Times Press.

Yi, Gang. 2011. 中国金融改革思考录 *[Reflections on the Financial Reform of China]*. Beijing: Commercial Press.

Yi Gang. 1996. '中国金融机构的资产结构和政策含义' ['Asset Structure of Chinese Financial Institutions and its Policy Significance']. 经济研究 *[Economic Research]* 12.

Yu, Yongding. 1999. 'China's Macroeconomic Situation and Future Prospects'. *World Economy and China* 3: 15–26.

Yu, Yongding. 2012. 'Rebalancing the Chinese Economy'. *Oxford Review of Economic Policy* 29(3): 551–68.

Zelin, Madeleine. 1988. 'Capital Accumulation and Investment Strategies in Early Modern China: The Case of the Furong Salt Yard'. *Late Imperial China* 9(1): 79–122.

Zeng, Jinghan. 2014. 'Institutionalization of the Authoritarian Leadership in China: A Power Succession System with Chinese Characteristics?' *Contemporary Politics* 20(3): 294–314.

Zhan, Xiangyang. 2000. 论中国不良债权债务的化解 *[On the Dissolution of Bad Debt and Obligations in China]*. Beijing: China Financial Publisher.

Zhang, Gaoling. 2004. 中共领导人与中国现代化 [*CCP Leaders and China's Modernization*]. Beijing: Central Documents Press.

Zhang, Ming. 2012. 'Chinese Stylized Sterilization: The Cost-sharing Mechanism and Financial Repression'. *China & World Economy* 20(2): 41–58.

Zhang, Shu, and John Ruwitch. 2018. 'Exclusive: Ant Financial Shifts Focus from Finance to Tech…'. *Reuters*, June 5, 2018.

Zhang, Ming, Haihong Gao, and Dongmin Liu. 2014. *Revealing the Chinese Shadow Banking System* [透视中国影子银行体系]. Beijing: Chinese Academy of Social Sciences Press.

Zhao, Suisheng. 2017. 'Whither the China Model: Revisiting the Debate'. *Journal of Contemporary China* 26(103): 1–17.

Zhao, Suisheng 1993. 'Deng Xiaoping's Southern Tour: Elite Politics in Post-Tiananmen China'. *Asian Survey* 33(8): 739–56.

Zhao, Tingyang. 2007. '身与身外－儒家的一个未决问题' ['Self and Other: An Unresolved Issue in Confucian Theory']. 中国人民大学学报 [*Journal of Renmin University of China*] 21(1): 15–21.

Zheng, Shiping. 1997. *Party vs. State in Post-1949 China: The Institutional Dilemma*. Cambridge: Cambridge University Press.

Zheng, Yongnian. 2001. 'Ideological Decline, The Rise of an Interest-based social order, and the demise of communism in China'. In *The Nanxun Legacy and China's Development in the Post-Deng Era*, edited by John Wong and Yongnian Zheng. Singapore: Singapore University Press.

Zheng, Yongnian. 2010. *The Chinese Communist Party as Organizational Emperor: Culture, Reproduction and Transformation*. Abingdon: Routledge.

Zheng, Yongnian, and Lance Gore. 2015. 'China Enters the Xi Era'. In *China Entering the Xi Jinping Era*, edited by Yongnian Zheng and Lance Gore. New York: Routledge.

Zhou, Xiaochuan. 2006. '中国货币政策的特点和挑战' ['The Characteristics and Challenges of China's Monetary Policy']. *Caijing* 175 (26).

Zhu, Ling, and Zhongyi Jiang. 1997. *Credit Systems for the Rural Poor in China*. New York: Nova Science Publishers.

Zhu, Min. 1998a. '东亚金融动荡引发的思考 [Reflections Provoked by the Asian Financial Upheaval]'. 人民日报 [*People's Daily*], 26 January.

Zhu, Mingchun. 1993. '加快金融体制改革，建立竞争性金融制度' ['Accelerate Reform of the Financial System, Establish a Competitive Financial System']. 经济体制改革内参 [*Internal Reference of Economic System Reform*] 4:13–16.

Zhu, Rongji. 1991. 'Clearing up Triangular Debt Must start with the Source: Fixed-Asset Investments'. In *The Road to Reform: 1991–1997*. Beijing: Foreign Languages Press.

Zhu, Rongji. 1992. 'On Comprehensively and Correctly Understanding the Spirit of Deng Xiaoping's Talks in Southern China'. In *Zhu Rongji on the Record*, edited by Rongji Zhu. Beijing: Foreign Languages Press.

Zhu, Rongji. 1993. 'Some Comments on the Current Economic Situation and Macroeconomic Controls'. In *The Road to Reform: 1991–1997*, edited by Zhu Rongji. Beijing: Foreign Languages Press.

Zhu, Rongji. 1998b. '深化金融改；防范金融风险；开创金融工作新局面' ['Deepen Financial Reform; Guard Against Financial Risks; Create a New Phase for Financial Work']. In 新时期经济体制改革重要文献选编 *[A Selection of Important Documents on Structural Economic Reform in the New Period]*, edited by Document Research Center of the Chinese Communist Party Central Committee. Beijing: Central Document Publisher.

Zhu, Rongji. 2000 [1997]. '深化金融改革，防范金融风险，开创金融工作新局面' ['Deepen Financial Reforms, Guard Against Financial Risks, and Open Up a New Phase of Financial Work']. In 十五大以来重要文献选编 *[Selection of Important Documents Since the 15th Party Congress]*, edited by Document Research Center of the Chinese Communist Party Central Committee. Beijing: Central Document Press.

Zhu, Rongji. 2011. *Zhu Rongji Meets the Press*. Oxford: Oxford University Press.

Zhu, Rongji. 2011 [1993]. '整顿财税接续，严肃财经纪律，强化税收征管，加快财税改革' ['Rectify the Fiscal and Tax Order, Restore Strict Budgetary Discipline, Strengthen Taxation Collection, Speed up Fiscal and Tax Reform'] w. In 十四大以来重要文献选编 (上) *[Selection of Important Documents Since the 14th Party Congress]*, edited by Document Research Center of the Chinese Communist Party Central Committee. Beijing: Central Document Press.

Zhu, Rongji. 2011 [1994]. '跨出金融改革关键性的一步 [Taking a Critical Step Forward in Financial Reforms]'. In 朱镕基讲话实录 (全四卷) *[Zhu Rongji on the Record (Four Volumes)]*, edited by Zhu Rongji. Beijing: People's Press.

Zhu, Rongji. 2013a. *Zhu Rongji on the Record*. Beijing: Foreign Languages Press.

Zhu, Rongji. 2013 [1993]. 'Thirteen Measures for Strengthening Macroeconomic Controls'. In *Zhu Rongji on the Record*, edited by Rongji Zhu. Beijing: Foreign Languages Press.

Zhu, Xufeng. 2013b. *The Rise of Think Tanks in China*. London: Routledge.

Zwan, Natascha van der. 2014. 'Making Sense of Financialization'. *Socio-Economic Review* 12(1): 99–129.

Index

Note: 'n' after a page number indicates the number of a note on the page.